The Kintsugi Poet

Mirella Di Benedetto

writing as Anna Verduci

A Memoir-Blood Memory, Family Secrets, and Identity

First published in 2025
Copyright © 2025 Mirella Di Benedetto
mirelladb25@outlook.com
Published by Verduci Fili d'Oro Press

Edition 2 – The title has been slightly changed, photos have been added, and errors have been corrected.

The moral right of the author has been asserted.
All rights reserved. No part of this publication may be reproduced, stored in a retrieval system, or transmitted in any form or by any means – electronic, mechanical, photocopying, recording, or otherwise – without prior written permission from the author, Dr Mirella Di Benedetto (writing as Anna Verduci).
This is a work of creative nonfiction. Every effort has been made to honour the emotional truth of my experience. My (biological) Father's real name is used with his permission. Most other living individuals have had their names and identifying details changed to protect their privacy. In some cases, characters are composites, or events have been reordered for narrative clarity.
The voices in this memoir speak from memory, silence, and blood. While I have written what I remember, what I have been told, or have read, I acknowledge that others may remember differently.
This book is intended for general literary purposes only. It is not a substitute for professional advice. Readers should consider its relevance to their own situation before acting on any reflections it may evoke in areas such as mental health or identity.
Cover design by Dr Mirella Di Benedetto and Eli Affram
Internal layout and design by Mirella Di Benedetto
Typeset in Georgia
Edited by Mirella Di Benedetto
ISBN: 978-1-7641323-1-2

Parts of this work were developed using AI-assisted tools under the creative direction and final authorship of the writer.

Table of Contents

Dedication i
Epigraph Poem ii
Author's Note on Narrative 1
Prologue: Seven Enigmatic Fragments 5
Part I The Cursed Bastard Child 9
1. The Confessional Bus – Shattered Identity 13
2. The Madhouse of Secrets and Lies 23
3. Blood, Shame, and Shattered Glass 40
4. The Brief Calm 61
5. The Intruder 73
6. Falling into the Gap 83
7. Alchemy of Identity 95
8. The Great Escape 109
Interlude 1 121
Part II: Mothers – Scattering 123
9. 26 - 'Giuseppe' (1990) 127
10. Ursula: Final Rejection 148
11. The Second Orphaning 163
12. Life After Loss 183
13. Meeting Siblings 197
14. Fading Hope 227
Interlude 2 235
Part III: Sinful Fathers - Kintsugi Poet 237
15. DNA Detective 239
16. Dr Rosemary: The Historian 263
17. Giuseppe: The Meeting 281
18. My Sinful Father: The Shadow Archive 290
19. Sinful Uncle Andrea 301
20. The Compassion of Strangers 320
21. Casting the First Stone 334
22. The Kintsugi Poet: Giovanni 'John' Verduci 347
23. Papà: The Philosopher and the Father 356
24. Diego – The Reckoning 371
25. A Seat at the Christmas Table 377
26. Carpe Diem! 387
27. Redemption 397
Interlude 3 407
Author's Interlude 408
Epilogue: Blood Memory 411
Author's Note on Structure 419
Glossary of Italian - Sicilian Terms 421
Acknowledgements 425
About the Author 427

Dedication

Dedicated to my Mother, Michelina Di Benedetto, and my Father, Sebastiano Di Benedetto – the parents who gave me a home, an education, and a future.

These pages are dedicated to all tortured souls seeking refuge and solace – including the Kintsugi Poet – Giovanni 'John' Verduci. Those who are navigating their own unique path in life. To the many clients who have shared their stories and healing journey with me. To the many thousands of students I had the opportunity to teach, and who taught me much more in return.

Was mich nicht umbringt, macht mich stärker. (Nietzsche)
(What does not kill me, makes me stronger)

Epigraph Poem

This poem is woven from the epigraphs of each chapter – fragments of voice and memory, refracted into verse.

Memory scatters, but fragments never forget.
The revelation – sudden, irreversible.
The house whispered louder than the people inside,
The body remembers what the mind chose to forget.
Even calm hummed with what had come before,
A porcelain vessel splintered without a sound.
Lost, fragmented, swirling in a cave.
Transformation began in the shadow of uncertainty,
Holding stillness between jagged edges.
What is hidden, always leaving a trace,
Silences echoing across generations.
A second rebirthing of sorrow,
Rising from scattered ashes.
Blood memory stirring, refusing to be still.
Hope, vanishing, resurfacing, calcifying.
Unearthing golden threads through a labyrinth,
Archival puzzles holding ghosts,
Answers arriving in unsettled ambiguity.
Sinful legacies staining ancestral marrow,
Then, welcoming a familiar shame.
Outsiders mending wounds kin dare not touch,
Familial blood dripping from unforgiving stones.
A broken heart, refusing to betray.
Musings reflected in enigmatic eyes.
Unsettled by mirrors too heavy to bear.
Building a bridge between theft and reckoning,
wounds carved in the chambers, where wisdom dwells,
Fractures mended with golden seams.
Every ending, a new beginning.

Author's Note on Narrative

This is not a story told once and for all.

It is a vessel of fragments: scattered, gathered, held.
You may read it beginning to end – fracture to grace.
Or begin with the gold and walk backward through time.
Or pick up each part in your own order, like a mosaic assembled by instinct.
This work does not begin with a plot, but with a descent – beneath surface, beneath language.
It resists the neat arcs and resolutions, that too often flatten complex lives.
Think of it as an excavation site: layered, recursive, uneven.
Each fragment matters as much as the whole.
Each seam is golden, made luminous through its breaking.
Adoption does not offer a single story.
It offers rupture and return, forgetting, and remembering.
This book asks you to read slowly.
To feel the pauses.
To listen where language falters.
You may read it in sequence. Or not.
Each part reshapes the whole.
This is not a provocation, or not only that.
It is a cartography of return.
Identity is not a destination.
It is the ritual of becoming – again and again – through what is broken, buried, and brought into the light.
These fragments weren't just stories.
They were the terrain. And I have traversed every one.
However you choose to journey, you will arrive at the same truth:
That identity is not found.
It is made – seam by seam, memory by memory, hand over hand.

Me at 26 years old (1990)

Prologue: Seven Enigmatic Fragments

Memory scatters, but fragments never forget.

After 1990

Each morning, dark honey eyes peer back at me from the bathroom mirror – questioning, constant. These eyes, unchanged since childhood, hold a story waiting to be told – memory coursing through blood vessels I've never fully fathomed. *What secrets lie buried in the deep wells of those eyes, shimmering with unspoken histories?* This was the first fragment of my identity puzzle – one of seven enigmatic pieces scattered across a terrain I'd spend decades mapping. Scattered by upheavals that weathered my life like storms across fragile terrain.

Near the mirror sits a photograph: me at 26, the same age my Father was when I was conceived. *Did I inherit his features – the arch of my brow, the angle of my jaw, the curve of my mouth, the restless flicker behind my gaze?*

His name, Giuseppe, was the second fragment, offered reluctantly by my first mother decades after I discovered the secret of my relinquishment. A man who lived in Carlton, worked in a nameless business – a shadow with hazel eyes and brown hair, known to the world, unknowable to me.

The third fragment: biological heritage – the invisible strand of DNA linking me to ancestors scattered across continents I had never seen.

The fourth: a medical history – its pages remained crucially blank whenever doctors inquired about family conditions. I would confess, 'I don't know. I'm adopted.'

The fifth: cultural origins that resonated within me in ways I couldn't articulate – an inexplicable gravitational pull toward certain foods, music, intellectual pursuits, phrases, and instincts that seemed to rise from some subterranean well of memory beyond conscious knowing.

The sixth fragment haunted me most viscerally: family history – birthdays, Christmases, weddings, births, and deaths I had missed. Moments that should have been woven into the tapestry of my life, but instead floated like phantom constellations – visible, unchanged, already extinguished, yet still casting their light.

And finally, the seventh: my psychological self – the person I had become in this constellation of absences, forged in the crucible where nature and nurture collided, tempered by both love and abandonment.

Who am I?

The question echoed through the decades, a secular prayer whispered into the void.

Melbourne, 1980

Broken at 16 on a Melbourne bus, my identity felt splintered – each shard a piece of memory, biology, and culture. Pieces scattered across decades, awaiting alchemy to fuse them. In the Japanese art of *kintsugi*, broken pottery is repaired with gold, transforming damage into beauty. Each fracture is traced with shimmering golden lacquer. The breaks are not hidden but illuminated – the very points where the vessel becomes most precious.

My life, like the vessel in kintsugi, would crack and gleam with gold in time, perhaps under a fig tree.

Each golden seam telling a story of shattering and reconstruction, of vulnerability transfigured into strength.

Could I, too, be transformed by breakage – remade by golden seams rather than undone by the shattering?

We inherit more than chromosomes. We inherit silences, unspoken traumas, and psychic wounds long unacknowledged. This is the blood memory – coursing through generations, a current of unresolved sorrow.

In my case, I inherited not just genetic matter, but the negative space of secrets: a cartography not of places, but of absences mapped across my veins.

For years, I subsisted on mere slivers of insight.

A southern Italian mother. An Italian Father's name. A suburb. A nameless family business, his hazel eyes and brown hair.

Fragments, like relics buried in an archaeological dig – too jagged, too sparse to reconstruct with certainty.

Calabria, 2024

When finally I set foot on Calabrian soil – travelling to the tiny village where my paternal ancestors had dwelled for generations – I carried with me the fragmented relics of my identity.

There, I unearthed more than heritage.

Identity, I discovered, is not a buried prize, but something quarried slowly from the stone of our own persistence. It is something we actively create and assemble across the arc of our lives.

This is the story of that arduous reconstruction – a rollercoaster journey toward understanding who we are when the stories authored by others prove to be fictions. It is a story of families: those who engendered me, those that reared me, and the one I ultimately fashioned for myself from the fractured remnants.

La figlia dell'amore è il prodotto di una gentil donna innamorata di un principe di grazia e virtù per destino di una sorte ingrata. (The daughter of love is the product of a gentlewoman enamoured of a prince of grace and virtue by fate of a thankless lot.)

So wrote my Uncle Andrea in one of our rare exchanges before his passing. A poetic gloss gilding a starker truth: I was the progeny of a young woman's ardour and a libertine's fecklessness, in an era when such unions invited shame and severance. A love child. A bastard. A fragile covenant between longing and despair. And now, four decades later, I begin to fathom both the devotion and devastation that conceived me.

To understand how these shards came to be strewn – how I arrived at that fateful bus stop on an unremarkable afternoon, an unsuspecting girl whose entire existence teetered on the edge of unravelling – you'll need to step with me through the fragments, in whatever order they reach you.

PART I

THE CURSED BASTARD CHILD - FRAGMENTATION

The 16-year-old before (1980)

1

The Confessional Bus – Shattered Identity (1980)

The revelation – sudden, irreversible.

On an ordinary spring school day in 1980, I stood alone unsteadily in the aisle of bus route 534, one hand gripping a chrome-coloured support pole, the other holding my schoolbag, as the vehicle bumped and lurched through the quiet northern suburbs of Melbourne. The acrid sting of diesel fumes curled into my nostrils. My light blue summer uniform hung on my skinny teenage frame. My battered brown Scampers were half-lost in the forest of restless schoolchildren's legs. Boisterous chatter and laughter rang around me. Though the chaos at home had long faded, I still flinched at loud voices.

Then came the words that would divide my life into before and after.

'*E tu sai ca tò patri, non era tò patri?*'
(And you know your father wasn't your father?)

My journey had begun earlier that morning at our modest clinker-brick home in Glenroy, a northern working-class suburb of Melbourne. The streets around us – Middle, West, North, and South – formed a perfect grid that had helped me learn compass directions at an early age. This neighbourhood had been my entire world for most of my 16 years: a world of Italian neighbours and subtle reminders that we were different from the 'real' Australians. A world where I had always felt slightly out of place, without understanding why.

A short, pudgy man – vaguely familiar as an acquaintance of my Father – interrupted this dreaded commute. His face emerged like a forgotten photograph – a flash of my Father in fragments. I was a shy, reserved 16-year-old, awkward when talking to adults and strangers.

The man smiled in recognition and asked in his Sicilian lingo:

'*Ciau, comu stai?*' (How are you?)

'Good,' I replied quietly, reluctant to engage and avoiding his gaze.

'*Comu sta tu matri?*' (How is your mother?)

'*Bona*' (Good).

'*E su maritu?*' (And her husband?)

My grip tightened with each invasive question. Feeling trapped and eager to end this conversation, I replied with an indifferent shrug. Thankfully, my bus stop was approaching.

With a sigh of relief, I tugged on the overhanging cord. The bus began to decelerate. I meekly moved towards the rear door. The balding man, with his wispy blonde-grey hair and an air of smug indifference, pulled me back with his words:

'*E tu sai ca tò patri, non era tò patri?*'

His words – casual, indifferent, tossed toward me like scraps to a stray – instantly hit me with physical force. A detonation in the quiet of my ordinary existence.

Adrenaline flooded my system as heat rushed to my face. The once familiar Glenroy suburb beyond the glass became foreign in an instant.

My surroundings dissolved into silence. Though I could see his lips moving, they formed soundless shapes.

Only the frantic pounding of my heart remained audible – *Ba-boom. Ba-boom.*

My throat constricted, and my gut clenched, as if gripped by an invisible fist. Disoriented. Unsteady. I grasped a pole, cold beneath my touch.

Oblivious to the bus decelerating, the driver changing gears, passengers swaying as it lurched to a stop.

My world had stopped completely, cleaved in two – my world before the revelation, and my world after.

The girl, at once, splitting.

Abruptly, 16 years of fragile identity began to crumble – fragmented and uncertain. A vessel fracturing from the inside out.

Feeling panicky, I vaguely nodded and quickly turned away, not wanting to reveal the red-hot burning shock of the words he had indiscriminately thrust in my direction.

I couldn't breathe. *Stop the bus!* I screamed into the void within.

In desperation, I eagerly scurried down the metal exit steps – the hissing sound of hydraulic hinges louder than usual. The bi-folding back doors parted like curtains, revealing a world newly alien to me. I stepped out onto the bone-dry nature strip. The scent of diesel was overpowering.

With a gentle whoosh, the bus doors settled back into place behind me, and the bus – a conveyor of secrets – rolled on.

I momentarily paused, gasping in the warm afternoon air. I felt utterly overwhelmed by this stranger's cryptic message.

Had he revealed a massive, hitherto-hidden family secret?

Dismayed. Confused. His words swirling around. Teenage mind fractured. Deep crevices. His casual revelation – a cyclone. Havoc. Mayhem. Nothing solid beneath my feet now.

What did he mean – Tò patri, non era tò patri?

Stepping off the bus, I found the usually stable and familiar earth instantly uprooted. Foreign.

Slowly turning to cross West Street, heading east, the bitumen wavered like black water under the hammering sun.

This well-trodden road now seemed to have wobbling, snaking cracks across it, that could've easily swallowed me up in one gulp if I stood for too long.

My fragile foundations continued to crumble – like the cracking of an egg dropped from a great height onto hard concrete.

As I walked one street block towards home, a strange outward calmness began to conceal my increasing agitation. My head was tightening, but I felt a lightness.

The very ground beneath me had cracked open, hairline fractures spreading outward from each footfall.

The girl I had been for 16 years began to dissolve – like a photograph in acid – replaced by a drifting collection of jigsaw pieces I couldn't yet name or understand, sharp-edged and impossible to reassemble with hands that suddenly seemed unrecognisable.

The stranger's voice echoed, widening the cracks beneath my teenage skin.

Fragment by fragment, my sense of self was dismantling – like a New York skyscraper folding in on its own foundation. I tried to keep it upright and unified, but the collapse was inevitable. Each step toward a home that no longer felt like mine chipped away at something I hadn't realised was breakable.

The cloudless bright blue southern sky overhead concealed the shadow cast over my world.

Nausea turned to numbness. The world became strangely still. The occasional Holden or Ford drove by soundlessly. Everything blurred.

His words reverberated inside my skull with increasing loudness –

'Tò patri, non era tò patri.'

Uncertainty and disbelief clung like a sticky veil.

More confusion flooded my already turbulent young life.

As I approached home, thoughts and questions relentlessly interrogated me.

If I'm adopted, then my parents aren't my real parents. My Mother isn't my real mother, and my Father wasn't my real father.

Everything is a lie.

A charade.

A façade.

As I reached the corner, I anxiously pondered, confusion seeping into every crevice of my being.

My aunts, uncles, grandparents, and cousins aren't my real family either.

Deep within, I just knew that they weren't of my flesh. Nor was I of them.

How did I know, almost intuitively that he meant that I was adopted?

Flashes of the past, subtle comments, crystallised into a new, jolting clarity.

Growing up, I had often felt like an outsider in my own family – quieter and more introspective among the louder, boisterous, arm-waving relatives. I was shyer, a deeper thinker, more studious, and creative. I always had to know how and why.

A 'just because' dictum was an insufficient and lame response for my all too inquisitive and curious mind.

These people, these biological strangers weren't my tribe. I was not of their blood.

We didn't share a single drop of DNA.

Never doubting the stranger on the bus – who had revealed a truth that wasn't in any way his to reveal – my gut knew he wasn't lying.

Reluctantly, I stepped into our small, modest family home and pretended that it had been just another ordinary school day.

I quietly disappeared into my bedroom, as I often did, to be alone with this troubling revelation.

The interrogation didn't stop.

Who else knew that I was adopted? Other than the person I'd always thought was my Mother?

Conflicted anguish began to rise. I couldn't just approach my Mother about being adopted.

Since she had remarried, we now had a strained and increasingly distant teenage rage-filled relationship.

Her second marriage had shattered our once-close bond.

The wounds still raw, still unhealed.

There was a quantum vastness between us now.

After her marriage hurt and loneliness had moved in, where there once had been peace and joy.

I rarely spoke to my Mother other than out of necessity. I rarely spoke to my stepfather. I loathed and despised him for taking my Mother's love and attention away from me.

He tried to take my Father's place – and I wasn't having a bar of it. He was an unwelcome stranger in our home and our once serene, blissful life.

It took a few days for my Mother to reluctantly admit that I was indeed adopted. That is, after I had spoken to two maternal cousins using our 1970s green phone. The same shade of green that had once matched my Father's 1960s Holden Special. The dial-up phone was plugged into the wall with a thin green cord, as it sat lonesomely in our small entrance foyer on a specifically made small phone table stand.

Hands shaking, I rotated the heavy plastic dial, releasing it with each number. I dialled the long-distance number to an older Australian born cousin, now living in Staten Island. Her family had migrated to New York from Australia in the late 1960s. I clutched the heavy green receiver tightly to my ear.

I croaked into the line, my voice barely above a whisper, 'Am I adopted?'

She promptly lied in her Italian-Brooklyn accent, 'I honestly don't know.' A lie, intended to keep me safe from the sharpest edge of harm.

Another much older cousin, who still lived in an outer northern suburb of Melbourne, told me a bigger lie in her Aussie-Sicilian accent: 'Sometimes people make *fings* up. You shouldn't listen to *dem*.'

I wondered if they had all been sworn to secrecy. Perhaps some old pact, woven years before I was even aware.

A few days later, my Mother's younger sister, who had also migrated to New York, rang my Mother and instructed firmly: *Tu ci l'haiu a diri.* (You must tell her.)

Later that day, my Mother finally told me what she should have confessed years ago – considering that everyone seemed to know except for me, the adoptee.

This deep, dark, shameful family secret was now confirmed, as we sat in our family room, surrounded by the chunky orange-brown Italian-style leather lounge suite.

To my great disappointment – and greater anger – my stepfather was present. I sat, seemingly calm, while inside my head I seethed.

He shouldn't be here!

My loathing for him grew even deeper that day, especially as he butted in with details that were not his to share.

My Mother confirmed what I already knew: I was adopted in 1964, when I was a very young babe.

It now made more sense that there were no neonatal photos of me.

The neighbours had known. The extended family had known. Even the stepfather had known.

The rage inside me swelled like a tidal wave, threatening to split the seams of my careful exterior.

I wanted to scream – *Why didn't you tell me?*

Why did I have to find out from a stranger?

Instead, I sat mute – burning.

My Mother's first words to me were not apology or explanation. She said, in a flat, reluctant voice, *'Ora tu lu sai.'* (Now you know.)

With those words, the fruit that had believed itself firmly attached to its tree, fell and rolled away – tumbling down a rocky slope into a deep, dark ravine.

Then came another lie: that my biological parents had 'died in a car accident.'

Another fiction, designed to quell questions, to still my searching heart before it could even begin the quest.

Later, I would learn that this was a common practice, during the era of closed adoptions and 'White Stolen Generations', where governments and churches colluded to sever children from their origins.

'It's for the best,' they said.

Best for whom?

Not for the children, plucked from their mothers like forbidden fruit, labelled as shame, hidden away.

And so it was, on what became the worst day of my life, I discovered I was an illegitimate *bastard* – my very essence revealed not by those who should have loved and protected me, but by a stranger.

Plucked from obscurity and surreptitiously grafted onto a foreign limb.

On a crowded, lurching, exhaust-fume-filled bus.

The white bus with a green stripe across it – the bus that still haunts my dreams.

The bus that turned my world upside down and inside out.

The bus that carried me into a lifetime of questioning, searching, and yearning for truth – and for a home that could hold all my broken pieces.

A life suddenly shattered. An identity bleeding out invisible onto the suburban pavement.

The stranger's words left a wound. One that would take decades to understand.

That single, careless question shattered something sacred and sealed.

My body remembered before my mind could catch up.

To understand how I arrived at that fateful bus ride, let me take you back to the life I lived before the revelation – a life built on fragile foundations and family secrets.

A house of cards.

A house already trembling before the stranger's revelation brought it down.

Prep – Hadfield Primary School (1970)

Netball Team (1976)

2

The Madhouse of Secrets and Lies

The house whispered louder than the people inside

That spring morning in 1980, as I walked toward the bus stop, a strange foreboding settled in my chest – like smoke curling inward. I exhaled into the spring air, watching the mist dissolve – as if the certainties I once held were evaporating too. Beneath my feet, the concrete pulsed with latent truths – each crack a whispered revelation. My schoolbag felt heavier than usual – not from books or pens, but from an invisible weight I could not yet name. I was already becoming fluent in contradiction – a child raised by whispers, taught through omission.

Walking past the second-to-last house, I always noted it had once belonged to my *Zia* and her family, before they migrated to the United States in the late 1960s. That modest home still stirred echoes of family history and culture – fragments of a story that stretched across oceans.

In America, they joined my maternal *Nonna*, Gaetana, and her only son, Sebastiano – known within the family as Sammy. Names in our family folded back on themselves like mirrors in a narrow hallway – distorting, multiplying, erasing identity. A tapestry stitched in misrecognition, where each thread whispered a different name for me. I was already a vessel of substitution – my true name floating somewhere in another woman's mouth. My Father's name was also Sebastiano, though he was known as Vastiano or Sammy to his Aussie mates. Every

Sicilian carried a *li 'ngùria* – a nickname that translated literally as an insult, but functioned more like a signature woven from geography, habit, or feature. These names were shorthand for belonging – a kind of oral identification system. Some examples: *Test'i lignu* (wooden head), *Facc'i trippa* (tripe face), *Nasuni* (long, arched nose). My Father's family bore the li 'ngùria *u Petre Loru* – the Stonemason.

Nonna, born at the turn of the century, was denied entry to Australia on health grounds – a bureaucratic refusal that would shape the trajectory of our family's dispersal. Her husband, *Nonno* Giuseppe Carfi, had sailed to Buenos Aires shortly after my Mother, Michelangela – known as Michelina – was born, seeking work to feed his growing family.

There, he joined two of his brothers, who would eventually make Argentina their permanent home. Five years later, Nonno returned to the village, and his next three children were born beneath the same Sicilian sun. The Italian diaspora, like a great tide, scattered our bloodline across continents – its DNA dissolving into saltwater and soil, memory and myth.

Zia Diana's birth name was Sebastiana, but to add to the naming confusion, she was also known as Yanni to her relatives and *paesani* (townsfolk). She embodied migration itself – a young woman transformed by geography, her very name a palimpsest of cultural translation. From Vizzini to Melbourne to New York.

Her crossing haunted my childhood imagination – a 14-year-old girl alone on the Sorrento in 1949, the ship slicing through weeks of darkness, peeling her from the only world she'd ever known.

Zia Diana had always been brave, adventurous, and independent, unlike my Mother, who was mostly afraid, dependent, and clingy. Two sisters, planted in the same soil of southern Italian culture, yet blooming into radically different flowers – one reaching toward the horizon, the other curling inward.

My Mother's terror of severance shaped my own inheritance of fear. She didn't want to leave her Mother. She married my Father, five years her senior, in 1950 at the chiesa di San Giovanni Battista, in their small hilltop village of Vizzini – shaped like a seahorse clinging to the mountainside. A perfect metaphor for migration's tenacity.

Vizzini lies in the southeastern section of Sicily, in Provincia Catania – a landscape etched by conquest, where each stone tells a story.

At 24, my Mother relented and followed her sisters to Australia. Migration wasn't a choice – it was a choreography. Survival's dance.

Tears soaked her departure. She left her long-widowed Mother and youngest sibling behind at 21 Via Levante.

Nonno had died when my Mother was 10, leaving Nonna with five children and no pension. Poverty followed.

Hunger sculpted my Mother's childhood – six bodies pressed into a single bed, each breath a prayer for fullness, each dream a fragile map of escape. She was taken out of school, and made socks on a small machine to help financially support the family. Child labour transformed into survival's thread – each stitch a small rebellion against poverty's crushing weight.

Nonna had *a bottega* (a little shop), selling goods such as rice, coffee, sugar, and oil. This modest storefront became her economic sanctuary, a tiny kingdom where survival was measured in grams of coffee and spoonfuls of rice.

At night, when hunger stalked the village like a wolf, my Mother and her siblings became swift-footed thieves, scaling walls to neighbouring orchards. Mum would tell me stories of their nighttime raids, their bare feet darting through shadows, snatching fruit to stave off gnawing hunger.

In Australia, Mum never threw any food away. Dried-up spoonfuls of homemade tomato sauce on saucers could be found lurking in the recesses of our fridge. Each hoarded morsel – a fossilised memory of scarcity.

My parents made the long sea-sickening trip on the TSS Cyrenia to the Lucky Country. It departed Piraeus, Greece, in February and arrived in Melbourne in March 1952, during the pinnacle decade of Italian migration to Australia. They were among 194,000 southern Italians – previously not white enough – now permitted to call the southern continent home, following changes to Australia's White Australia policy. Zia Diana recalled that Australia was seeking 'white' migrants. Calwell, Australia's first Minister for Immigration, declared that Australia had to 'populate or perish.'

My parents stepped onto Australian soil as strangers in a foreign land, their tongues heavy with words no one understood. Upon their arrival, they lived at 120 Peel Street North Melbourne, a stone's throw from the Queen Victoria Market, with my Mum's maternal Zia Maria and her husband, who sponsored them and many other relatives during this bustling migration period.

A few years later, after much hard work and saving, my parents bought their first home, an old single Victorian terrace, in Coppin Street, Richmond. A few years later they bought their newly built home in Glenroy, the place that I now called home.

Having experienced subtle and not so subtle racism from a young age, I was quite familiar with all the racial slurs hurled at us from the purer whiter Aussies or Skips as they were referred to: The Dagos. The Wogs. The Wops. The Greaseballs. The Eyeties. The Eye-talians. These new Australians were hard working, determined, tough migrants who went to more prosperous lands – so their descendants would have a better life than the one left behind in destitute, war-torn southern Italy, where there were few jobs, less food, and less opportunity for a formal education and home ownership.

Their departure tore families apart like fragile sepia photographs – bloodlines unspooled across vast oceans, memories fraying at the edges, identities suspended between what was lost and what might be found. Often never to be reunited. Some family members remained in their villages, while others sailed to other, unknown and distant places, on other sides of the world. They sailed toward alien landscapes, hearts heavy with melancholy, aching for the soil they had been forced to leave behind.

'*Terra straniera, quanta malinconia,*' Luciano Tajoli achingly lamented – a line carved from my Mother's marrow. It drifted from the scratchy, warbled 78 spinning on our all-in-one 1970s record player most Saturday mornings, as she sang along – out of key.

These waves of migrants carried homeland in suitcases – seeds wrapped in handkerchiefs, recipes memorised, soil still embedded in boot treads. Each journey was both an ending and a beginning, a cartography of loss and potential. The Dagos brought with them their once strange low-status food and customs, which were initially regarded with scorn by the not-so-new Aussies: homemade sauce, winemaking, garlic, olives, artichokes, eggplant, zucchini, pasta, gelato, cannoli, and bitter coffee – once strange and scorned, now staples of the Australian table.

How ironic it is that cappuccino, Parma, pizza, and pasta are now proudly claimed as *fair dinkum* Aussie food. Even more ironic – that dinkum has Chinese origins. Fair dinks.

In my childhood lunchbox, shame was the meat between thick crusts of belonging. As a school kid, in a vain attempt to fit in, I wanted to take vegemite sandwiches to school, instead of the smelly mortadella in between two big fat chunks of crusty white Italian bread that my Mother made for me.

From Merlynston Station, it was a short 15-minute walk to my junior high Catholic girls' school, Mercy Diocesan College, in Coburg. On these walks, I was usually lost deep in thought, often daydreaming and easily distracted.

After primary school, I had to attend an all-girls' high school as my pubescent, good Catholic Italian self couldn't possibly be allowed to mix with boys. So, I insisted on attending Mercy College. At the time, I believed that a private high school education was better than a public one and I didn't want to wear the tan and brown uniform of the local girls' Catholic high school, where the girls were known as Santa Sofia 'brown cows.' Not wanting to be a brown cow, I opted to be a Mercy mole instead.

In 1980, I was in year 10. Although I liked school and I was a bright, conscientious student, I was very mentally troubled. At the time, I had no words for what I was experiencing – only later would I come to understand it. I was already afflicted with bouts of melancholy, periods of sadness, and growing sense of unease in social settings – emotions that would later be compounded by the fracturing revelation of my adoption.

My mind was a haunted house – rooms filled with shadows that had no names, only voices. In many social settings, I was terribly shy, tense, and awkward, especially around adults – particularly those in authority. They caused me the most angst. These adults were often unpredictable and too critical for my sensitive nature. Socialising became difficult.

During this time, my closest friend at high school was Jaz. She lived in Fawkner, another outer northern suburb of Melbourne. Her family were originally from Naples, Italy. A region I didn't yet know I had deep roots in. She became my first love interest. My adolescent confused sexuality added yet another layer of complexity to my omnipresent feelings of being uncomfortable, strange, and different, just like our very Italian house and garden.

Concrete encased our house like an exoskeleton – shielding secrets, trapping breath. The side and back of our little house formed a vast, desolate concrete landscape – typical of migrant homes built after WWII in the area. Italians seemed devoted to concrete – a hard promise beneath foreign skies, smooth on the surface but fractured beneath, like secrets waiting to break through. In summer, these slabs radiated heat long after sunset; in winter, they remained stubbornly cold – a permanent reminder of the hardness required to survive transplantation from one world to another.

On these great slabs of concrete, I would spend endless hours riding and doing tricks on my skateboard, shooting basketball, or hitting a ball with a tennis racket against our large back brick wall – smashing out my teenage angst.

The house sat on a corner block, with huge front and side nature strips – endless grass. From the age of nine, I had to mow all four areas of lawn that surrounded the house. The front garden had a large rectangular expanse of green lawn and was bereft of flowers, shrubs, or trees. A few thorny rose bushes sprung up from the hard, dull-grey, lifeless clay soil that edged the lawn on three sides.

Each tree in our backyard was catalogued in my mind according to its climbing potential, its fruit, and its capacity to hide me from adults' watchful eyes. The backyard also had a large area of lawn to one side – dotted with trees, sweet-smelling, edible fruit trees: nectarine, almond, apricot, peach, pear, and, my favourite – a huge old fig tree.

I still love the sticky, fruity aroma of home-grown figs. The fig tree was my 'Faraway Tree' – and I believed I was one of its fruits, firmly rooted in its limbs and leaves. My solace. My hideaway.

As a child, I would climb my Faraway Tree and sit in it for hours – sticky white sap clinging to my hands, its distinctive earthy-sweet scent becoming part of me. The rough bark left faint imprints on my thighs as I straddled a favourite branch, hidden behind by the broad, hand-shaped leaves that rustled with secrets in the slightest breeze.

I would drift off to enchanted places – imagining a different, safer, and more adventurous life, as the naughtiest girl in school.

Alongside the fence – dividing us from our Calabrian neighbours – was a high hedge of twisted, succulent, and menacing olive-green Indian prickly pear plants. They stood like contorted old men. Once transported in suitcases, now found dotted across Melbourne's wastelands or pastures.

In springtime, a sunburst of yellow, orange, and red-coloured, plump, ripe fruit – covered in little bunches of thin, short spikes – stuck out like stumpy fingers on the ends of the palm-like prickly nopales.

Whenever my parents picked this strange-tasting, dark, blood-red fruit – dotted with hard black pips, and rarely eaten – those tiny, pesky prickles would invariably end up in my little fingers.

Our garden resembled the southern Italian countryside – dotted with edible plants, not the ornamentals found in barren neighbouring Aussie gardens.

The garden was southern Italy transplanted to Australian soil – memories of home cultivated alongside food for the table, beauty secondary to survival.

Ours was a typical Italian migrant backyard. A large, sometimes fallow vegetable patch sat in front of our concrete-cladded garage. More concrete.

Sometimes, I would climb onto the peach tree to get to the garage roof top, to jump off and land in the bare veggie patch – just for the thrill of being airborne for a few seconds – much to my Mother's dismay and ineffective, hand-waving admonishments.

Our garage was half temple and half tomb – housing a concrete wine-making press like an open sarcophagus.

My friends, cousins, and I would climb into this contraption and pretend it was a sailing ship – imagining voyages to distant shores.

When I was around three years old, one sunny spring day, my Father placed some potato peels into the loose, grey soil of our veggie patch.

Some weeks later there were large dark-green potato shoots magically sprouting out of the earth. My child mind was surprised and thrilled. I smiled and clapped my hands in excitement.

How did the plants grow from potato peelings?

My love of fruit and vegetable gardening goes back to that day, if not further rooted in my DNA.

My Father was a man of paradoxes – nurturing seedlings with infinite patience yet shattering peace with a single beer.

He wasn't much of a gardener – unlike many other Italian men I knew, whose backyards overflowed with vegetable abundance.

My Father preferred chain-smoking, chatting with the neighbours, or heading to the pub to spend time with his Aussie workmates.

He chose beer over wine – as his stomach couldn't handle copious amounts of red. The smell of home-brew was more familiar to me than homemade wine.

Signor (Mr) Garisto's garden across the fence was everything ours wasn't – a living Mediterranean oasis. His entire backyard was a luscious, green food-producing machine: tomatoes, zucchini, eggplant, corn, beans, peas, basil, parsley, oregano, fennel, chillies, garlic, onions, capsicum, and lettuce.

Signor Garisto also made his own wine, tomato sauce, pork sausages, salami, and *giardiniera* (pickled vegetables). His was a much more typical Italian garden of that era.

He was married to the much taller Caterina – a tough, strong, hardworking, but uneducated woman. She spent most of her time yelling at her many children or washing clothes by hand in a large concrete laundry trough and then putting them into the washing machine to be washed again.

Their four youngest children were among my close friends during my teen years. Occasionally she would bring over her signature dish – baked eggplant stuffed with tomato, minced beef, and rice.

The brown front door stood like a portal between two realities – outside we were newly Australian, inside we were Italian.
Our modest, working-class home staged both joy and terror – wallpapered rooms filled with contradictions that shaped my understanding of family.
The centrally placed front door, with its built-in screen, opened into a small entrance foyer. Opposite it stood the only built-in cupboard in the house – always overflowing with blankets, coats, and odds and ends. It remained in disarray unless I re-organised it.
To the left, two white-framed doors with square, rough-edged, textured glass panels led into a formal living room. Its walls had once been light green.
A petrol-fuelled heater sat on the eastern wall, surrounded by a glossy black-and-brown brick hearth. Above the white mantelpiece hung a gold-gilded oval mirror. On the mantelpiece sat a black-and-white framed photo of my Father, beside a mostly naked, silver-grey Jesus nailed to a shiny brown wooden cross – about 40 cm high.
The old, worn-out grey carpet, patterned with curved red, orange, yellow, and white stripes, led into a smaller dining room. Both rooms were now dressed in floral wallpaper – gold, red, brown, and tan – more suited to a Rococo church than a suburban home.
The living room housed an ornate Italian Baroque glass cabinet, a record player with built-in speakers, and our big, brown, chunky 1980s colour TV – sans remote.
The dining room, equally Baroque, featured an oval glass-topped table surrounded by plastic-covered chairs. A glass cabinet

displayed sparkling drinking glasses – tall, short, coloured, and patterned – always reminding me of *Rose-Coloured Glasses* by Johnny Farnham.

Large black-and-white portraits of Dad's stern-looking relatives once adorned the furniture. Curiously, there were none of Mum's family. Only my elder cousin's wedding photo was allowed.

As a child, I was captivated by arranging those glasses with meticulous care. It soothed my compulsive, autistic-like tendencies.

The adjacent kitchen, facelifted in the early 1970s, remained chaotic – a mirror of Mum's hoarding.

Unlike the stereotypical Italian housewife, she thrived in disorder. Overflowing drawers and crowded benches testified to her belief that nothing should be wasted.

At the yellow-topped kitchen table, Dad taught me maths – colourful wooden Cuisenaire blocks lined up like peace offerings between storms.

Memories doubled in space – each room a stage for repeated scenes: Dad teaching me numbers at the same table where, hours later, he would rage at Mum.

The kitchen led southward to an enclosed, sun-filled veranda – a later addition – where our fridge stood beside a dark green and gold-framed dowry chest.

A light pink, glossy paint coated the rough cement-clad walls, which rose about a metre high. Above them, large glass panels and the occasional jalousie window formed the upper wall. I would carefully remove the louvre panes when I needed to break into our house as a youngster.

My bedroom sat nearby. It was both sanctuary and prison – the door a thin membrane between belonging and exclusion. I spent more time in that cocoon than anywhere else, surrounded by the ever-growing murky shadow of myself.

The pale yellow walls were papered with KISS, Queen, and Suzi Quatro – all torn from *TV Week*. My love of music, pinned up like prayer flags. A white writing desk sat beneath the window. Rearranging furniture calmed me – a habit I carried into adulthood.

Most of my bedroom furniture had once belonged to Nonna, my Father's Mother, who lived with my parents until, to my Father's displeasure, his conniving younger brother, *Zio* Giovanni, took her away – supposedly to help with childcare, but mostly to collect her aged pension. Zio was far more money-focused than Father ever was.

Cold grey lino – poorly laid – once covered the original floorboards. Its pattern resembled short, crooked ladders, with scattered coloured blocks of white, red, blue, green, and yellow – shapes that could've been lifted straight from Kandinsky's *Komposition VIII*.

When nightmares clung to me like damp sheets, I'd play guitar in the veranda, letting music trickle into the garden like a cleansing stream. One Christmas, when I was seven, Father gave me a small guitar. My fingers were too tiny to press the metal strings. I didn't learn properly until years later, but I first played on that little guitar, grateful that Father had planted the love of music in me.

Before the modern fridge, we had an old, chunky 1950s model with a pale yellow single door. Its edges were rounded, not square, and inside hung a tiny, stainless steel, doorless freezer compartment.

Mum once worked at the Nestlé factory in Campbellfield. Back then, the fridge was always stocked with boxes of chocolates, which she handed out to any young visitor. That was before my time. After I was born, she worked at the Yakka factory in Broadmeadows. I got non-trendy, daggy jeans instead.

From the veranda, you could access the small indoor laundry, where remnants of the old copper still lingered. It had since been replaced by a top-loading Westinghouse washing machine. This was where I first began handiwork as a child – under my Father's attentive supervision.

My four-year-old hands trembled with pride as I painted the architrave – each brushstroke an act of creation, not destruction – quiet evidence that his hands could guide without harm. Father always encouraged me to do and try things – to be bold, brave, and adventurous. My Mother, by contrast, was overly anxious and tightly wound. She taught me to fear the world, to shrink from it, always saying, 'Be carefulla, *fidya mia*' (Be careful, my daughter).

It was Father who emboldened me. Yet it was Mother's voice that echoed for decades after she was gone – warning, worrying, looping through my mind like a scratched record. Her words kept me vigilant, anxiety-ridden, alert to the dangers she believed were everywhere.

Between them, they planted opposing seeds – her caution, his daring – each taking root in my psyche and warring underground.

Ours was a typical 1950s house in Melbourne's outer, working-class belt – 133 Middle Street, Glenroy – twelve kilometres north of the CBD, surrounded by asphalt and absence. A house set in the middle of a suburb many called wasteland.

As I crossed West Street that day, the revelation – like all those before – didn't just shift what I knew. It reshaped who I was, one fragment at a time. The house I returned to still whispered its secrets – louder now, as though it too could no longer contain the lies.

The first truth: an abusive alcoholic Father, with undiagnosed mental health issues – a reality I navigated long before I knew the truth about my beginning.

Dad (1930s)

Dad, me, and Mum (1964)

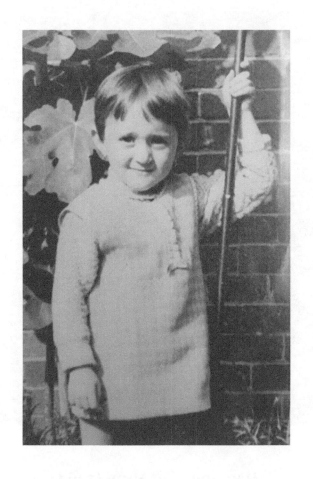

Me, 2 or 3 years old (1966)

Me, Mum, Dad (1973)

My Painting – Shattered (2017)

3

Blood, Shame, and Shattered Glass

(1964–1973)

The body remembers what the mind chose to forget.

Growing up with an alcoholic Father was a rollercoaster of conflicting emotions. The highs of his sober affectionate moments clashed jarringly with the lows of his drink-fuelled rages, leaving me perpetually off balance – never knowing which version of him I would encounter from moment to moment.

One memory stands out as a perfect encapsulation of the stomach-churning drop and fleeting elation of life with my Father. It was a bright afternoon, heavy with unseen storm clouds. He had built a Billy-cart for me, pushing me on it, up and down our long driveway. In those moments, he was an adventurous, attentive Father that I loved. In these shining moments, I basked in the pure, fleeting joy of his undivided attention.

Inevitably, the monster would return…

I want to run and hide. I want to go somewhere safe. I want you to take me away, Mother, thought my 7-year-old self.

Rereading an old journal, it takes me back to when my Father was still among the living. In the vexed topography of my relationship with my beloved Father, my memory of him is a landscape saturated with the acrid chemistry of cigarettes and stale beer, where volatile, jealous rages carved geological fault lines through my childhood.

Glass didn't just shatter. It embedded itself like shrapnel in memory – glinting each time I tried to forget. Early in life, I had developed a pattern of watching adults carefully, sensing danger before its arrival. This hypervigilance – born in the chaos of my Father's alcoholic rages – would later serve me as I pieced together fragments of my identity. I learned early to listen for what wasn't being said, to notice contradictions, to question official stories. These were survival skills then, but would become the very tools I needed to uncover my truth decades later.

These silent companions had walked with me long before I knew I was adopted. The house on Middle Street held more than just the normal challenges of growing up – it was a battleground where my Father's demons regularly took centre stage.

Due to his vices, Dad looked much older than his years. He had a mostly bald head with grey hair at the sides and back. Deep crevices lined his face. A small beer belly protruded from his medium build. He was 41 when I arrived. Dad had been a soldier in the Italian army during WWII. One of five children. The wayward middle child. Born to his Father, Nonno Giovanni's second wife. Nonno died in Italy before my parents migrated to Australia. I know little about him. He looked serious and stern in old family photos.

There weren't many times when Vastiano didn't have a cigarette in his hand. He'd light up one after the other with his strong khaki-tipped fingers and forward curving fingernails. Lighting up the next cigarette with the butt of the one he had just finished, smoking day and night. In the house. In the car. His other hand often held a smoothly curved conical-shaped beer glass filled with golden Foster's Lager or Melbourne Bitter with a thick layer of white foam at the top.

In those days, beer was commonly sold in large 750ml brown bottles. The Melbourne Bitter emblem was a crimson, royal blue, and white label, with a large crimson M in the middle. Twelve bottles in a cardboard crimson box. The same crimson as the

Fitzroy Football Club's jumper. A full box of beer always sat in our garage, near the side door – a constant in the house, like the trepidation and the looming dread of when the monster would appear.

The whiff of beer triggers unwanted childhood memories... Instead of being asleep, feeling safe, feeling nurtured, feeling loved, an intense emotional turmoil builds within. My Father, the monster, is roaming the hallway outside my bedroom. I'm sobbing in my bed, terrified, gasping at each breath.

S-stop. P-p-please... someone... make h-h-him s-stop...

Volume. Deafening. Cannot breathe. His voice – incessant – merciless – rage without end. Words lost meaning. Only hate remains. Jealousy. Morbid. Unfounded. Me. Small. Shrinking. Disappearing.

Go away! Leave us alone! Screaming in my child's mind. Tears cascade down my child's cheeks. Din continues. Helplessness chokes me. After a few years, the stinging harsh reality eventually sank in.

No one can help me. No one will come and save me. No one will hold me and make me feel safe.

I'm repeatedly left alone to endure this ritualistic nightmare. During these unpredictable rages, my Mother regressed into a childlike state, wounded, she sobs and wails, while a cold chilling loneliness seeps into my veins, freezing my heart along the way. I suppressed and buried my feelings deep inside the emptiness. The vast, growing void within. Into the vault.

Worse than this constant rage is the constant lies I'm made to tell. No one must ever know what happens in this madhouse. I would later wonder if my desperate need to uncover truth – no matter how painful – began in those years of enforced secrecy. Beneath the silence, I sensed pressure – fissures forming in our family's carefully tiled narrative.

'You mustn't tell anyone!'

The shame has been seeded. With each passing year, it grows.

Who would I tell? Who could I tell?

Who would have believed a child in the late 1960s – early 1970s?

It was on one of those nights that my Mother entered my bedroom, as I lay distressed, crying in my bed. This poor pitiful battered woman. The torment and terror etched into her face. In her brokenness she was reduced to a child again. Sobbing. Frightened. Bewildered, I stare at her.

You are supposed to protect and comfort me, the voice whispering in my despairing mind.

Drowned in her own anguish, through battered eyes, she has no room to see the helpless desperation in mine. She has no capacity to comfort or soothe me. In these moments, her daughter doesn't exist.

She climbed into my bed and helplessly, desperately cries out in vain, '*Mamma, Mamma.*'

The sad vapour of her tears seeped into my skin, blanketing my emptiness. Myriad droplets enveloping the pain, the sorrow, the despair, casting out my childhood innocence, and replacing it with a dark void.

What am I supposed to do?

She wiped between her legs and cried herself to sleep. A battered wife and her forgotten child.

Finally, silence crept through the madhouse, soothing my invisible wounds. The silence is precious. I felt exhausted. Drained. The silence plunged me to sleep, the images imprinted into my brain.

The next morning, the monster was gone. My loving, attentive Father reappeared. I had sat at the yellow kitchen table many times with him, and he helped me with my readers. Reading books such as *Dick and Jane*.

As the day wore on, I watched his demeanour shift, his steps becoming unsteady, his speech changing, becoming louder and more erratic. The clack-clack-clack of the rollercoaster chains had begun, slowly pulling us up to the peak before the inevitable plummet. By the time night had fallen, the monster had emerged, hurling insults with ferocity.

Later that night, I walked into the hallway and found him face down, motionless on the floor. My breath caught. 'What's wrong with him, mamma?' I asked. 'He's just tired. Let's get him into bed.'

I adored my Father by day, but usually at night he turned into this horrible rage-filled person, an unreachable and out of control monster. A Jekyll and Hyde. Ranting and raging. Every night. I became increasingly terrified. Each episode eroded my trust in adults until people in authority became scary and unpredictable.

I sobbed and cried, salt tears burning channels down my cheeks, the cotton pillowcase growing damp beneath my face. No one ever comforted the child. Eventually, my tears dried up – not because the pain lessened, but because the child that was me-but-not-me retreated deeper inside, like a sea creature withdrawing into its shell at the first tremor of danger. My chest still heaved with phantom sobs, but the reservoir had emptied, leaving only the hollow echo of grief in a suddenly too-quiet room. I began to observe myself through thick glass: small hands clutching the bedsheet, shoulders hunching with each inhale, voice falling silent. My body grew numb while my mind floated above it all, finding safety in this strange separation.

At night, and sometimes during the day on weekends, our solid seemingly homely clinker-brick house turned into an alcohol-fuelled infested nuthouse. At the time, I didn't understand that the beer and alcohol turned my Father into an angry, raving, uncontrollable lunatic. I just thought he was unpredictably crazy and angry.

My early childhood was an up and down of contrasting unpredictable emotions. This was the exhausting rhythm of life with someone who abused alcohol – brief glimpses of the attentive, loving Father I craved, followed inevitably by the terrifying tyranny of his addiction.

Love wasn't a sanctuary – it was a double agent, offering safety one moment and betrayal the next, its tenderness laced with shards.

Over the years, with the limited awareness and insight a child can have, I learned to brace myself for the drops, to not trust the highs, as I knew it was only a matter of time before the ride plummeted again.

In between the madness, I also have some joyful, carefree childhood memories – fast horse rides, riding around in a hand-me-down metal toy car that Dad had repainted in his Holden-matching light green, day trips with extended family to the old ricotta cheese factory in Sunbury, or the lion safari at Bacchus Marsh, but most of all, I vividly recall instances of shattered glass and blood. Lots of blood. Followed by lots of lies.

This incident remains a vivid marker of the sudden drops on the rollercoaster, the moments in which any illusion of safety or stability would shatter along with the flying glass. One sunny day, firmly etched in my memory like a scar that won't mend. I was about five years old.

The memory flickers like an old film reel, images stuttering, sound distorted. A soft pack of Peter Stuyvesant lay on the yellow kitchen table.

As a scrawny kid, I'd walk to our local milk bar on the West Street shopping strip. Sent to buy my Father's cigarettes. A white pack with gold writing. Lined with silver paper and sealed with a light and dark blue tag at the top. My timid voice would politely ask for the cigarettes and lollies, my small hand reaching up on tiptoes to place 20 cent pieces on the counter...

Dad was sitting at the table wearing a well-worn dirty white Bonds singlet and light brown shorts, his forearms grey-haired, rope-muscled, and sinewy. Mum wore a light modest floral summer dress, already wilting in the heat. I stood frozen still in our kitchen feeling small, as if I was watching Skyhooks' 6:30 News, from a great distance, everything happening on a screen lacking an off switch.

Glued to the madman who appeared at the kitchen table, beer glass catching afternoon light, cigarette between yellowed fingers, smoke curling upward like a malevolent spirit.

The volume of his voice increased as he spat out his words and thumped on the table, making the clear glass ashtray bounce up and down with each impact. The cigarette butts inside dancing a macabre jig. With each booming thud, the dreaded anticipation charged through my veins like ice water. The pounding in my chest furiously increased like a wild caged animal seeking escape. There was only one exit point. Slowly, I floated up toward the ceiling. A safer viewing point. Cornered yet again, Mum stood with her back to the sink. Her arms folded like armour across her chest. Head slightly lowered in that familiar submissive posture. Inverted lips pressed together. A deep furrow between her eyebrows, forced to listen to another of his rants, waiting for the storm to worsen.

As the horror movie unfolded frame by predictable frame, I shrank into the corner. Two worried little eyes peered into this murky scene from a face trying to make itself invisible. Frozen in time. Images imprinting themselves on my developing brain. Madman. Ashtray. Movement razor-sharp. Spinning. Ash scattering. Butts floating. Air trembling.

Trajectory: Mother's forehead.

Blood. Red. Flowing. Red rivers down white face.

Couldn't move. Couldn't help. Couldn't breathe.

Couldn't be here, but nowhere else to go. Small. Smaller. Disappeared but still able to witness.

Blood kept coming. Coming. Coming.

'*Mamma mia!*' Piercing the air.

The stills turn to motion. I quickly averted my eyes to my Mum and back to the ashtray. Now a projectile weapon, the ashtray spun in slow motion, cigarette ash and cigarette butts twirled and cascaded into the air. My Mother's forehead, just above her eye suddenly stopped the trajectory of the airborne ashtray. Pierced her skin and my heart simultaneously. Thick red blood trickled down over her left eye, down the side of her nose, and invisibly down my cheeks. The all-too-familiar pitiful and helpless cries followed, '*Mamma mia, Mamma mia,*' shocked me back into my tiny body.

...Before we left for the nearby doctor's surgery, I was told the lie. Mum clumsily walked into a door...

Like a wounded and scared animal, my Mother was lying on a sterile medical bed at the local medical clinic. The old grey-haired, stern-looking male doctor wore a white coat. My Mother let out a piercing scream with each stitch. Mum's eye was puffy and red. Inside, I became lifeless and dead. The relentless bloody melodrama continued.

Each unpredictable outburst was another jarring turn on the rollercoaster of my childhood, leaving me disoriented and clinging to any semblance of stability. Long after the wounds had scabbed over, the shards of that memory remained – not swept away, but reassembled in a shape I didn't yet recognise.

And then, despite the turmoil, moments of genuine joy would return – the exhilaration of learning to ride my first bicycle on our driveway with his careful directions and guidance. From these precious moments I developed a sense of adventure and self-confidence. These fleeting highs were almost more painful than the lows, as they held the promise of a different life, a different father, one that was always just out of reach.

1971

In my seventh year of life, on another hot summer's day. A rare daytime visit from the madman. The green monster sat on our old dark green couch, the light-green-walled lounge room a backdrop as he sits in front of a thick glass-topped coffee table. The ever-present chalice in his hand filled with the blood of his God. He drank his golden fluid again. Ranted and raged. The child learnt to quickly retreat. It felt numb and small. It levitated and watched yet another horror scene unfolding. He accused Mum of having an affair because a man sat next to her on the bus. She recounted this story many times later when I was an adult.

Mum was on the bus coming home from work. The grey-balding man sat next to her. They engaged in idle chatter. My Father boarded the bus. He sat near my Mum and this man. Later, at home, he interrogated her in a jealous rage for the umpteenth time.

'Why did you talk to him?'
'Why did you look at him?'
'What did he want?'
'Why did he sit next to you?'

He wanted her to admit that she was having an affair with him, when she wasn't.

His tirade gathered momentum and volume. His pulsating veins bulged on his forehead as he fired out the angry, baseless words. The irrational madness had taken over.

The child silently watched, with anticipatory doom, chest hurt with each thump. Nowhere to go.

My Mother sat silently. Pouting. Like a child being scolded. Anything she said would make the situation worse.

The madness can't be stopped. There is no reasoning with the unreasonable.

The glass in his right hand was forcibly lowered onto the glass-topped coffee table, it sent the beer to the top of the glass. Motion slowed. Then, like the crescendo of voices, cymbals and drums in *'O Fortuna from Carmina Burana'*, the beer glass smashed into the table as he punctuated his last words. *Boom! Boom! Boom! Clash! Clash! Clash!* Over and over again I saw the glass crashing down, down, down and shattering. Shattering. Shattering. Tiny shards of thin beer glass rocketed off the table. The thick, frothy puddle on the table began to turn a swirly orangey red. Blood red. Thick blood spurted out like a small Roman fountain from Dad's hand through multiple cuts.

My Mother, always useless in the company of blood, ran around the house, in her now familiar refrain, *'Mamma mia, Mamma* mia! (My God!). *Dio aiutami!* (God help me!)'

My Father found a bath towel and wrapped it around his blood-dripping hand.

Somehow, he drove himself to a hospital, but not before I was told another elaborate lie... 'My Father was cleaning a glass light fitting in their bedroom and it fell, cutting his hand...' The lie morphed into reality when my Father had later taken down the light fitting in their bedroom and hidden it.

Some days later, I sat in my classroom. My now cheerful and normal looking Father dropped me off at school. His arm was wrapped in thick white bandages from his right elbow to his right fingertips. The teacher – not my usual one – stood in front of the class and asked, 'What happened to your father's hand?' It doesn't initially register that she was talking to me because she was cross-eyed.

She repeats, 'What happened to your father's hand?'

When I realised, she was speaking to me I wanted to sink into the floorboards that we were sitting on. I want them to swallow me up. Meekly, I replied with the lie I had been told to tell.

A burning hot flush covered my innocent young face. Naked shame filled my tiny body. The lies. The secrecy. 'Don't tell anyone.' Shame became embedded in my every sinew and tattooed on my forehead. With each episode, new layers of shame and terror.

It was lunchtime and the three of us were sitting in the kitchen eating.

He had been drinking, again.

He had started up with his wild delusions, again. His morbid jealousies. No, not again. The familiar shrinking feeling. Mum wore the familiar helpless look. The battle lines, etched on her face, tell of the horrors that she had been through for the past 20 years since they were first married. She was silently trapped. If she spoke, he said she was lying. If she said nothing, he said, she was guilty.

She chose to say nothing.

The verbal onslaught escalated.

My chest thumped. *Ba-boom. Ba-boom.* I froze. He had a bottle of beer in his hand. He flung it from the table in the kitchen through the back door into our veranda. It somersaulted through the air and then smashed, like the sound of distant thunder, onto the pink wall of the veranda and exploded into pieces. Foamy beer dripped down the wall and collected in a frothy puddle on the ground. Just another madhouse day.

School as Solace

In between the unpredictable chaos at home, school was one of my saviours. My safe space. It was my solace and provided my salvation. I could momentarily forget what happened in our secret madhouse. My life soon became a cycle of intense nighttime dread and then daily reprieve.

I went to Hadfield Primary School (PS476/87), now a housing estate. Each morning I'd walk or ride my bike, the one-kilometre trek to school. I was then still able to immerse myself in my surroundings. Along the way, I would delight at seeing my favourite big English oak tree, its curly brown leaves and the cute acorns it dropped in late winter. I memorised the names of all the streets between home and school: Tassell to Davies streets.

I simply loved going to school. I engrossed myself in reading, learning, writing, drawing, and doing maths. My mind was a sponge, absorbing it all. My intellect was my saviour, as was my intense need to burn that pent up terror.

Before school, during lunchtime, and recesses, I excitedly ran around on the grey bitumen that surrounded the grey-clad box-like classrooms with white-framed square awning windows and I played various sports and games with my many school friends. I had boundless nervous energy to expend.

I rarely sat still at playtime, unlike many of the other girls.

The boys and girls were segregated, and we had to keep to our separate sections of the large school grounds. It was grossly unfair that the boys had the whole, green-grassed footy ground, at least a third of the school area, to run around in, while the girls were restricted to a tiny section on the hard grey asphalt that included a cream-coloured wooden shelter shed. We invented games. On the wooden benches, we ran back and forth through the dark brown posts that held up the shed roof. The fastest won.

One of the few times that I dared venturing into the boys' section, I played kick to kick with a male friend. The teacher on yard duty caught my serious gendered transgression and promptly sent me to my classroom.

Resentfully, I wrote out one hundred times in a small exercise book, 'I must not play in the boys' yard.'

From a young age I learned that there were distinct differences and privileges between males and females, which were reinforced at home in my Italian upbringing. Not much changed over the ensuing decades.

I liked being active and I enjoyed running; and soon discovered that I was a good middle-distance runner. In my final year at primary school, we had a sports day. I ran the fastest 400 metres for the boys and the girls. Then, I ran as a teenager, and I kept on running as an adult. I even ran in my dreams. Constantly running away from the madman and the demons he left behind. From a young age, I vowed to be no man's woman. Especially a violent, drinking man like my Dad.

As I grew older, the rollercoaster's peaks and valleys only intensified. The good times felt higher, as I clung to any scrap of normalcy or affection. But the bad times plunged me into ever darker depths, as my Father's rages became more volatile and my sense of helplessness more acute.

Despite his alcohol-fuelled craziness, I loved my Father greatly, unlike my Mother who felt more like the home help when my Father was around.

I don't recall much interaction with her, except for the single Pebbles-like ponytail she'd roughly tie on the top of my head.

She insisted on embarrassing me with as a young child.

Mum wasn't a physically affectionate kind of person until I was a teenager, when I no longer wanted her hugs. I couldn't have known then how dramatically our relationship would change after my Father's death, or how those changes would shape my understanding of family.

As a child, I felt that I had to choose between my Mother and my Father. Dad's insecurities and jealousies wouldn't allow my love to be shared between them. Besides, he was much more fun to be around. He would spend quality time with me, and we did exhilarating things together.

On weekends we got into his light green box-shaped Holden Special. I would sit in the passenger side or in the middle if Mum was with us – and we would roam around Melbourne visiting his many relatives: brothers, cousins, nieces, and nephews. His Mother, Nonna Ninfa lived with his brother, my Zio Giovanni, his wife, my two cousins. They lived the closest – just 1.2 km away, walking distance in Princess Street, Pascoe Vale.

But even in the darkest moments, there were glimmers of the man he could be when sober – the father who loved music and bought me my first guitar at age seven. My Father liked to listen to a variety of music, from Italian folk and contemporary music, pop, rock, to classical, and opera music. *La Bohème. Barber of Seville.*

He once purchased an old reel to reel tape player. On this he would record music from records, so that you could listen to music for hours on end and not have to flip a record every 15 minutes. My Father's version of streaming.

Our house was filled with the sounds of music, when it wasn't filled with the sounds of lunacy or despair. The first single I bought was *'Raindrops Keep Fallin' on My Head'* (1970) by Johnny Farnham. The B side was *One*. I still have this record.

My Father was a good, kind, loving Father, brother, son, cousin, friend, neighbour, and workmate, but an insecure, jealous, lousy, and abusive husband. I never saw any affection between my parents. Instead of calling her by her name or some term of endearment, he called her '*Signora*' (Mrs). He abused my Mother verbally and physically.

It started long before I was born – back in Sicily. I never witnessed the violence my Father inflicted on my Mother, but I would hear about it years later. What I heard was worse than anything I had seen. She would often be left black and blue. She would escape to her sister's house, but after a day or two, they would always sent her back to her abusive husband. Divorce was not an option.

As an adult, I would often look back and wonder if my Father was physically or sexually abused as a child, or he suffered trauma during WWII as a young soldier. His self-medication indicated that he probably had suffered repeated trauma, abuse or both.

Often, in my presence he would talk to himself, as if he was deep in conversation with someone else. *Was he hallucinating, alcohol affected, or both?* None of these excused his violence, but they might explain his excessive drinking and smoking. He was a troubled man. I only knew him through a child's mind – the why was always just out of reach.

As I grew older, his alcohol rages caused me deep and lasting trauma. His rants kept me awake at night, when, as a young child, I should have been safely asleep. During his alcohol fuelled rages, my child's needs were unmet. There was no love, no nurturing, no care, and definitely no comforting. My little mind was left to fend for itself: To interpret, to make sense of the madman and the chaos he inflicted.

One day, sometime after my ninth birthday, I was walking through the back veranda. I vividly recall wishing that my Father was dead. Soon after that, he died.

December 1973

It was December 1973. My Father had bought camping equipment. A huge cream-coloured canvas tent. Matching cream-coloured wooden camp cots. A camp table and chairs. A small portable gas stove. Dad put up the tent in the back yard. A new excitement filled the air. We were going to go on our first big family adventure, along with Zio's family who had recently bought a caravan.

Before that fateful summer, we often went to Phillip Island. I remember sitting on the sand beneath the night sky, watching the little fairy penguins waddle past on the soft, cold, orange beach. I saw my first koalas in the tall eucalypts overhead. We'd stay for a few days, sleeping overnight in the car. The single front seat of Dad's Holden folded down flat into a makeshift bed, just big enough for the three of us.

One dark night as we slept amongst the trees, a police officer tapped on the window as he shone his flashlight into the car. 'Hey, move along! You can't sleep here!'

My love of nature and adventure extends back to those happier days.

The last time I saw my Father alive was Christmas night, 1973. I was almost nine and a half years old. He was almost 51. We had come home from a large Christmas family gathering. I found a large rubber dinghy under our small light-green tinsel Christmas tree.

By this stage, I knew there was no *Padre Chrisimissa*, as we'd leave home Christmas eve with nothing under the tree for me. Dad would disappear during the night, and when we got home, there would be a big present under the tree. Perhaps the rubber dinghy was intended to come along on our impending camping trip.

As I gazed up at the clock on the wall, the small hand pointed to 12 and the large hand was 11. The house was unusually quiet. My Mother, my Father, and I stood around our kitchen table, with its shiny chrome frames. Chunky pieces of silky white Italian bread with a light-crunchy crust and hard peppered pecorino cheese lay on a wooden chopping board, next to a bowl of salty dried black olives. There was no ranting or raving on what would be our final night together – our last supper. I happily kissed my parents good night and went to bed.

It was a rare quiet night.

The next morning, I awoke to my Father's absence. This was quite unusual for a weekend or public holiday. As we stood in our bathroom, next to the blue basin, I asked my Mother, 'Where's *Papà*?'

'He's in hospital. He couldn't breathe during the night, last night. He asked me to open the windows to let in the air so he could breathe. He said, *'Michelina, aiutami! Sulu tu mi poi aiutari!* (Help me! Only you can help me!). I called Zio Giovanni, and he came and drove him to the hospital, as Papà gasped for air.'

Later that morning, Mum and I walked the short distance to Zio's house. As the adults – Mum, Zio, his wife, and Nonna Ninfa, who was still customarily dressed in black, mourning her long-dead husband, sat in sombre silence around the kitchen, I quietly played with my younger cousin outside, oblivious to the severity of the unfolding situation.

Dread, anticipation, sadness hung in the air. Zio Giovanni and my older cousin went to visit my Dad at the Royal Melbourne Hospital that morning. He solemnly asked about me. Later that day, the older cousin went into their hallway to call the hospital to see how my Dad was doing. He was the one amongst us with the best grasp of English. We all sat around in the kitchen waiting for the news.

My cousin slowly walked around the long dark hallway, towards the well-lit kitchen. As his body came into clearer view, tears were streaming down his sad and young contorted face. He entered the room and gave a thumb's down. His favourite uncle was dead. My Father had died alone, around 2:30 pm on Boxing Day, in a hospital bed. His death certificate would list chronic bronchitis as his cause of death. In truth, he died of chronic smoking.

Dad was a stonemason back in the old hometown, he started his smoking habit as a young boy. He had been told by his doctor many times to quit but couldn't. His demons, whatever they were, were too powerful. The nicotine addiction too entrenched. His lungs ravaged by emphysema would have resembled the crumbled-up buildings of Gaza, rained upon by bombs that I'd seen on TV recently.

That day, I learned death is quiet, sudden, and forever. Shortly after the phone call, we all returned to our home in Glenroy. The adults were dressed in obligatory black mourning outfits. Then the never-ending stream of shocked and distressed relatives, friends, and neighbours arrived. My inconsolable Mother sat outside, shaking and wailing uncontrollably. Later, a doctor would inject her with something to medicate her grief. From that moment on, she took Valium or Serapax daily.

The adults moved and spoke around me, seemingly oblivious to my shock, pain, and confusion. I didn't cry and from then on, rarely cried in the front of others. I stuffed away my emotions, along with the others I had carefully buried over the years. I never made a scene in public. I didn't draw attention to myself. My older Cousin, Francesca, arrived. She came over to me and gave me a warm, knowing hug – the only adult who comforted me and acknowledged my grief. I cried on the inside. From then on, I cried myself to sleep – on nights that would soon become eerily quiet.

The Funeral

The last time I saw my Father's body was at the Tobin Brothers funeral home in North Melbourne. The large strangely quiet viewing room was packed with relatives dressed in black. My Father's modest light brown coffin lay open in the centre of the room. I walked up to the coffin. He lay stiffly. Quietly. He was wearing a new pale purple blue suit, a much lighter shade than his dark purple-red lips. I went outside. The hot sun beaming down. I threw up in the bushes. Nobody noticed or cared.

The last time I saw my Father's coffin was on a hot summer's day, as it was being lowered into his grave at the Fawkner

Cemetery. He was the third eldest child, but the first of his adult siblings to die. Many of the adults were crying and the women were wailing. Italians do grief well. They don't hold it in, but they do hang onto it for years. Nonna Ninfa still wore black for her long dead husband, and now for her eldest son.

Soon after the funeral, Dad's Holden Special was sold. The brand-new tent and the camping gear were returned to the shop to my great disappointment.

Though I never went camping with my Father, I later came to love the outdoors. I carry my Father's legacy in many ways.

My Mother eventually went back to work. I would go to my Uncle's house to be looked after by my stern, ancient looking Nonna Ninfa for the remainder of the summer school holidays. One day my male cousin and his younger sister and I were swimming in their round above ground swimming pool with a neighbour Jonah. My cousin decided it would be fun to swim around with our pants down. I felt uneasy watching their appendages bob in the blue plastic water. This was a strange game.

Then, my older, taller, stronger male cousin took me to the side of the house, out of view of the others. He scooped me up and momentarily rubbed his erection between my legs.

One day, he had me in the garage. He locked the door so his younger sister couldn't come in. He sat me on his lap. My pants were down. He was touching me between my legs. He put my tiny hand on his erection and motioned it up and down. I was confused. Not knowing what to make of what was happening.

I felt helpless in these situations. I froze. I was unable to scream or call out. Already, conditioned to believe that no one would help me, and I didn't know at that time that what he did was wrong and inappropriate.

One day after these events had happened, my Mother said 'Don't let him or any boy touch you in your private parts.'

A burning sting engulfed my tiny body. Her words were far too late. I froze and said nothing.

Now I knew what he had been doing was wrong and shameful. Soon after my Mother's warning, the cousin and I were standing near his garage door entrance. He was trying to coerce me into being sexually molested again.

As frightened as I was, I bravely said, 'No, I don't want to do this anymore.'

The sexual abuse that I wrongly believed was child's play, which had lasted only a few months, thankfully stopped, but the shame lived with me for at least the next 40 years.

Despite the trauma of my Father's death, what followed was an unexpected period of calm. The chaos that had defined home evaporated with my Father's last breath. No more waiting for the monster to emerge after his fifth beer, no more listening for the subtle change in his voice that signalled danger approaching. The silence that descended wasn't just the absence of his voice – it was the absence of fear itself. It was a silence that left the first hairline fracture in the glass that had held my childhood together.

My Father and me (about 1965)

4

The Brief Calm (1974–1978)

Even calm hummed with what had come before

December 1973 marked both an ending and a beginning. My Father's sudden death at 51 shattered our family narrative – yet paradoxically, it ushered in the only true stability I would know as a child. The chaos that had defined our home disappeared with his last breath. No more waiting for the monster to emerge after his fifth beer, no more listening for the subtle shift in his voice signalling danger. The silence that followed wasn't merely the absence of sound – it was a void so profound it became a presence.

In the vacuum left by my Father's volatility, a different kind of existence began to take shape. Our small clinker-brick house, once a pressure vessel of tension and unpredictability, gradually transformed into something unfamiliar, a tranquil haven. The very walls that had contained years of terror now sheltered a fragile peace.

Nights that had once been punctuated by shouting and raging became quiet enough to hear the gentle ticking of the kitchen clock, the distant calls of neighbourhood children, the rustle of leaves in the trees in our garden. I marvelled at ordinary domestic sounds I'd never noticed before – the TV in the background, or the comforting creak of floorboards under familiar footsteps.

Games and Creativity

Necessity made me resourceful and inventive – a child learning to channel my hypervigilance and hyperactivity into creativity. I transformed the neglected space between our garage and back fence into a miniature shop – my first act of world-building. This invented world gave me what I needed most: control, order, rules that didn't change. I pinned up the posters I had pulled out of the *TV Week* on the walls around me, assigning a price to each, usually 10 or 20 cents. The local children would join this elaborate game and, to my surprise, bought them.

My creative endeavours extended beyond play. I dismantled my bicycle, painted it light purple, and rebuilt it – a quiet triumph. The chain clicked, the paint shimmered, and for a moment, the world made sense. When I tried the same with a transistor radio, I couldn't put it back together, but the attempt taught me more than success might have. I learned that some systems, once disassembled, resist easy reconstitution – that wholeness, once shattered, demands more than mechanical reassembly.

The creative instinct that drove me to these projects wasn't merely distraction but salvation – each construction an island of order in a sea of uncertainty. I arranged my bedroom with almost ritualistic precision, positioning each object according to some internal logic that brought comfort.

I decorated the walls with posters torn carefully from magazines, creating a visual landscape that reflected my adolescent tastes. It reflected my desire to surround myself with images of worlds beyond our suburb, lives different from my own.

Weekends and holidays revolved around visiting relatives scattered across Melbourne's sprawling 1970s suburbs. We often took public transport to North Melbourne to visit Zia Maria, who now lived alone in the same house she'd occupied for decades. The journey itself became an adventure – trams lurching along tracks laid before my birth, buses navigating streets whose names I memorised like incantations, trains offering glimpses into backyards, colourful graffiti, and lives usually hidden from view. Each journey was both a geographical and psychological displacement.

The Vic Market became a source of wonder – its kaleidoscope of colours, mingling aromas, vendors' melodic calls, and constant movement of shoppers creating a sensory tapestry that seemed to contain the entire world within its boundaries.

I would walk beside my Mother through the bustling crowd, marvelling at the oceanic abundance of the seafood section, the aroma of the sea, the jewel-like displays of sweet-smelling fruits and vegetables, the seeds in hessian sacks, the smell of flesh and blood, and the hanging carcasses in the meat hall that simultaneously repelled and fascinated.

Above all, I enjoyed and looked forward to staying over at my eldest Cousin Francesca's place, the only maternal cousin who lived in Australia, in another flat and desolate northern suburb of Lalor. Her Mother, Zia Concettina, was my Mother's eldest sister. Zia came to Australia in the late 1940s with her Sicilian husband and their 3-year-old daughter, Francesca, known as Franca. From a young age, one needed mental acuity to keep up with our convoluted naming traditions. I never met this Aunty, as she tragically died at 29 from breast cancer, adding to my Mother's grief-stricken family montage. I had been told that Zia was a good scholar, more like me and unlike my Mother. She liked to read and recite poetry. As the eldest, she oversaw the four younger ones. In every single old family portrait, she looks solemn and sad, and much older than her young years.

Perhaps her gaze in photographs already contained the cancer that would claim her, death's shadow visible in her eyes years before diagnosis. *What grief was she carrying?*

Zia's daughter eloped in her late teens, with a Sicilian man, Francesco, known as Cicciu or Frank. They were now married with three young children. Amongst other things, my cousin, Francesca, introduced me to Chinese fried rice, bean sprouts, and pancakes. This was a welcome reprieve from the almost constant Italian cuisine punctuated by the occasional Aussie fare of fish and chips, pies, and pasties, which had been my culinary experience up to the age of 10.

In her home, I discovered what family could be when undistorted by rage and beer – a circle of warmth with me drawn into its centre rather than hovering at its ragged edge. At her place, I felt like I was finally part of the happy family I had longed for. I joyfully played with my two younger cousins outside, never supervised by adults. We played chasey under vast blue skies across sunburnt fields where lilac artichoke thistles stood like sentinels. It was freedom. We gleefully and forbiddingly jumped on beds, rather than the trampoline in the backyard, suddenly stopping when an adult walked into the bedroom to see what the ruckus was about.

We rode on roller skates on bumpy concrete pavements. Whenever we fell and scraped our knees, bloodied and bruised, we got up, and cheerfully continued.

Beneath beaming hot summer suns, we swam in a neighbour's pool, often getting sunburnt.

In the evenings we'd all sit around the dining table and enjoy an Italian feast. Pasta was almost always on the menu. Life was peaceful. Simple. Carefree.

I was happy and my Mum smiled more often.

1974–1977

Mum and I grew increasingly closer during these years, our relationship transforming from the fearful co-dependency of my Father's era to something warmer and more genuine. Our house became the neighbourhood hangout for local Italian kids – my Mother's natural warmth, infectious laughter, and the perpetual offer of food drawing them like moths to a flame.

She would feed whoever appeared at our door, setting extra places at the table without comment, extending the bounty of our modest means in the way of women who have known scarcity. This open-door policy created a kind of extended family, a community of children and adolescents who drifted in and out of our home following the ebb and flow of hunger, boredom, and the need for company.

Life felt more carefree without my Father's volatile presence, though his absence created its own burden. I felt increasingly different from my peers. All my friends had fathers and family cars; they took holidays and enjoyed family outings that remained beyond our means as a single-parent household. I sometimes missed him despite not missing his alcoholic rages – a confusing emotional tangle that taught me early how love and trauma could become inseparably interwoven. This paradox – mourning someone whose presence had caused such damage – was an early lesson in the complexity of human emotion, in the ability to hold contradictory feelings simultaneously without resolution.

1st Trip to New York (December 1975)

In late 1975, I discovered we had more family in New York – a fact I'd completely forgotten, or perhaps never fully registered in the self-absorption of early childhood. My Mother, illiterate and possibly dyslexic, relied on our neighbour to read letters from her Mother and sisters. After one such reading, Mum announced we were going to New York because her 77-year-old Mother, Nonna Gaetana, was ill. The news sent excitement coursing through me – a journey to the other side of the world by plane, to family I barely remembered, through airports and skies I had only seen in movies.

This revelation of extended family was like discovering a missing puzzle piece I hadn't known was missing – another realm of belonging that had existed parallel to my life in Melbourne, invisible yet consequential. The knowledge that I was connected to people in distant places expanded my sense of possibility, suggesting that identity wasn't limited to immediate geography but could stretch across oceans and continents.

In late December 1975, we boarded a Pan Am plane to New York – our first flight. The journey took a gruelling 32-36 hours, our bodies suspended between time zones as we crossed the International Date Line, a liminal experience that seemed to physically enact the psychological suspension I would later experience between identities. The airplane itself was a marvel to me – an enormous metal container somehow defying gravity, carrying hundreds of strangers united only by their temporary displacement.

I marvelled at the long, deep sea of lights as we approached John F. Kennedy International Airport. Upon disembarking, three aunts, three uncles, Nonna, and seven cousins greeted us warmly. Arms intertwined, bodies hugged, kisses on both cheeks, tears, laughter, and joy. I was overwhelmed by all these loud, joyful, funny-sounding strangers, who were simultaneously family.

The airport scene remains vivid in memory – the flood of faces sharing features with my Mother, the hurricane of Italian dialect and American-accented English that enveloped us, the embraces that seemed to physically reconnect us to a family line that had been stretched thin by migration.

In that moment of reunion, I glimpsed what biological connection looks like when acknowledged and celebrated – the unspoken recognition in similar gestures, the familiar cadence of shared laughter – the casual recognition of shared traits, the unquestioned belonging that would later become the object of my most painful yearning.

New York dazzled me with its abundance and variety. Everything seemed magnified: skyscrapers casting long shadows across streets teeming with unprecedented diversity, oversized automobiles gleaming with chrome and confidence, and expansive houses filled with appliances that seemed to belong to a different century than our modest Melbourne home.

These American Italians differed notably from the Aussie-Italians I'd grown up with – their accents, fashions, and lifestyles transformed by different patterns of assimilation. There were no vegetable gardens or fruit trees, no chicken coops, or rabbit hutches. Their multi-storey houses featured large basements, staircases, and colour TVs instead of backyard produce. No one made homemade wine, tomato sauce, sausages, or salami; everything came from oversized stores in packaging that seemed unnecessarily elaborate.

Being there during winter allowed me to experience snow for the first time – a phenomenon I had only seen in Christmas cards and Hollywood movies. A thick white blanket transformed everything, rendering the familiar strange and the strange magical. From Nonna's bedroom window, I would stare mesmerised as snowflakes drifted gently down through the streetlamp's glow, watching squirrels scurrying about. Part of a collective beauty that transformed the urban landscape. The snow seemed to muffle the city's usual cacophony, creating a strange acoustic intimacy that made even busy streets feel momentarily still and private.

We shared countless family meals and celebrations filled with joy and clamour but without the drunkenness and volatility I'd known at home. The food was abundant and varied – plates of antipasto, pasta dishes in sauces I had never tasted, meats prepared in ways that differed subtly from our Melbourne versions, occasional desserts that combined Italian tradition with American excess. These shared meals were more than nourishment; they were ritual reinforcements of family bonds, tangible expressions of love, care, and belonging.

I was surprised to observe how my Mother transformed in this setting, how she blossomed – without my Father's coercive, controlling ways – among her own loving family, in the presence of her beloved Mother, how her posture loosened, her raucous laughter came more readily, her gestures expanded. This was a woman, transformed back to her days before marrying my Father. A woman I had never seen or known.

One dark, wintery night, Nonna slipped on icy pavement and broke her wrist. Soon after, she fell in her bedroom while getting out of bed, breaking her hip. Each evening at mealtime, a nightly ritual, I would help her walk from her bedroom to the kitchen, offering my small frame as support for her now fragile one. I once heard her remark strangely to my Mother, 'Thank God you have this child.' The comment passed without explanation, but its peculiarity registered somewhere in my consciousness – a pebble dropped into still water, creating ripples that would only become visible years later when I understood the context it lacked at the time.

As we shared many family gatherings in Staten Island, I was witnessing the result of what historians called 'chain migration' – the process where one family member establishes a foothold in a new country, then brings others across the ocean, one by one creating a transplanted village. My Aunt's journey at 14, my Mother's reluctant crossing at 24 – these weren't isolated choices but links in a human chain stretching across continents and decades. As I passed dishes at the dinner table, I was participating in the final acts of a migration story that had begun long before my birth.

We stayed in New York until Easter 1976. Our departure was tearful – the family gathered at the airport, embraces that didn't want to end, promises to write and visit that everyone knew would be difficult to keep given the vast distance and expense of travel. It would be the first and last time I would see my beloved Nonna – the kindest, gentlest presence of my childhood. My Mother inherited these traits, along with a wild temperament. We returned to Australia, where I finished my last year of primary school with an American accent, cursive handwriting, and a heavy heart that ached for the warmth and chaos of my extended family.

The New York experience had shown me something profound: what family could be at its healthiest. Not perfect – there were still arguments, tensions, and the occasional raised voices – but fundamentally secure, unshakably rooted in mutual recognition and unconditional belonging. The contrast with Melbourne was stark – a silent benchmark for future reckonings.

Mother and Daughter

As the years passed, Mum and I grew even closer. I don't recall any heated arguments during this time.

During this period, a door-to-door encyclopaedia salesman convinced my Mother that I needed the Encyclopaedia Britannica. Though the expense was significant for our limited budget, she signed the contract – investing in my education in a way that reflected her values despite her own limited schooling.

I devoured the volumes along with dictionaries, thesauruses, manuals – anything with spine and purpose.

I collected books of fiction and non-fiction as others collected stamps and swap cards.

I lost myself in worlds created by Enid Blyton, experiencing midnight feasts and boarding school escapades far from my suburban Melbourne reality. I soon graduated to Agatha Christie, drawn to stories where chaos resolved into pattern, where the incomprehensible became – through logic and observation – suddenly clear.

In fiction, I found maps. Ways to shape fragments into form, to impose story on disorder.

I happily spent hours in my room, blissfully immersed in books that transported me beyond the limitations of my circumstances. The characters became friends and teachers – blueprints for possible selves.

Heroines who overcame obstacles through intellect rather than beauty, especially captured my imagination: Elizabeth Bennet's independence, Jane Eyre's quiet determination, and Nancy Drew's sharp-eyed enquiry. These fictional girls and women offered models of femininity that differed from those around me – expanding the boundaries of what a girl from Glenroy might dare to become.

In school, I flourished academically, my natural intelligence finally finding proper channels for expression now that the constant anxiety of my Father's years had subsided. Teachers noticed and encouraged my abilities. For the first time, I began to develop a sense of self based on achievement rather than survival – an identity anchored in what I could do rather than what I could endure.

This shift was profound, laying groundwork for the professional self I would later construct as a psychologist and academic, a self defined by intellectual exploration and contribution rather than mere reaction to circumstances.

Music provided another avenue for self-expression and connection. The soundtrack of these years ranged from classical music, Italian folk songs my Mother hummed while cooking, to the latest pop hits. I'd listen to these on my small record player in my bedroom, staying awake past bedtime to catch the top 40 countdown. I saved pocket money for months to buy my first record player, a modest unit that nevertheless represented tremendous luxury to me. The physicality of records fascinated me – the grooves that somehow contained music, the ritual of carefully placing the needle, the warm crackle before the first notes emerged. Music offered both escape and belonging, connecting me to a wider creative world while also providing solitary comfort during introspective moments.

Late at night, I would sometimes awaken with a start, disoriented by the silence. My ears strained in the darkness, waiting for footsteps that wouldn't come, or for a door to slam that remained closed. The quiet itself became unsettling – too complete, too undisturbed. My shoulders remained tense even in sleep, my jaw often sore in the morning from clenching through dreams I couldn't remember. The peaceful days stretched into months, yet my body remembered what my mind tried to forget. It would take decades for this physical memory to fade, for my limbic system to accept that danger had passed.

These years between my Father's death and my Mother's remarriage represent a rare plateau of stability in an otherwise tumultuous landscape – a temporary respite that allowed for development and exploration rather than mere survival. Though the plateau would eventually give way to new upheavals, the growth that occurred during this period was real and lasting, creating a foundation that would help me weather future storms.

Even stillness collects dust – on the bookshelf, on the encyclopaedia spines, on the mirror frame. Each particle a memory waiting to be disturbed.

These were the quiet years, held by something less than gold, but enough to keep me intact.

As this interlude ended with my Mother's unexpected interest in the man who would become my stepfather, I couldn't yet recognise the pattern that was forming: cycles of stability and disruption, belonging and displacement, integration and fragmentation that would characterise my life's journey.

Each cycle would bring both loss and discovery, each disruption creating space for new understanding. The peaceful years had provided essential nourishment for the lost years that would follow – a reservoir of security I could draw upon when everything else seemed uncertain.

5

The Intruder (1978–1982)

A porcelain vessel splintered without a sound

The five years following my Father's death had given my Mother and me the opportunity to develop a different kind of relationship – one built on shared activities rather than shared fear. I discovered the joy of simply being a child – unburdened by the constant anticipation of chaos, shoulders lighter from a weight I hadn't known I carried. I became a curator of small orders – rearranging my bicycle like a puzzle, building a shop from empty space, organising my Father's tools into silent defiance.

This interlude of quiet bliss all came to a sudden halt when my stepfather – an unwelcome stranger – thrust himself into our lives at the beginning of my teenage years.

This period of relative peace was shattered when my Mother uttered the words that would begin another chapter of upheaval: 'He's a good man,' she told me with an unfamiliar excitement. 'He has a steady job. He doesn't drink.' These qualities – being employed and sober – seemed to constitute her entire criterion for a worthy partner.

Mum was introduced to him around mid-1978. They had a snap engagement two months later and married soon after. The stranger came to visit one day. Then, suddenly, he was there every night – a thorny presence where serenity used to live.

I recall the first time I saw him. He looked like a relic from the 1960s. He was wearing an old dark blue suit that was his station master's uniform. He smelled of mothballs and Brylcreem – the staleness of another era clinging to him. His stench was repulsive. His handshake was weak, hot, and sweaty. He had none of my Father's charisma, cheeky smile, or warmth that appeared when my Father wasn't being taken over by the monster.

He was boring and uninspiring. His arrival was tectonic – imperceptible shifts gradually destabilising the psychological foundations I had meticulously reconstructed after my Father's death.

How could I tell her that her craving for stability threatened the fragile peace we had only just begun to trust? I had finally found my place in our small two-person family – I wasn't ready to be displaced again.

The first time he entered our home, I watched him with the quiet intensity of a child who's learnt that safety can shift with the slightest change in tone. He was quiet, unassuming – nothing like my Father's explosive personality. That should have reassured me. Instead, it made him harder to read, more unsettling in his ordinariness.

'*Che pensi?*' (What do you think?), my Mother asked after he left, her voice hopeful.

'He seems nice,' I lied, as cracks crept beneath the surface of everything we'd just rebuilt. I would come home to find his car outside, his coat on a chair, his voice reverberating through the house that used to be ours. With every item he brought, a piece of me was pushed out. I became quieter, more withdrawn. I took longer routes home from school. I lingered at the corner milk bar or loitered at the library, delaying my return.

His attempts to bond with me were clumsy and unwelcome. He spoke to me like I was a child, even though I was already a teenager. The garden of my childhood withered beneath his shadow, despite his intentions. I didn't want a new father. I wanted my Mother back and the close bond we had created during the blissful years.

Their relationship escalated quickly. Within months, she announced their engagement. They would marry in September. I was shocked. Betrayed. The wedding was small. I wore a forced smile. My Mother looked radiant, relieved. She had found someone who could provide stability, a future. I felt like a ghost at the ceremony, haunting the edges of a new life that did not include me.

His presence was the rollercoaster taking a sudden, stomach-churning drop, upending the fragile peace I had come to rely on. Just before my Mother's engagement, she told Nonna, my paternal Grandmother, that she was getting married.

We were shunned. Thereafter, I never saw my Father's large family until 13 years later at Nonna's funeral. In an instant, I lost one half of my extended family including my Grandmother and the cousins I had been close to. A new darkness enveloped me. Joy melted away, superseded by irritable teenage petulance. A tiny lone vessel, thrashing about in a turbulent ocean. Withdrawn and conditioned to ignore my feelings, I distracted myself from wanting to snuff out my life and by immersing myself in my first relationship with Jaz.

After they were married, his presence filled our home like an invasive fog, seeping into every corner, altering the atmosphere in ways I couldn't articulate but felt viscerally. The mathematics of family had changed – from a perfect two to the awkward triangle of three, with all its inherent imbalances and shifting alliances. The stranger wasn't actively malevolent; that would have been easier to resist.

Instead, his very ordinariness was the threat – the way he casually occupied spaces that had been ours alone, the casual presumption of permanence in his careful placement of his tools and car in my Father's garage. His old furniture in our house, his clothes smelling of mothballs and mustiness replacing the reek of beer and cigarette smoke. His control of what we watched on TV. The channel firmly fixed to SBS and foreign-language subtitled movies.

Instead of our home being filled with music, now all I heard was the Italian radio station. The food at the dinner table changed. My Father had more exotic tastes: snails, tripe, liver, *involtini di carne* (Sicilian rolled meat dish) *arancini* (rice balls), *pasta al forno* (baked pasta), *pasta e mudicca* (spaghetti with fennel fronds, breadcrumbs, or almond meal), *salami*. Now we ate *polenta*, broccoli, and *i favi* (broad beans).

My stepfather would usually sow only one vegetable crop at a time, and I mostly recall the dreaded legume season. Rows and rows of dull green pods, some left to dry on the plant, ensuring a superabundance of their starchy contents. This humble bean dominated our sparse menu. There was pasta with them, soup made from them, and often just a plain, steaming bowl. They became a shorthand for monotony – blandness masquerading as nourishment. Although my Mother was a good cook, her home cooking was usually a plain affair. Hence my dislike of simple food. *Was that also in my DNA?*

He expected obedience. Respect. Gratitude. I gave none of these. He wasn't violent or cruel – just ever-present, disapproving, critical in small ways that wore me down. He complained to my Mother about the way I spoke, the way I dressed, the music I listened to.

My Mother never defended me. The man was always right. We began to argue more often. She yelled. He intervened, which infuriated me even more. Inwardly, I was sad, resentful, bitter, and angry. Intellectually, I told myself it was a good thing that she had found a new mate, to take away her sadness and loneliness. Her attention had, overnight, turned from me to this stranger.

I was conveniently tossed aside.

Discarded.

No longer useful or wanted.

I had thought the house was settling after the storm of grief, but now it quaked in smaller, more insidious ways. Cracks that had started to heal, reformed not from one great blow, but from the slow pressure of being ignored – the kind of stress that makes porcelain split without a sound.

Loneliness itself became my roommate, breathing quietly beside me in the darkness. I'd often skip school because I just wanted to be even more alone with my aloneness. I'd roam the local streets and sometimes end up at Fawkner Cemetery where my Dad was buried or going on long solitary bike rides. Once I ended up on Hoddle Street, Collingwood, at the overpass bridge to the Eastern freeway. I have no idea how I made it home safely. My teachers didn't seem to care much that I skipped lots of school. I'd often forge my Mother's signature on notes of absence. No one noticed. No one cared.

Once my Mother remarried, I was constantly admonished for playing cricket outside with the boys, especially when a tennis ball was hit against our dining room window with a loud thud. '*Disgraziata! Si ti acchiappu, ti ammazzu!*' would ring through the quiet neighbourhood, with dramatic emphasis on the first and last words – loosely translating to 'You little shit! If I catch you, I'm going to kill you!' Thankfully, I could easily outrun my short, plumpish Mother, who possessed little athletic ability.

Eventually, I reluctantly surrendered to these demands and stopped playing outdoor games with the boys. Instead, I retreated indoors to endless hours of television or isolated myself in my bedroom.

At home, I grew increasingly bored, morose, and sullen. The dark shadow of adolescent melancholy tightened its grip, squeezing out the joy that had briefly flourished during our years together.

This second loss, after the peaceful connection I'd established with my Mother, created a template for how I would later experience the loss of my assumed identity: as a sudden, inexplicable severance from something that had seemed secure and foundational.

Away from home, activities kept me emotionally balanced. At school, I joined the netball team and played softball on weekends. Team sports provided the camaraderie I craved. I was still chasing balls, still running – perhaps from something I couldn't yet name. In these physical activities, I found metaphors for my life's central challenges: maintaining balance while in motion, finding my position within larger patterns, recognising when to advance and when to retreat.

The netball court offered momentary structure – rules, positions, patterns I could rely on. As wing attack, I moved with rhythm and purpose, a stark contrast to the confusion at home.

In these 60-minute games, I experienced what was increasingly elusive elsewhere: the certainty of belonging somewhere specific, being needed for a defined purpose, contributing to something larger than myself. My body, moving confidently through these structured spaces, remembered what it felt like to be unquestionably present, while at home I was becoming increasingly ghostlike, fading into the background of my Mother's new life.

After my Mother's remarriage, I began taking acoustic guitar lessons at the Oak Park Guitar School with Bob Petts and his daughters. Perhaps music was my way of remaining connected to happier memories of my Father and his positive legacy. He had bought me my first guitar and his music had filled our home during the peaceful times. My Mother bought me a new, larger acoustic guitar, and years later, a bass guitar and amplifier.

These instruments were among the few significant gifts I remember receiving from her. Music offered another language, another way of expressing what I couldn't articulate in words.

The overnight stays at my cool cousin's house that I had cherished abruptly ended. Suddenly, we were visiting complete strangers – my stepfather's relatives and friends. During the first couple of years after their marriage, I was reluctantly dragged to these gatherings across Melbourne's suburbs in my stepfather's prized 1966 dark blue Chrysler Valiant – the car I would learn to drive in at 18, which later became my first car.

These weekend excursions felt like forced marches – a betrayal of my Father's memory and everything we'd shared. Surrounded by unfamiliar faces with strange expressions and jokes I didn't understand, I would sit sullenly and watchful, a reluctant anthropologist observing an alien culture. These strangers shared no blood with me, no history, no memories – yet I was expected to perform familial warmth, to laugh at their references to events I hadn't witnessed, to care about the health concerns of elderly relatives whose names blurred together in my mind. In these suffocating living rooms that smelled of unfamiliar cooking and furniture polish, I became expert at the minimal engagement necessary to avoid reprimand: the perfunctory smile, the noncommittal nod, the strategic bathroom visit when conversation became unbearable.

After enduring several years of these obligatory weekend visits to strangers, I finally rebelled. One day, as Mum and my stepfather prepared to leave, I defiantly announced, 'I'm not coming. I don't want to see these people anymore.'

With her now familiar sudden rage, my Mother replied, 'Yes, you are,' her stern expression having little effect on my determined independence. She chased me through the house and out the back door, biting her lower lip and hurling her Sicilian insults.

I quickly scaled the side timber fence and leapt onto my neighbour, Mr Garisto's concrete driveway, safely beyond her reach. In frustration, face contorted with rage, she bit the web of skin between her thumb and index finger before thrusting her hand toward me – a characteristic Sicilian gesture of threat, which translated to, 'I'm going to kill you! *Disgraziata!*'

Despite her melodramatic display, I was pleased with my rebellion. I never again accompanied them on these visits unless they were seeing my Mother's relatives, and then only if I felt inclined. The victory was small but significant – my first real assertion of independence, my first conscious rejection of imposed identity, my first refusal to pretend belonging where I felt none.

1980–1982

In the years following the adoption revelation, arguments with my Mother increased. The distance between us widened until we hardly spoke to each other. In frustration and underlying sadness, I slammed doors, making our house shake. Screaming at her, 'Leave me alone!' A new rage, I could barely contain.

As an introvert, I needed solitude and quiet, while my Mother, an extrovert, found isolation unbearable. Our contrasting needs and characteristics increasingly created tension – a fundamental mismatch in temperament that would later make me wonder if my psychological makeup might be explained by genetics rather than nurture.

I completed Year 10 and then Years 11 and 12 at Geoghegan College, then located in Broadmeadows. The school grounds contained an old historic mansionette that was the former St Joseph's Foundling Hospital.

I couldn't understand why this building had called to me so persistently, why my fingers would trace its weathered contours with something approaching reverence. Years later, the revelation of its identity would create a perfect circle of meaning – my body had recognised what my mind could not, had been drawn back to its first home through some cellular memory that transcended conscious knowledge.

This physical connection to a place I didn't yet know I belonged revealed something profound about identity itself: that we exist beyond our own awareness, that recognition precedes understanding, that our cells carry histories our minds haven't yet discovered. My attraction to this building wasn't random coincidence but biological magnetism – matter recognising matter across the divisions of time and consciousness. In these moments of inexplicable connection, I glimpsed how fractured identity might eventually heal – not through intellectual discovery alone, but through allowing the body's wisdom to guide the fragmented self back toward wholeness.

Year 12 was a struggle. The stress of completing high school led to sleepless nights. My sense of self was falling apart. I was drifting in a sea of mixed teenage angst, none of which I yet understood. I became increasingly withdrawn and my social anxiety worsened.

I managed to scrape through the year and decided that I would take a gap year, in 1983. I wanted to fly back to New York and reconnect with happier times and with my extended adopted family. The story I'd told myself of safety was already fracturing – not with a bang, but with silence, substitution, and the slow erasure of certainty.

Nonna Gaetana Costantino Carfi

6

Falling into the Gap (1983)

Lost, fragmented, swirling in a cave

Over the summer of 1982–1983, I dated a Hungarian refugee. We took day trips in his green panel van. As much as I liked him, there was no shagging in his wagon, the same shade as my Father's Holden Special. It was the early 80s, and it was still deeply shameful for a single Italian-Australian woman to fall pregnant outside of marriage. I carried this truth like a talisman; I was always mindful that I was the product of shame. Sometimes, when my Mother was angry at me, she would scream, '*Fidya di puttana!*' (Daughter of a whore). Its sting was permanent.

I had no desire to bring any further shame to my family. The weight of being '*illegitimate*' hung heavy around my neck, dragging me down through every conversation, every silence, a constant reminder of the circumstances I could never escape. Each time my Mother hurled those words at me – '*Fidya di puttana!*' – another crack formed in my tenuous sense of self, the 'unwanted child' fragment growing larger, edges sharper with every insult. I didn't need to add to it. Not yet.

The relationship provided a welcome distraction from the confusion I felt about my identity. Our connection was simple, and undemanding compared to the complex questions I was avoiding about my origins.

June 1983

My second trip to New York was markedly different from my first experience with my Mother. I was now a young adult carrying a burden of undiagnosed mental health issues that shadowed every experience like a persistent fog. The fragments of my identity that had shattered completely on that bus seemed to drift further apart with each passing month, leaving me increasingly hollow at my core. Though I suspected I experienced anxiety and depression – I'd sometimes borrow books from the Glenroy library about these topics – I had no framework to understand my struggles. In New York, I once mentioned to an Uncle that I was depressed.

He replied, 'What do you have to be depressed about?'

His words landed like a stone dropped into still water, ripples of shame expanding outward. This simple dismissal drove my feelings deeper within, reinforcing my belief that I was innately defective rather than someone whose upbringing had shaped my psychological challenges. Each denial of my emotional reality was another small crack in my already fragmented self – another piece that would eventually need to be gathered and restitched.

To my Mother's credit, when I was around 15 and had withdrawn into a sullen state where I just watched endless television, she had taken me to see our local GP, Dr Irish – a pale, stale, male of his generation. My Mother, in her broken English, told him she was worried about me because all I seemed to do was watch TV all day.

He asked me, 'Is the television talking to you? Do you hear voices?'

'No,' I meekly replied.

'Your daughter is fine. She's just a typical teenager.'

That brief exchange effectively slammed shut the only door that might have led to help. The moment remains crystallised in my memory – sitting in that sterile office, the doctor's dismissive tone reverberating off the walls, my Mother's worried face, and my own crushing realisation that my inner turmoil would remain unnamed and unresolved. I stared impassively at the faux wood panelling. The antiseptic in the air stung more than any wound I could name.

If only he had given me a thorough mental health examination, I might have been spared decades of anguish. I was overly anxious and depressed, but I didn't hear voices – the bar for receiving help was set at psychosis.

In many ways, this pattern of dismissal was familiar – another echo of the invalidation I'd experienced when questioning my origins. My feelings, like my identity, were treated as inconvenient intrusions rather than essential truths deserving attention. Each silencing reinforced the sense that my inner reality was somehow less legitimate than others'. The dissonance I felt was a personal failing rather than a reasonable response to profound disruption.

In New York, I gravitated toward the one thing that could temporarily silence the persistent question of who I really was: alcohol. Each drink created a momentary sensation of wholeness, the edges of my fractured identity blurring into something that felt less jagged, less painful. This was the beginning of a pattern that would define much of my twenties – seeking chemical means to fabricate the integration I couldn't achieve naturally.

When I arrived in New York, the familiar embrace of my extended family initially provided comfort. These were people connected to me through my Mother – a family I could trust, unlike the uncertain terrain of my Father's family.

It was the northern hemisphere summer of 1983. Being with extended family offered a temporary reprieve from my inner turmoil. My cousins moved through the world with an ease I coveted – their certainty about who they were and where they belonged only highlighted what I lacked – they had never questioned their place in the family narrative, never wondered about the blood that ran through their veins.

I went to see Simon and Garfunkel at a huge football stadium in New Jersey, where silence also became my closest friend. I spent a week with my Uncle's family at a place in upstate New York called Pine Ranch. There we ate abundantly, lounged by the pool, and rode fast horses. On one early morning ride with a small group, we were galloping through a lovely green picturesque forest when the horses made a sudden turn through the trees. Had I not been hanging on for dear life, I would have been thrown headfirst over my horse.

I frequently visited my favourite Chinese restaurant, Jade Palace, for egg rolls and plum sauce – a Chinese-American invention. These were huge spring rolls filled with chunky bits of cabbage, carrots, eggs, pork, and prawns, something we didn't have in Australia. At this Jade Palace, my cousin and I would have delicious, fruity cocktails called Zombies. I still have the tall ceramic jade-green glass, carved with the head of a monster, that I stole from there one night, along with a few ornate Chinese teacups.

Alcohol quickly became my self-medication of choice, the only balm that soothed the persistent ache. Each Zombie cocktail I consumed at Jade Palace temporarily filled the void where a sense of self should have been. The sweet liquid coursed down my throat like liquid courage, a temporary armour. I can still recall with visceral clarity the sweet, fruity taste masking the strong alcohol beneath – a perfect metaphor for how I moved through the world in those days, a pleasant exterior concealing a dangerous emptiness within. The jade-green monster glass I stole seemed appropriate; I, too, was becoming a vessel containing something monstrous – a growing addiction that would nearly consume me in the years ahead.

That stolen glass became my unintentional talisman – grotesque and strangely familiar. Like it, I had been shaped by unseen forces. Its monstrous face mirrored the strangeness I felt rising within – a self both filled and hollowed by forces I barely understood. The monster's frozen expression – half-grimace, half-smile – mirrored my own contradictions. I was grateful for my adoption, yet resentful. Belonging everywhere and nowhere. I would keep this glass long after other possessions had been discarded, its green opacity gradually acquiring a symbolic meaning. Years later, I would understand that I had been drawn to it precisely because it embodied the central paradox of my fractured identity: that sometimes we recognise ourselves most clearly in what seems most alien, that the monstrous and the familiar are not opposites but complex reflections of the same divided self.

The nightclubs of Staten Island became my sanctuary, places where identity didn't matter, where the pulsing lights and thundering music drowned out the insistent questions that plagued my quieter moments. Under strobing lights, I became nobody and somebody simultaneously – a paradoxical freedom. Each night followed the same ritual: awkwardness softened by alcohol, numbness setting in, sickness following like clockwork. My body purged what my soul could not.

We went dancing at least twice a week. It was the early 1980s, and the electronic dance pop music of that era was my favourite. I loved music and I loved to dance. My cousin, her best friend, and I would go to nightclubs and dance for hours. My favourite place was one called The Caves on Staten Island, where they lived. It resembled an underground cavern, musty smelling with water dripping down the walls. A long bar stood in the centre of the venue, surrounded by small dark, cave-like rooms jutting out around it. We danced the night away to 80s synth-pop beats.

One of my favourite songs was *Safety Dance* by Men Without Hats. The song's refrain felt like a temporary permission slip to exist freely, a sensation I rarely experienced in my daily life. For those brief minutes on the dance floor, the fragments of my identity seemed to move in harmony, synchronised to the music, creating an illusion of wholeness that vanished when the song ended. I felt safe to dance, and I only felt safe and free when I had been drinking. The alcohol was both a key and lock – unlocking my capacity for joy while locking me into dependency. The alcohol washed away my demons.

I was searching for something to make me feel normal, whatever 'normal' meant – a state I imagined others experienced naturally that remained elusive to me. The morning-after emptiness was perhaps the truest reflection of my emotional reality – hollowed out, fragile, my mind searching frantically for the scattered pieces of myself that had drifted even further apart during the night's chemical escapism. Silence lingered in my body like a shadow – dense, low-lying, impossible to shake. I wanted to be hugged and held. I wanted to feel safe and warm. I was in no way ready for the adult world.

My life up to that point had been an ongoing series of survival modes, each day another exercise in simply continuing to exist while carrying the unbearable weight of not knowing who I truly was. The adoption revelation had created a chasm within me that daily threatened to widen, to swallow me entirely. Every social interaction, every quiet moment alone became treacherous territory where the question, *Who am I really?* might suddenly surface, leaving me stranded once on the shores of my own uncertainty.

The only exception had been the five blissful years I had with my Mother after my Father died. My life might have turned out differently if subsequent events hadn't happened. I may have had the opportunity to recover from the turmoil of my childhood years with the drunken monster. But things didn't unfold that way.

The adoption revelation had only deepened my isolation, transforming it from a vague childhood discomfort into a yawning existential abyss. I moved through the world like a ghost – present but not entirely real, visible yet unseen. I walked around with a dark cloud hanging over me, my shoulders bent beneath the weight of not-knowing. In social settings, I often became mute, not because I had nothing to say, but because speaking required a certainty about who was doing the speaking – an 'I' that felt increasingly fictional to me.

I didn't know how to be a proper functioning, emotionally stable adult. The adults in my immediate world had offered only damaging models: alcoholism, drug dependency, emotional volatility, unpredictability. Each had demonstrated different ways to escape from oneself rather than how to become oneself. I didn't understand at that time that my mental state was anything but normal – that most people didn't feel as though they were constantly performing an identity rather than living one.

I just assumed there was something deeply and fundamentally wrong with me. This core defect seemed to explain both my biological mother's decision to give me away and my persistent sense of disconnection from everyone around me. None of these family members seemed to understand the impact that growing up with an abusive alcoholic Father, my Mother's remarriage, and being adopted had on me.

I was a shattered vessel, carelessly reassembled – all the pieces present, but none fitting quite right, the cracks visible from every angle. I was on the edge of life, barely hanging on by my fingernails. I wanted to let go, but thought I couldn't do that to my Mother. These early childhood experiences were the first dizzying drops on the rollercoaster of my life, the psychological equivalent of being thrown for a loop before I even understood the ride I was on.

Even in these darkest moments, some deeper instinct for self-preservation kept me going – a stubborn spark that refused to be extinguished despite the howling winds of confusion and pain. Perhaps it was this same resilience that had enabled my survival through my Father's alcoholic rages and my Mother's emotional abandonment. Or perhaps it was something more – an unconscious drive to discover the truth of my origins, to find the missing pieces that would make sense of the fragments I carried. Whatever its source, this persistence would ultimately prove my salvation, though the path forward remained invisible to me then.

Then I discovered marijuana.

My first encounter with pot created a moment of profound significance that would reshape my relationship with my fractured self for years to come – another turning point in my ongoing attempt to either reconnect the fragments of my identity or numb myself to their separation.

My eldest Australian-born American Cousin had given me a bag of pot soon after my arrival in New York. I decided to have my first big joint on the 4th of July, when the three families celebrated together. My drinking cousin and I had started the day's festivities with orange juice and vodka. Around midday, after the other relatives had arrived, I stood on the balcony of my Uncle's two-story house in Sunnyside.

The multi-level house sat on a hill that sloped towards the Staten Island Expressway. It was a bright, sunny day. The sky was a brilliant northern-hemisphere New York blue – different from the blue we have in the southern hemisphere. This blue was more assertive, less apologetic – everything America seemed to be. Green conifers lined the street in front of mostly identical box-like houses. There was no comforting perfume of eucalyptus. Standing on the balcony, I lit my first fat joint. I shared some with my younger male cousin, who showed me how to take deep drags.

Some of the other cousins were shocked to see me smoking and said they could smell the weed from the back of the house, where the older adults were gathered, warning me to stop. It didn't take long for the effects to hit me, accentuating the alcohol already in my system. I felt a sudden rising dizziness and nausea. I bolted to the upstairs bathroom, just making it in time, locked the door, and promptly threw up orange-coloured liquid into the toilet bowl. I hadn't eaten anything all day, which was probably a good thing at this point.

The cream-tiled bathroom transformed into a spinning chamber of nausea and revelation. As the room revolved around me, I experienced a terrifying dissolution of self – a complete untethering from the anchors of personhood I'd managed to maintain even through my worst moments of identity confusion. This wasn't mere dizziness but an existential vertigo, my consciousness spinning through emptiness, untethered from any sense of who I was.

The bathroom was spinning like a spinning top, whirling for hours. The cold tiles beneath me were also moving, as if I were simultaneously in a top-loading washing machine. I spent most of that time hugging the toilet bowl – we became intimately acquainted. Like a good Aussie tourist, I was chundering spectacularly.

My desperate attempt to either integrate the pieces or escape their separation had left me clutching cold porcelain, my world spinning out of control, nothing solid to hold onto. Each revolution of the room was another orbit around a central truth I couldn't yet face. The bathroom's hard surfaces refused to stay still beneath me, just as the foundations of my sense of self had been unstable since that moment on the bus three years earlier. Each heave into the toilet was an expulsion of something poisonous that nonetheless left me empty rather than purified.

The next day, I gave the bag of weed to my younger cousin, who just laughed.

The aftermath of this experience didn't deter me from marijuana in the long term. Instead, it became a preview of what would eventually become another form of self-medication – another chemical attempt to either integrate or obliterate the persistent question of who I was. What had been a terrifying loss of control in that bathroom would, with practice and increased tolerance, transform into a more manageable form of escape. The spinning would eventually slow to a pleasant orbit, the nausea replaced by a numbing calm that felt, in its own way, like peace.

Despite these misadventures, I found something in this extended family that I craved: a sense of belonging, however tenuous and temporary. The daily rituals of shared meals, the insider jokes, the physical resemblance between relatives – all offered a simulacrum of what I had lost through adoption: connection within a lineage, and a place in a continuing story.

These moments were puzzle pieces I collected – incomplete but precious, hinting at a picture I couldn't yet see. These moments at the family dinner table were precious fragments that I gathered carefully, storing them away as evidence that belonging was possible, that perhaps someday I might reassemble enough pieces to feel whole.

I was staying with my Uncle Sam, who had three children – my drinking buddy and his two younger teenage sons. I enjoyed sharing large family meals together. Although my Uncle was a heavy drinker at the time and would get mildly intoxicated most nights, he was never violent or loud like my Father had been. He didn't get along well with his wife or his kids during this period. It wasn't the happy household I remembered from my childhood visit.

Feisty Zia Diana had three daughters who didn't get along with their Mother, creating frequent tension in their house. Her eldest child was now married and expecting her first child. Nonna was no longer with us. There was tension between the families.

Much had changed. Even in this imperfect family setting, I recognised what I lacked at home: a tangible web of connections, a place where I fit into a larger picture. These people might argue and struggle, but they did so within the security of knowing exactly who they were in relation to each other. Their arguments were rooted in solid ground; mine always occurred in quicksand.

Even their conflicts were rooted in a certainty I couldn't claim – the certainty of blood, of shared history, of undisputed belonging. Life was no longer carefree. Even so, I wanted to stay in New York with my extended Italian American family. I didn't want to return to my lonely existence back in Australia with my Mother and stepfather.

The prospect of leaving this family – imperfect as it was – filled me with a grief disproportionate to the length of my stay.

When my Uncle told me I couldn't stay and that I had to go back for my Mother's sake, I wept uncontrollably at the loss of family, belonging, and tranquillity. And so, in November, after having stayed for five months, I reluctantly flew back to the house that no longer felt like home. Grief lodged in my sternum like a splintered rib – something once whole now poking inward.

Seeing my extended family only highlighted what I'd lost through adoption – the natural web of connections that others took for granted. The cousins who complained about family obligations couldn't understand the luxury of their certainty – the unquestioned knowledge of where they came from and thus who they were. To know your origins is to possess a compass I had been denied. My identity remained divided between the person I was raised to be and the unknown person whose DNA I carried. I brought this wound back with me across the Pacific. Another fragment to add to my splintered identity, another piece of what might have been.

As the plane lifted off from Newark, I pressed my forehead against the small window and watched the Statue of Liberty recede. The distance growing between me and my extended family felt like another piece of myself being torn away, another fragment I would need to retrieve someday when I finally understood how to make myself whole. The clouds below resembled the fog in my mind – patches of clarity surrounded by vast unknowing. The questions that had driven me across the ocean remained unanswered, but now they had new urgency. *If I couldn't find belonging even among relatives, where would I ever find it?* The revelation that family itself offered no automatic salvation from my fractured identity left me even more adrift, heading back to Australia with less certainty than when I'd left.

Back in Melbourne, the familiar landscape of my childhood seemed simultaneously more real and more alien than before, as though my time in New York had adjusted the lens through which I viewed everything. Streets I had walked a thousand times appeared subtly altered. The quality of light different, the horizon somehow shifted. This wasn't merely jet lag, or culture shock, but a deeper perceptual change – I was seeing my surroundings through eyes that had glimpsed alternatives, other possible lives, other configurations of belonging.

The following year, I started university. There, I found another connection, a different sense of belonging among new friends and like-minded people.

7

Alchemy of Identity (1984)

Transformation began in the shadow of uncertainty

Since discovering I was adopted, the fundamental question *'Who am I?'* had become a mantra, following me from Glenroy to RMIT, from my Mother's house to the Royal Children's Hospital – where I found temporary work as a clerk at the end of 1983.

Alchemy of Identity: The Laboratory of Self

My first trip to New York at 11, with my Mother, had shown me what family could be at its best – boisterous gatherings where no one feared sudden violence, where connections felt secure rather than fragile. Now, as I embraced the escape of alcohol and marijuana, I was seeking something of that same feeling – temporary release from the hypervigilance that had become my default state.

Shortly after returning home from New York, I reconnected with a high school friend who introduced me to her boyfriend – my first pot dealer. Despite the terrible ordeal I'd had on that 4th of July, I decided to give pot another go. Alcohol alone couldn't bear the weight of broken origins and a Father's ghost.

The first-time pot fully enveloped me, I was bunkered in our garage, watchful as a wounded animal, my back pressed against the cold metal of the vintage Valiant, eyes fixed on the back door like a sentinel wired for betrayal. As I inhaled deeply, a silent rush of unusual calmness permeated my typically anxiety-ridden body. It was as if someone had finally silenced the cacophonous Greek chorus of doubt that had been screaming in my head since that bus ride.

My overactive sympathetic nervous system – perpetually wound tight like a spring ready to snap – suddenly relaxed. The constant negative self-doubting chatter ceased its relentless interrogation: *Who are you really? Where do you belong?* I felt like I was floating, suspended between memory and possibility, momentarily carefree.

What I couldn't recognise then was the profound psychological mechanism at play: I wasn't mending, only masking. The cracks weren't healing; I was simply turning away, painting over the fissures with a temporary chemical veneer.

Starting University at RMIT

RMIT sat on the northern edge of the city – primarily a vocational tertiary institution, not yet a fully-fledged university. Science beckoned me as a subject of study, but also as a metaphorical sanctuary. I was drawn to it partly because it promised certainty, clear answers – everything my personal history lacked. In the lab, elements obeyed. Reactions made sense. Nothing exploded without reason. How utterly unlike my life, where the ground could shift beneath my feet with a stranger's casual words on a bus, where identity itself was a hypothesis waiting to be disproven.

I was enrolled in a Bachelor of Applied Science, Medical Laboratory Science, majoring in Medical Microbiology. Despite my newfound mind-altering sedative, insomnia and social anxiety were still problems, so I missed many of my early morning classes. When I did go in, I thoroughly enjoyed learning pathology, anatomy and physiology, biology, and biochemistry.

Science gave me the logic my life had denied – a place where each piece fit, each name had meaning.

The laboratory classes were interesting and sometimes dangerous. Each experiment became a controlled version of my internal chaos. One day, my friend, Bee, spilled some acid on the chemistry bench. She quickly threw a sponge on it. The sponge then rapidly vapourised into the air. Another time I was trying to light a Bunsen burner, but I had turned on the wrong tap. Suddenly the tap burst into a large roaring flame. I must have jumped a foot high. These were controlled explosions, unlike the emotional detonations that had defined my childhood and the identity revelation that had blown my life apart – here, at least, chaos followed predictable scientific laws.

Hockey – 1984

At the start of 1984, searching for something solid to anchor myself to, I joined the RMIT hockey club.

Highly competitive and with an energy that seemed to burn from some internal nuclear reactor of unresolved emotion, I found in hockey both physical release and a peculiar form of belonging. The sport allowed me to channel my well-hidden aggressive streak, while giving me somewhere to run – something I was doing more often in my dreams, pursued by unknown, murky assailants I couldn't escape.

Sport came easily to me. But that ease was haunted by questions: *Who had passed this down to me? Was I tracing the outline of an unknown legacy every time I struck the ball?* Hockey gave me both answers and questions – and, for a while, that was enough.

Unlike my unstable sense of self, my body on the hockey field moved with innate certainty. My muscles carried truths my consciousness couldn't access – genetic inheritance encoded in sinew and reflex, a physical connection to unknown origins that both comforted and unsettled me. I was learning to play with broken parts – rearranging them into something functional, if not yet beautiful.

Once I had settled into university and hockey life, I felt like I'd finally found my tribe away from the narrow-minded life I had lived in Glenroy. Back there the now young women I had grown up with seemed only interested in getting married and having children – ambitions furthest from my mind. But even as I found this new intellectual community, I recognised the irony: I was setting myself apart from my adopted family while having no connection to my biological one. I was crafting an identity in opposition to the only roots I knew, with no knowledge of the roots I didn't know.

I was the only one in my neighbourhood of friends to complete Year 12, HSC, and the only one of my maternal Australian Italian relatives to go to university. This also set me apart. Mum had never pushed me to go to university. I just didn't want to be a secretary, hairdresser, or shop assistant – the usual narrow occupational choices for girls in that time in my local circles. I had decided that I wanted to go to university mainly because I loved to learn, and my high school teachers at Mercy College had mentioned and encouraged it. University sounded interesting and exciting. I straddled a fault line – between working-class Italian culture and academic pursuits, between the family I knew and the blood I didn't. I belonged nowhere completely but found momentary footholds in this shifting terrain.

On Saturday afternoons, after hockey games, some of our club members would go to a small dingy pub, the old Royal Hotel on Flemington Road, near the Royal Melbourne Hospital. Surrounded by teammates, drinking beer, I could temporarily forget the hollowness I carried. For those hours, I wasn't the adopted girl without a history; I was just another uni student celebrating a win or mourning a loss.

Animated men and women smelling of sweat and Dencorub would be packed into the hotel, and we'd drink lots of pots of beer, which arrived by the jugful. The pub pulsed with post-game chatter – triumphant or grim, depending on who'd won. Many of my hockey mates were drinkers and some smoked pot too, so I fitted right in. I was able to drink, smoke, and forget my social anxiety for a while. The Royal became a sanctuary where identity required no documentation – a warm cocoon of belonging created by shared experience rather than shared blood.

I was also developing a sense of belonging. I was drawn to this environment – part sporting, part intellectual. Some days I felt almost whole here. Connected. Present. Then memories would intrude. Reminders. Questions without answers. I'd drink another beer. Smoke another joint. The questions would recede. For hours, sometimes days, I could pretend I knew who I was. Then I'd catch my reflection in a window or hear someone mention their family, and the cracks would reappear. But here, with these people, the cracks seemed less important. Or maybe just less visible. I learned to wear alcohol and later marijuana like armour – chemicals that temporarily quieted the persistently negative mind chatter. In those social moments, enveloped in laughter and acceptance, I could almost forget the hollow space within me.

I went to my first intercollegiate hockey tournament in the nearby former gold rush town of Ballarat where I scored my first hockey goal, on a typically bitterly cold and grey Ballarat winter's day, on a wet sand-filled ground. The ball was crossed in from the right wing, bobbing along over the bumpy sand, and across the face of the goals. In succession my teammates swatted at the white ball as it rolled towards me. I was last in the line, as left wing and I gently tapped it into the net.

The joy of that first goal contained its own peculiar melancholy – a celebration lacking witnesses who shared my blood. As teammates surrounded me, I felt both embraced and isolated.

Somewhere, unknown to me, was there a biological father who might have recognised his own technique in my shot. A mother who might have seen herself in my competitive drive. Siblings who might have felt a strange pride in a sister they'd never met. It was the first of hundreds of goals that I would score over an amateur hockey career that spanned the next three decades.

I soon had a tight circle of hockey friends. We'd play hockey on Saturdays and then go out for dinner after having spent a few hours at the pub. I was introduced to several new cuisines for the first time: Vietnamese, Malaysian, Indian. It was a different world to the insular Italian world I had grown up in Glenroy. I now had uni friends who studied engineering, architecture, or graphic design. Most came from an Aussie-Anglo background. I felt more at ease and at home with them. They weren't as critical, judgmental, nosy, or close-minded as my Italian-Australian neighbourhood friends and their parents had been. Their boundaries were more permeable than the rigid confines of my Italian upbringing – allowing exploration rather than dictating conformity. Despite my internal struggles, I found liberation in this new social landscape.

With my social group, we'd often end up at someone's place after dinner, continuing to drink into the night. Sometimes a spontaneous party would erupt. We'd put on records or CDs and dance the night away to the latest 80s music. *Johnny* by the Fine Young Cannibals captured the mood of that time in my life – restless, repetitive, and edged with melancholy.

The reasons I drank weren't mysterious. Alcohol dulled the persistent ache of not-knowing, the constant reminder that half my identity remained a void. Drinking wasn't just social – it was medicinal, an attempt to fill the hollowness with something, anything.

There were never any hard drugs. No fights. No tension. And thankfully no social media or phone cameras to record our mischief. We all got along; we just wanted to have fun.

The fragments of self I'd been collecting since the bus revelation – adopted daughter, university student, occasional drug user – seemed to find their most coherent expression when I stepped onto the hockey field or sat surrounded by teammates at the pub. While I was running around on the pitch, there was no time to ruminate. There, at least, the pieces fit together without contradiction.

But off the field, the questions remained, waiting for me in quiet moments – in reflected windows, in family photographs, in the search for familiar features in a face that was still a mystery to me.

The contrast between my vibrant outer life and hollow inner existence created its own dissonance – another split in an already divided self. Outwardly: the university student, the hockey player, the social butterfly. Inwardly: the rootless adoptee, the pharmaceutical experiment, the genetic mystery. I lived across these parallel realities, moving between them with increasing skill but never fully resolving their contradictions.

The club and team camaraderie, my hockey mates, other uni friends, along with the alcohol and pot were my saviours, as I weaved my way in and out of relationships. Apart from hockey and fitness, which kept me grounded, I floundered through my 20s – my academic life trailing far behind. Surviving, but still feeling largely lost and aimless, and completely unprepared for the discipline and seriousness of adulthood.

More Madness

Towards the end of my first uni year, just before my first exam, impeccably timed, my stepfather decided to have a psychotic episode. While my own identity crisis continued its slow burn, my home life was about to erupt into its own form of chaos.

Mum and her husband became involved in a fundamentalist Italian Catholic group, which they attended regularly. My stepfather quickly became fanatical and decided to stop taking his medication. Unbeknownst to Mum and me, he was on Lithium, usually used to treat bipolar disorder. His behaviour became bizarre. At night, he didn't like having the lights on. So, we sat and watched TV in the dark. He didn't like the TV sound being up, so we started to watch TV with the sound down, while sitting in the dark. He became aggressively erratic. Mum reluctantly told me that he had torn up some of our family photos – those precious artefacts of my constructed family narrative, further erasing what little sense of history I had. On an outing with their religious group, he tore off a man's glasses and said, 'You don't need these. Just pray to God and he will heal you!'

My first father hadn't been quite this mad.

As my stepfather's psychosis worsened, our family reality became distorted – a grotesque mirror of my own internal disintegration.

One day, he insisted that I drive his old Valiant, that was now mine, to the back of our house. I obediently drove the car down the driveway. He then slowly and surreptitiously snuck out the back door, as if ASIO had him under surveillance and was simultaneously being scrutinised by aliens. He crept along the back of the house, carefully, quietly on tiptoes, slinking his way into the back seat of the car. With a deranged look on his face, he lay down on the back seat, away from the prying eyes and hurriedly, *sotto voce*, told me to 'quickly drive,' gesturing with an anxious sweeping away motion of his hand toward the front of the car.

I started to drive out of the driveway and onto Middle Street, but I didn't know where he would be safe from those pesky prying aliens. Luckily, after about five minutes into our drive to nowhere, he soon fell asleep on the back seat, neatly tucked up in a foetal position. I did a U-turn and drove back home. Parked the car in the garage and left him there to sleep.

Mum and I had no idea what was going on. As the days drifted into each other, he became increasingly dishevelled and unshaven. He was starting to morph into Jack Nicholson in '*The Shining*,' not knife-wielding insane, just unpredictable, and crazy-looking.

Mum finally called his only son, who lived on the other side of town. The son who rarely called and never visited his father. She told him that his father was acting strange and had refused to see a doctor, and who now thought we were also part of the Devil's conspiracy. His son spoke to his father on the phone and encouraged him to see a doctor.

In language uncharacteristic of my stepfather, he became enraged, thick blue veins creeping across his temples, gesticulating wildly down the phone line to his son, '*You-a fukin-ah bust-ard-ah*' and forcibly slammed down the phone receiver into its cradle. In that deeply satisfying way when you could slam the phone down to abruptly end a conversation.

The final straw came when he was in my bedroom, lying on my bed on top of all his clothes that he had taken from his wardrobe and strewn onto my bed in a hobo heap. This left me with a creepy, icky, disgusting feeling. I had no idea what to make of this crazed behaviour.

Now a young adult, I wasn't as perturbed by these scenes as when I was a terrified lone witness to my Father's rages. I was more cognisant and more informed about mental illness. My stepfather was having some kind of mental breakdown. Nevertheless, my Mother and I were afraid and wary of this increasing erratic chaos unfolding before us.

We stood outside in the dark, stars dotted through the night's sky, near our side street, looking disbelievingly at the sequel to '*Madhouse 1*'.

I watched this disintegration with déjà vu's cold finger tracing my spine – another father figure losing touch with reality, another household descending into chaos. Unlike my Father's alcohol-fuelled rages, my stepfather's psychosis created a different kind of alienation. His madness wasn't directed at us but seemed to pull him into a private reality where we existed only as peripheral characters – neither seen nor unseen, merely irrelevant. This peculiar invisibility resonated with my own sense of being fundamentally unseen in my identity.

Once again, the stability I so desperately sought was crumbling. The parallels to my childhood – watching my alcoholic Father's outbursts – were striking, but this time I wasn't a helpless child. I was a young adult with the vocabulary to understand what was happening, even if I couldn't stop it.

We spoke to a neighbour and decided to call a doctor.

The doctor arrived and tried to examine him, but my stepfather became verbally abusive. He waved his fists and hissed angrily at him, 'Piss-ah off-ah!'

The doctor said the only thing we could do was to have him certified insane. We would have to call the police, so we did.

My brave new world had rapidly turned into a cuckoo's nest.

The darkness around us soon flashed like a blue light disco hall, as the police arrived, alerting the neighbourhood in the process. Two friendly but stern male officers entered the house. There was no tasering or pepper spraying. Apparently, my stepfather bit one of the officer's hands as the officer tried to take him outside. He was hauled outside, handcuffs behind his back. By this time, my stepfather was totally out of it. He had lost touch with reality. I had no idea what he was going on about. I was in a calm state of bewilderment. Now I was an adult. I had friends I could later talk to about this incident and drugs that I could take to escape and wash away these surreal situations.

The police put my stepfather in a divvy van and drove him to Larundel Psychiatric Hospital on Plenty Road, Bundoora. We followed.

Larundel was a large two-storey red brick mental asylum. It would become one of the last asylums to be closed in Melbourne in 1999. Unbeknownst to me at the time, it used to house some of the most severely mentally ill criminals in our town.

As birds started chirping and the night greeted the morning, I drove into the extended driveway and parked the Valiant in front of this imposing old building. It was the first time I'd set foot in a psychiatric hospital. The next time would be as an inpatient. At first, the admission people weren't going to admit him. The certifying doctor had written the wrong date on the paperwork, and when the psychiatrist, wearing a white overcoat, examined my stepfather he was now perfectly calm and softly spoken. To our dismay, the examiners thought there was nothing wrong with him and wanted to send him home. My Mother and I were then interviewed, and we recounted all the strange events that had happened over the previous few weeks. We managed to convince them that he needed to stay.

The hospital admission process created yet another surreal layer to our unfolding family drama. My stepfather's ability to appear perfectly normal to strangers while harbouring private delusions mirrored my own daily performance. He presented a coherent exterior while internally navigating chaos, moving between worlds of appearance and reality, never fully inhabiting either.

My stepfather stayed there for about two weeks. We visited this strange foreboding place every day. One day we turned up and my stepfather was in a padded cell. A heavy metal door ensured there would be no escaping. A bare mattress lay in the middle of the floor. He wasn't eating the hospital food, so we'd brought him fish and chips at his request – I'd never seen him eat fish and chips. I gave him the butcher paper-wrapped warm parcel, salty grease oozing out, and he ravenously devoured its contents.

As I walked through the open ward, I met someone who told me he was Jesus and another deranged fellow who had a direct line to God. I had traversed a time warp onto a bizarre and wackadoodle old movie set. The scene was bare and sterile. A dry, rum-like, sweetish odour hung in the air, along with the stench of urine. Paint peeled off hard cold lath and plaster walls, cracked in places. Busy looking people in white jackets carrying clipboards scurried about, inpatients sitting in chairs rocked back and forth. Others stared piercingly with ping-pong ball wide-eyed gazes and suspiciously in my direction. I quickly averted my gaze. People standing motionless, staring blankly into space. People dribbling and making disturbing repetitive twitchy motions with their hands, mouths, and faces. Nurses roamed around in funny hats. Bars on windows kept the inmates safe from the dangers lurking about the outside world.

Strangely, I didn't feel afraid. It was just another experience to add to my anything but normal life.

The treating psychiatrist told us that my stepfather had had a psychotic episode and paranoid schizophrenia. I didn't have much of an idea about what he was talking about, other than what I had seen in movies. My stepfather was heavily medicated when they released him. Initially, he seemed high as a kite on the antipsychotics he was taking. He'd walk around the house with a silly grin, laughing to himself. The medication was later altered, and he became zombie-like, heavily sedated, and hardly ever talking. He would never be the same again, nor would their lives. Their friends and relatives immediately shunned them. Mental illness was taboo. People were largely ignorant back then.

Prior to this, Mum and my stepfather had an active social life. They went to three Italian social clubs every week. There, they played cards and bingo, had lunches, and took day trips across the border to Albury, NSW, to play the one-arm bandits – which my Mother loved. They went visiting friends and relatives and lots would visit them in return. After this episode, everything stopped. Few relatives came to visit. My stepfather lost his driving licence, and my Mother became his carer and was home bound. Her world shrank to the four walls of our home. Life, once again, dramatically changed for my long-suffering Mother, and I absorbed the stigma that surrounded mental illness.

Watching his identity disintegrate, and then be partially reconstructed through medication, I wondered why no such process existed for the rupture I carried within me.

Somehow, through this new madness, I managed to pass my first year of university exams. Science, at least, still made sense when nothing else did.

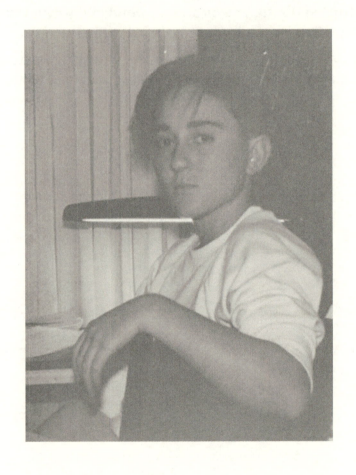

Me at 20 years old (1984)

8

The Great Escape

(1985–1989)

Holding stillness between jagged edges

The years from 1980–1985, following my adoption revelation, were marked by a desperate search – not yet explicitly for my biological roots, but for any sense of belonging, a deep connection that might fill the void their absence created. At this early juncture in my long journey, I did not understand that the happenings during my critical early years of life had caused the fracturing. I believed I was born faulty – inherently broken. I struggled to comprehend my fluctuating emotions and erratic behaviour. Awareness was not yet tangible. I was simply in a reactive survival mode, using drugs, running, and distraction to quell the inner turmoil. Life had been a series of upheavals. I was a tightened coil, bracing for the next rupture. Unity might have healed the shatter, but I was still splintering.

University life at RMIT and the hockey field had become twin refuges where I could temporarily escape the central eternal question that haunted me and perhaps all adoptees and others who have experienced intense trauma that ruptures sense of self: *Who am I?*

The year, 1985, began fulfilling the thrill-seeker in me – perhaps an inherited trait from biological parents I couldn't name – I got my motorcycle learner's permit and bought my first motor scooter, a blue and white Yamaha 80cc – a thrill and a rebellion, to my Mother's horror. I was studying and working part-time at Dorevitch Pathology on Burke Road, Camberwell, in the microbiology department processing samples. Another labelled slide in the mosaic of me. Budding laboratory scientist, small but definable, concrete in a way my origins were not.

I sprinted across fields, buried myself in textbooks, counted every dollar – each motion a decoy, each achievement a getaway car speeding me away from the wreckage of my past. Escape wasn't a destination; it was a velocity. The decision to leave came slowly – then all at once. I couldn't keep piecing myself together beneath a roof that still whispered someone else's name. I wasn't just leaving a house – I was fleeing the myth of who I was expected to become. I needed space to imagine who I might be. I stood trembling in my bedroom, my single bag hastily packed and waiting by the door.

Her face contorted. 'If you leave, I'll never speak to you again.' Her voice was raging with an emotion that fell somewhere between genuine hurt and calculated manipulation. Desperately, she yelled, 'I'll take you out of my will.' Her fists clenched, veins bulging at her temples.

Her words – meant to tether me through guilt – only strengthened my resolve. Yet underneath my defiance lay a deeper fear: that perhaps the real problem wasn't my circumstances, but something fundamentally broken within me – something that made me the kind of person people left behind or pushed away.

Tears streamed down my face, my body shaking. 'I'm still leaving.' My actions steadier than I felt – as though someone else, someone stronger and more certain, had momentarily taken control. The bag felt heavy in my hand – filled with more than just clothing. It carried the weight of this choice, another fragment to add to the pile.

I didn't know if leaving would help reassemble – or break what little was left. But the compulsion to move, to change, to seek was stronger than any fear – stronger than the slow tearing of staying still.

In those days, an unmarried Italian daughter leaving home was scandalous – second only to falling pregnant out of wedlock. My cousin and aunts acted as if I'd committed a mortal sin, bringing shame on the family.

'*Hai fatto una grande mala figura,*' they said. The accusation stung but it couldn't override my need for independence. In an odd way, this act of rebellion against my adoptive family's expectations was my first real assertion of self – a quiet declaration that I would define my own identity rather than accept the one assigned to me.

In their collective minds, it meant that I didn't love my Mother – which was grossly untrue, despite our differences. Years later, she told me they tried to convince her of this.

Despite the backlash, I'd wanted to move out of home before marriage and motherhood, which I imagined might come in five years' time. More than anything, I needed space – space away from the constant reminders of who I was supposed to be, to explore who I might be.

My Mother's narrow-minded, small village worldview was suffocating. Her emotional volatility and our turbulent relationship made home unliveable.

Leaving against her wishes felt less like rebellion and more like necessity – the first step in owning my story on my own terms.

The first night in my new home remains etched in memory: standing alone in a cold, sparsely furnished room, lino-covered floors, surrounded by boxes that held the tangible fragments of my life so far. The silence was both terrifying and exhilarating. No Mother's voice calling out, no stepfather's shuffling footsteps, no thick air with unspoken tensions. Just emptiness – waiting to be filled with whatever self I might create.

I ran my fingers along the rough unfamiliar cream walls, claiming this space as the first that truly belonged to me. The floorboards creaked under my weight in unfamiliar patterns, a new language of movement I would need to learn. The air smelled of old wood and possibility – no lingering scent of my Mother's cooking or my stepfather's mustiness. Even the quality of light was different, filtering through uncurtained windows at angles that transformed ordinary objects into something slightly mysterious. The sound of trams in the distance.

That evening, I spread my possessions around the room – artefacts from my life arranged like puzzle pieces on the floor. A few childhood photos felt like they belonged to someone else – their narrative of family continuity growing more fictional by the day. The guitar my Father had given me before his death was the only connection that felt unquestionably real. School medals, sport trophies, science textbooks – fragments of achievement that hinted at capability, but not identity. As I looked around, it felt like I was piecing someone together – someone I was still trying to find.

As darkness fell, I sat cross-legged on the floor, in front of the unlit fireplace in the lounge room where the freedom I'd sought suddenly felt hollow in its realisation. The silence I'd craved now swelled with all my unanswered questions:
If I was no longer my Mother's daughter in her house, who was I in this empty room?
What self could I assemble from these scattered pieces?
The independence I'd demanded now unsettled me with its implications – I was truly on my own, both practically and existentially.

First Serious Relationship

In mid-1985, I'd met a blonde-haired, quietly spoken, handsome young man at a party – sensitive, with a familiar haunted quiet. He was a sparkie, originally from the other side of Australia –

athletic, played bass guitar, and sang. He would become my first serious partner.

After leaving home, we went on a date around September, and by December, we were living together in his tiny one-bedroom flat in Clarke Street, Northcote.

A few years later we bought a house together in Queen Street, Coburg. I was 23 at that time. My Mother and stepfather had taught me that rent money was dead money.

Queen Street was off Moreland Road and was within walking distance to Sydney Road, Brunswick. I often did my shopping at the Coburg shopping area near the corner of Bell and Sydney Roads, or sometimes at Barkly Square in Brunswick.

In this relationship, I tried to assemble another fragment of identity: partner, potential wife, future mother. Our domestic routines and shared home seemed to promise stability – a counterweight to the uncertainty of my origins. I hung on tightly to this relationship, seeing in it the possibility of grounding myself in a present and future that I could control, unlike my past, which remained largely a mystery. Every decision – from buying a house to planting a garden – was like placing down an anchor in the turbulent sea of my fractured self.

The day we signed the mortgage papers for our house on Queen Street was perhaps the most conventional day of my life – sitting across from a bank manager, officially committing to 30 years of payments, a future that stretched further ahead than my known past stretched behind. The solidity of the paperwork, the weight of the pen in my hand as I signed, the concrete plans we discussed for renovations – all created a comforting illusion of normality, permanence, and predictability.

'Home,' my partner said, as we turned the key in the lock for the first time, his voice warm with a certainty I couldn't fully share. Home had always been a provisional concept for me, its foundations suspect. But I smiled and nodded, wanting desperately to believe that belonging could be this simple – that it could be purchased, constructed, claimed through sheer force of will.

That night, standing in the empty living room of our new house, I experienced a moment of genuine peace. The water-stained ceilings, the peeling wallpaper, the creaking floorboards – all awaited our transformation, just as I awaited my own. Perhaps this is how identity worked after all – not discovered intact but built painstakingly, room by room, decision by decision, relationship by relationship. For the first time since that day on the bus, I felt the fragments of myself settling into a pattern that might eventually become whole.

Somehow, I managed to just scrape a pass and get my first degree. I stood on the podium accepting my degree as my Mother, stepfather, and the boyfriend sat in the auditorium and proudly watched the proceedings. A fleeting moment of belonging, tranquillity, and achievement. Each new pursuit – love, home, career – was a tile I laid atop the crack, hoping it might hold.

The hope was short-lived. Six months after we had moved into our run-down renovator's nightmare California Bungalow in mid-1988, he said he wanted to split up. That night, I sat alone on our half-refinished hardwood floors, my body physically unable to move, breathing in shallow gasps that couldn't seem to fill my lungs. He moved out the next day. I stopped eating, stopped answering the phone, stopped opening curtains.

The house we'd planned to renovate together became my cave – dark rooms with dust-covered tarps, exposed beams, and unfinished projects that mirrored my own incompleteness. In bed each night, I'd press my palm against my chest, trying to physically hold together what felt like it might crack open.

To cope, the only way I knew how then, I self-medicated – not treating symptoms, but trying to numb my existence. The fragments of my identity that I'd so carefully assembled were scattering again, leaving me searching for connections that might hold me together.

The house we had bought together – meant to be our foundation – became instead a mausoleum of failed belonging. Each room held ghosts of our plans, the garden we'd started now overgrown with weeds, the half-finished renovations abandoned mid-transformation. I wandered through empty rooms at night, touching walls we had painted together, my fingers lingering on the cracks in plaster. Sometimes I'd press my forehead against these fissures, feeling their jagged edges against my skin, as if greeting a familiar face.

Months later, 'Maybe we could try again,' he suggested, standing awkwardly in the hallway. The hope that flared in me was almost painful in its intensity – for reconciliation and continuity, for the possibility that at least one broken thing in my life might be repaired.

We reunited towards the end of the year. But something had shifted. My sense of safety had been breached, and trust no longer came easily. I was wary – the rupture had reinforced my oldest fear: that I was fundamentally unworthy and unlovable.

What had my biological mother seen in me – or failed to see – that made her give me up? What had my boyfriend seen that made him leave? The questions were different, but the deep wound felt the same.

Apart from my angry outbursts with my Mother and door-slamming episodes, I'd always been placid, easy-going, and non-violent. I avoided conflict. If people argued or raised their voices, I had to leave the room. Any hint of drunken violence made me feel on edge. It awakened the old demons.

It was a scorching afternoon in the summer of 1988–1989.

I pulled into the Oak Park pool car park, the small orange and brown Ford Escort panel van rattling to a halt under the glaring Melbourne sun.

The humid air was thick with the smell of chlorine and the high-pitched shrieks of children splashing in the water. I weaved my way past families sprawled on faded towels, following the gradual incline toward the upper lawn area where I knew my partner was waiting.

As I came into view, I saw them.

My boyfriend was sitting far too close to our neighbour, their knees nearly touching, their heads bent together in an intimacy that didn't belong.

And then – as casually as if they had done it a thousand times – he turned and kissed her on the lips.

For a moment, the world slowed.

The sun's heat seemed to vanish. The bright colours of towels and swimsuits dulled. All the splashing and laughter around me dissolved into a thick, muffled silence.

I stood frozen, blinking stupidly against the sun, unsure if I had really seen what I thought I had. A strange hollow opened in my chest, as if all the air had been sucked from my body.

Then the heat rushed back – volcanic, unstoppable.

'What the fuck?' I exploded.

I stormed up the incline, my towel clenched in a fist, and hurled it straight at him.

'What the fuck is going on?' I shouted, the words tearing from my throat louder than anything I had ever said in my life.

The controlled, contained person I had carefully constructed dissolved, revealing a rage I hadn't known I possessed.

I stormed home. I took a hammer to his motorcycle, methodically destroying everything he valued. I became unrecognisable to myself – a stranger inhabiting my body, acting out a destruction that mirrored what had been done to me.

The sound of glass breaking beneath my hammer mirrored the shattering I'd felt on that bus years ago – fragments flung outward by my Father's violence. In destroying his possessions, I was expressing something fundamental about how it felt to be displaced, discarded, deemed replaceable. Back then, I thought breaking his things would fix what was broken in me. But it only scattered the wreckage further.

In that moment of destruction, I became someone I barely recognised – violent, vengeful, out of control. The fragmentation wasn't just metaphorical anymore; I was literally smashing things to pieces, as if my inner turmoil and brokenness had found perfect explosive expression. The adopted child who had been conditioned to be grateful, to never make waves, to accept what she was given, suddenly refused these constraints. The fury wasn't just about betrayal; it was decades of suppressed questions, fears, and insecurities erupting all at once – the primal rage of a child who had been told her origins didn't matter, her questions weren't welcome, her identity wasn't hers to claim.

Hockey Days

In the aftermath of the second break-up, I continued to stumble through my uni course, far more invested in the community I'd found than the academic content. Hockey wasn't just a sport; it was my only salvation. On the field, identity was simple: I was a striker, a goal-scorer, a teammate. The rules were clear, the boundaries marked. The satisfying thwack of stick against ball created a physical certainty that my life otherwise lacked.

Each sprint down the field, lungs burning, muscles straining, anchored me in the immediate present – no past to question, no future to fear, just the ball, the goal, and the next move. The bruises on my shins, the calluses on my palms, the sweat soaking my uniform – these were concrete proofs of existence, undeniable markers of presence in a world where I otherwise felt like a ghost.

The downward spiral that began the day I stepped off the bus was gathering momentum.

My trauma vault was stuffed to bursting.

I doused it with alcohol and pot, while exhausting my body through excessive training – the physical exertion serving as pressure relief for psychological wounds I couldn't otherwise manage.

I was running faster and more frequently now. I became increasingly obsessed with playing hockey. I played in the summer and winter competitions and mixed hockey. Pushing my body to its physical limits became a way to outrun my demons, to temporarily escape the questions that haunted me. If I could just move fast enough, perhaps the fragments wouldn't have time to separate further. I could just keep myself together. The running in my dreams still haunted me – that sense of being pursued by something I couldn't name, couldn't escape.

By 1989, I was 25. I still didn't have a deep need to search for my birth mother. There had been too much going on. Too many distractions from the central mystery of my existence – or perhaps these distractions were precisely the point, ways to avoid confronting what might be found if I looked too closely into my origins.

Standing on our front porch, after another difficult conversation with my ex-partner – who was moving out for the second and final time – I had a sudden, crushing realisation: I had been trying to recreate family through romantic partnership, seeking in him a stable centre I hadn't been able to find in myself. The house we had bought together, the garden I had planted, the future I had planned – all attempts to construct something permanent to counterbalance the impermanence at my core. I wasn't yet ready for such an undertaking.

As he drove down Queen Street, I remained on the porch clutching myself. The evening air carried the scent of my neighbour's BBQ, someone else's life proceeding with ordinary certainty while mine unravelled. A distant dog barked, traffic hummed on Moreland Road, leaves rustled in the front yard – the world continuing its rhythms despite the rupture I was experiencing. The concrete step beneath me felt solid yet temporary, neither belonging to the house nor to the street, but to the space between – exactly where I existed now.

The house was now mine alone, a clean slate upon which I could continue my faltering attempts to construct an identity. But the silence that greeted me when I finally stepped inside suggested that real integration wouldn't come from external arrangements, no matter how carefully planned.

I was in and out of a couple of relationships with other men. None were father material or happily ever after material. I kept collecting fragments of connection – each relationship promising wholeness, but offering only a temporary illusion of belonging.

Despite feeling lost, my 20s were among the happiest of my adult life. I found a group that felt like family – we shared meals, laughter, and the kind of easy loyalty I'd longed for. Friends all completed their uni degrees and got professional steady jobs, while I kept aimlessly floating from job to job. In between lab jobs, I was a manager at the State Hockey Centre, a non-destructive tester of steel working with radioactive isotopes, and a courier, constantly drifting and searching for a professional identity that would resonate with me.

Various housemates drifted in and out of my home. Many alcohol-fuelled hockey parties were held at Queen Street.

But beneath the carefree exterior, questions about my origins continued to simmer. Without a solid foundation of biological identity, I was building my life on shifting sands. The older I got, the more I wondered about my biological origins – those missing pieces that would lead me back to the beginning.

My various jobs, relationships, and social circles were attempts to create meaning and connection in the absence of origins – to build an identity from fragments I could find or create, rather than the biological and cultural inheritance that had been severed at birth. Like a mosaic artist without a pattern to follow, I was placing pieces side by side, hoping that someday they might reveal a coherent image. That image remained elusive, but the search – though temporarily paused – was far from over.

As the 1980s ended, I stood at a crossroads – behind me, a trail of childhood traumas, shattered relationships, and fleeting achievements. Ahead lay new challenges, new fragments to gather, and the inescapable search for my biological roots. The foundation I'd built – education, friendships, athletic identity – would prove vital when I finally returned to the question that had launched everything:

Who am I, really?

The answer lived not just in what I had gathered,
but in the empty spaces –
where nothing and everything, remained.

Interlude I

Lacuna

*There is a stillness, ancient,
blood stitched by DNA.*

*I traversed it–
the betrayal of stamped documents,
whispers around a kitchen table,
the thundering silence of a birthright, a name.*

*In this space,
I paid attention to missing words–
between the mother and the not-mother–
deciphering the language of sorrow
passed down through dreams and withholding.*

*The lacuna did not kill me–
it made me stronger.*

*It is revealed in my speech,
it walks in my shadow,
its silence in my lineage.*

Part II

The Mothers

–

Scattering

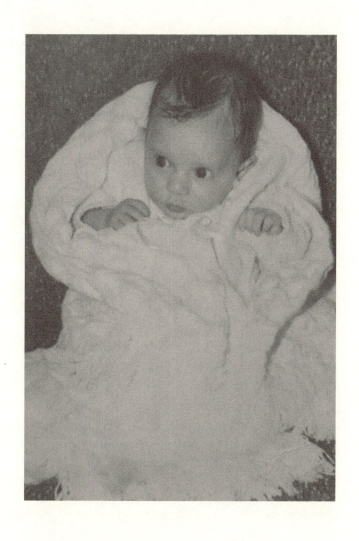

My first baby photo (5 September 1964)

9

26 - 'Giuseppe' (1990)

What is hidden, always leaving a trace

In 1984, while Reagan reshaped America, the AIDS crisis devastated communities, and as Australia moved toward economic deregulation, a quieter revolution was unfolding in adoption policy. Evidence began to emerge of the damage caused by closed adoptions – the psychological wounds that festered beneath policies of secrecy and separation. Studies documented higher rates of anxiety, substance abuse, depression, attachment disorders, and identity disturbances among adoptees denied knowledge of their origins. This research, emerging alongside broader social movements emphasising transparency and individual rights, slowly shifted legislative priorities. While Michael Jackson's *'Thriller'* album topped the Australian charts, adoption laws in Victoria changed with the introduction of the Adoption Act – legislation that would finally give me access to my real identity and origins.

One night after dinner, *A Current Affair* was on TV. Mike Willesee, on the softly glowing screen, spoke of a social revolution. Adoptees could legally access their real birth certificates. I felt relieved that my Mother, sitting with me in our baroque living room, couldn't understand English. My Mother's cousin was visiting at the time. Her daughter was watching the TV with me. After Willesee made his announcement she said, 'If that were me, I wouldn't want to see my real birth certificate'. She knew, like everyone else that I was adopted. I stared at the

TV and said nothing. The familiar burning warmth of shame crawling up my face. That night as I thought about what the adoption law change meant, a storm of conflicting emotions rose in my chest. Hope rose. Fear strangled it. Then silence returned.

The steel bars that had kept me from my origins were legally dissolving, yet I remained paralysed, unable to step through the door that had finally opened. For years I would drive past the government buildings that housed my birth records, my car slowing involuntarily before I accelerated away, thinking, *Not today. I'm not ready.*

My personal journey intersected with this historical inflection point, my individual search made possible by collective advocacy and an evolving social consciousness. The sealed records that had concealed my origins were cracking open, for me and for tens of thousands whose identities had been similarly broken by institutional practices now being questioned. There were fundamental changes in it that were highly relevant to me. I could now access my real, unadulterated original birth certificate, and associated adoption papers.

As I held my real birth certificate for the first time. The single, brutal stamp – 'ADOPTED' – tried to sever blood with ink. It embodied the era's cruel certainty – that a clean break was possible, the theory underpinning closed adoptions at the time that argued with little evidence, that nurture could completely erase nature, that my connection to my birth mother could be stubbed out as neatly as this document suggested. The same bureaucrats who had deemed single mothers like her 'unfit' had crafted this paper reality to replace my biological one, their typewritten certainty betraying none of the reality of human emotions beneath. They argued, along with the Catholic Church that, 'White, married couples were considered the 'ideal' family unit.' Any white married couple was deemed more fitting to be parents than a young unmarried woman. With evidence to the contrary, the post-1984 era led to what is now known as 'the open era of adoption'. Meaning the birth records are no longer sealed, in Australia.

A birth certificate is our first legal document, used to obtain many other documents throughout life: driver's licence, passport, Medicare Card, marriage certificate, bank accounts, credit cards. A birth certificate lists the names of our parents and connects us to our DNA, cultural heritage, ethnicity, and family and medical history. Mine was a falsehood. I had been deprived of this crucial knowledge.

I still cannot comprehend how entire systems – courts, hospitals, churches, societies – conspired to separate babies from their natural parents, severing ties with cultural and ethnic heritage, denying relevant biological or medical background, and giving innocent babies to complete strangers. Strangers who had not been adequately assessed for their mental stability or parenting ability. And to deny these children the fundamental truths of how they came into this world, and who their real biological parents were.

Who had made up these screwed up rules?

I was lucky to live during a time when the law governing these matters changed. Not so lucky for the tens of thousands of adoptees who died before 1984, either not knowing they were adopted or unable to track down their biological parents, if they wished to do so. In some parts of the world, as of 2025, these laws haven't changed, and real birth certificates and adoption records remain firmly sealed.

For the previous six years, since 1984, I had been too busy with starting uni, having relationships, socialising with friends, working, or playing hockey. Or so I thought and told myself. Perhaps what I'd truly found was temporary refuge – an identity and sense of belonging among my university peers and hockey teammates that allowed me to postpone confronting my most fundamental questions.

I had finished university, bought a house, had been in a relationship, and had now split up with the love of my life.

I was at an impasse.

Where was I heading in life? What was I doing?

I was 26 and many of my Aussie friends had partnered. Some were having children and starting families.

I was still struggling with my sexuality, compounded by all my other struggles. It was an even more difficult time to be gay during the 1980s than it had been previously. Homophobic slurs were par for course in Australian society: poofs, gays, poo jabbers, lezzos, dykes, carpet munchers. Australia, along with the rest of the world, was largely bigoted and anti-gay. The HIV/AIDS epidemic was lurking. It largely affected gay men, which gave the homophobes even more reason to be homophobic. In Australia we had the ominous Grim Reapers ad on TV to promote safe sex practices and to warn people about the evil dangers of HIV. Gay bashing was even more fair game. I didn't need to draw any more attention to myself. I already wore enough shame. My Catholic upbringing further reminded me that homosexuality was an 'abomination.'

Did the Bible say anything about women lying with women?

How much more could I burden my Mother and extended family with?

I wanted to play hockey at a higher level, so I moved to the Essendon Hockey Club at the start of 1990. I played in District 1, at the time the seconds to League 1.

It was the start of the 90s, but same-sex attraction was still a societal taboo. People whispered about the 'lezzos' at my new hockey club. Few celebrities were out. Gays and lesbians in films, TV, and earlier fiction were depicted as loners, mentally deranged, evil, or sinners. There had been no openly gay people at my high school, in my neighbourhood, at my workplaces, or in my friendship circles. I considered myself bisexual, and still do, but I now use the self-referring term gay, to avoid ignorant conversations about the fluidity or binary nature of sexuality. I was gay, adopted, and a child of an abusive alcoholic. I had hit the trifecta. Shame, shame, and more shame.

At the EHC, I met my first lesbian couples. I felt uncomfortable and an inexplicable shame in their presence. I wanted to run away from them. Shame being a state associated with too many unpleasant memories. I just wanted to be 'normal.' Instead, my life was an endless series of traumatic events and feeling anything but normal.

Then, I found myself involved with a precocious, blonde-haired, voluptuous, and attractive young hockey player. She, along with the lesbians in my hockey team, awakened what had laid dormant for the past nine years. It was a well-hidden but short affair. It was during this turbulent time that I decided to find my real mother.

Soon after I had stepped off that bus back in 1980, I had sought my real identity. I called Jigsaw, an organisation which helped adoptees track down their natural parents. It was still pre-internet. I found them in the phone book. To my aggravation, I had to be 18 years of age before I could start my search. In resignation, I had to put aside searching for my biological roots. By the time I was 18, I knew it would be difficult to trace my natural mother, as I was not allowed access to my real birth certificate. Perhaps to avoid disappointment, I never bothered to commence the difficult and emotional search.

After, the legal changes in 1984, if I confront the raw truth, it wasn't life's distractions that held me back from searching for my real mother – it was the suffocating weight of potential rejection. My self-esteem and self-worth had been too fragile. I'd had years of doubt, worry, fear, procrastination, and pretending not to care.

Sometimes the 'What ifs' take over and prevent us from reaching our full potential. Sometimes we believe that these imagined scenarios are real. More real than reality. I had imagined many such catastrophes in my mind.

What if she were dead? Or interstate? Or overseas?

What if I couldn't track her down?

What if she didn't want to see me?

What if she was a drunk or a sex worker? Or a criminal?

What if I was the product of incest or rape?

The 'what ifs' were crippling me.

'What ifs' only exist in our minds. Occasionally, the 'what ifs' might eventuate, but we won't know until we move out of our comfort zone.

What if I overcame the fears, the doubts? What if I took the risk and found out with certainty? Somewhere within I found the courage. Perhaps I was now mentally stronger to face any potential rejection.

What was the nature of my identity?

What was my nationality?

Were my natural parents alive?

Were they married?

Did they have children?

Did I have brothers and sisters?

Why was I adopted?

These questions would drift in and out of my mind over the years. In response, I imagined that my 'real' mother had been young and single when she became pregnant with me back in September or October of 1963. Although attitudes have changed, during the 1990s being pregnant and single was barely acceptable in Australian society. I imagined that back in the 1960s, death might have been a more favourable option, especially for a young Italian Catholic girl, rather than being single and pregnant.

Such a predicament would have brought great shame upon her family. Italians of that era, and perhaps even now, were into saving face and exhibiting *la bella figura*. Almost a mantra. According to *La Gazzetta Italiana*, July 2019, la bella figura means to make a good impression. To look appealing at all costs. An essential part of Italian culture, it is more than superficial chic looks, also representing dignity, hospitality, politeness, congeniality, and generosity. Good manners and good behaviour.

One would not want to be *mal' educato* (bad mannered, uncivil, or impolite). One needs to exhibit self-respect and decency. Proper decorum. Breaking the rules would mean making *una mala figura*, (a bad impression).

In terms of finding my real identity, my biological roots, these were superficial rules and concepts that I grappled with and fought against my whole life. I didn't want to care about what other people thought of me, an illegitimate, bastard child. I didn't want this way of thinking to interfere with or impede my quest to be my authentic self. Irrespective of how difficult and lonely that was at times. The concept of la bella figura seems even more prominent in small village mentalities, where everyone knows your business. Even though Italian villages were now spread out across the world, making a good impression was still paramount.

Italians can be comparatively incredibly rude when it comes to someone's appearance. Inevitably, I internalised elements of the la bella figura doctrine, but it didn't extend to being overly concerned about my outward appearance nor did I behave insensitively towards others.

The other reason that perhaps kept me from seeking my real mother was feeling intensely disloyal to my adopted parents. My curiosity made me feel guilty and torn. When my friends asked me if I had tried to trace her, I said no. Not really knowing why.

Any hint of negative feelings was quickly suppressed and shoved into the overstuffed box, buried deep within.

My fear of rejection was too great. I knew that I couldn't just step into my real mother's life, nor could she step into mine.

What would a reunion achieve?

In early 1990, I finally found the courage to fill out the forms requesting access to my real birth certificate. For nearly a decade, since learning I was adopted, I had carried the quiet burden of not knowing. Now, at last, I was ready to face whatever truth awaited me.

As I sealed the white envelope and slipped it into the red mailbox, my hand trembled slightly. *What would I discover? Would the knowledge heal or merely open fresh wounds?* The uncertainty made my stomach tighten, but the desperate need to know overpowered my fear. This was the first concrete step I'd taken since the revelation on that bus 10 years ago – the first conscious choice to pursue my truth rather than hide from it.

I soon received a letter from Community Services Victoria dated the 20 March 1990, acknowledging my application and assigning me a registration number. The letter explained I would need to attend an interview as required by the Adoption Act 1984, with a choice of individual or group sessions. It emphasized that adoptees could receive information to search for parties involved in their adoption, while natural parents and relatives would be assisted in their search by the Adoption Information Service.

The weeks of waiting felt interminable. I alternated between obsessive imaginings of what I might discover and deliberate attempts to distract myself with work and hockey. My dreams became vivid with nameless faces and distant voices. As the date approached for my group interview, I prepared myself mentally – or tried to. *How could anyone truly prepare for meeting the truth of their origins?*

The prospect of finally holding my real birth certificate in my hands filled me with equal parts terror and longing. *What name had I been given at birth? Who was the woman who had carried me for nine months? Did she look like me? Did she think of me? And perhaps most importantly, who was my father?*

On the appointed June day, I dressed carefully – as if my appearance might somehow affect what I was about to learn. The group interview took place in a nondescript government building in Melbourne's CBD. I sat among a facilitator and 10 strangers – other adoptees and a few relinquishing mothers – each with stories that mirrored aspects of my own. We heard stories of adoptees who had traced their mothers only to be rejected. Others who had discovered their mothers were alcoholics or living in poverty. Stories of successful reunions and healing connections. I listened intently, searching for clues to my own future in their experiences.

At the end of the session, clutching the yellow A4 envelope that contained my birth certificate and adoption documents, I felt strangely calm. The moment I had both dreaded and longed for was here. I quietly sat, and with a slight tremor, I slowly opened the envelope, not quite believing that soon my real mother's name would be revealed.

My eyes scanned the documents, initially passing over most details to find the name and missing fragments that would change everything. There it was – my real birth certificate – with 'ADOPTED' stamped across it in bold, capitalised letters: No. 38179/64. Born 25 July 1964, in Carlton. Anna Zunica; County Court Melbourne 30.8.65. was handwritten in the space next to father's details; Mother's name: ▉▉▉▉▉ ZUNICA; 18 years; Born in Italy; Address: ▉▉▉▉▉, Hawthorn; Registered on the 31 July 1964, in Melbourne.

When I saw 'Anna Zunica' printed starkly, the ink on paper swam before my eyes. It was a moment of reclamation – a quiet resurrection of an identity once buried. I splintered again, into the person I was, and the one I might have been.

My body trembling with the magnitude of that tiny print.

Something so small, so ink-thin, tilted the axis of my world.

I kept reading: my mother was born in Eboli, Italy. I am at least half Italian.

I read on, discovering that I was born at 11:40 am, weighed 2.89 kg, and that my mother's labour had lasted 32 hours. She had received ante-natal care from 33 weeks gestation – possibly code for put into a home for unwed mothers. I was admitted to St Joseph's Foundling Hospital nine days after birth, baptised twice, and six weeks later – on 5 September 1964 – handed over to my adoptive parents, who became my legal parents the following March.

For over 30 days, I was an orphan – lying in a cot among other crying babies, waiting for the scent, the voice, the heartbeat I knew to return. A recognition formed in the womb. A primordial attachment – innate, embodied, and preverbal.

Studies show that when infants are violently separated from their mothers, trauma, registers in the body – stress hormones surge through the bloodstream. My mother had experienced stress during pregnancy: I endured separation at the most vulnerable stage – moments after birth.

Even in the absence of memory, the body can retain a longing for the original connection – a preverbal grief, a cellular ache.

I learned more details about my mother – ▇▇▇▇ Zunica. She was a machinist from a large family – the fourth youngest of seven brothers and five sisters. Her parents were Luigi Zunica, a 55-year-old Catholic butcher, and Marianna Castiglia, age 54. The documents noted that my birth mother was five feet tall with dark hair, brown eyes, and 'average intelligence.' She 'seems certain re adoption.'

And then, the first mention of my father:

'P. F. 5' 7" Dark hair. Hazel eyes. 26 yrs Italian single. Has a share in father's business. Knew about baby. Decided against marriage. In good health.'

My father was Italian. He had a business connection. He had dark hair and hazel eyes. He was 26 when I was conceived. But there was no name – only five fragile threads linking me to him.

I was placed in care at St Joseph's Foundling Hospital, the same building at Geoghegan College, where I had attended high school. I looked up and noticed the lath and plaster surrounding me. The high ceiling and its large ornate ceiling rose. The same-coloured walls as the old mansionette that had always felt like the keeper of secrets. My mind drifted back in time...

The Mysterious Old Mansionette (1981–1982)

The old mansionette – its red brick walls held secrets more intimate than I could have imagined. Geoghegan College in Broadmeadows had been more than just another senior high school; it was a living archive of my own forgotten history. Its very architecture a palimpsest of abandoned childhoods and institutional memories.

It was a haunting intersection of my past and present. The imposing red brick building had loomed before me, its walls seeming to pulse with unspoken histories that ran deeper than mortar and stone. Each step I had taken across its grounds had felt like walking through layers of my own forgotten existence – a living archaeological site of memories I had yet to excavate.

My body had carried a knowledge that my conscious mind could not yet grasp – a cellular memory etched into my very being. Whenever I had approached the building, an inexplicable physical response would overtake me – a tightening in my chest, a slight dizziness that I had long attributed to ordinary teenage anxiety. But now I understood. This had been a cellular memory, a bodily inheritance of a place that had cradled me in my most vulnerable moments.

On the right-hand side, great tall cream-coloured bay windows shimmered with unspoken histories, their glass panes reflecting and refracting light like memory itself – fragmented, ephemeral, yet hauntingly present. An elaborate metal lace balcony surrounded the veranda, resembling the delicate neural pathways of memory, each curl and twist a connection waiting to be understood.

Somewhere beneath the architectural facade, a profound historical wound pulsed – the legacy of institutional violence against the most vulnerable.

The Catholic Church had established St Joseph's Foundling Hospital in 1901, later known as the Broadmeadows Babies Home. These were buildings, cathedrals of concealment – architectures designed to absorb shame, to transform human vulnerability into institutional silence. Each brick, each corridor held stories of mothers torn from children, of infants rendered invisible by societal judgment.

In a letter to *The Age*, the then Archbishop described the foundling hospital as created 'to assist erring but often innocent young women and their "illegitimate children",' a linguistic violence that transformed human complexity into legal erasure, reducing living beings to bureaucratic footnotes.

I would pause on the grand staircase between classes, my fingers tracing the ornate banister, feeling an inexplicable sense of déjà vu that transcended rational understanding. The cool wood beneath my teenage fingers had perhaps felt the same tiny hands that had once been mine – an eerie loop of contact across time.

It was a place where expectant unwed mothers could hide their 'stigma and shame.' After giving birth and relinquishing their babies, these women could go on to live 'respectable' lives. Respectability – that most insidious of social currencies – was purchased at the cost of detachment trauma, maternal grief, and infant identity.

Prior to the 1970s, having an illegitimate child was a cardinal sin against social morality. Mothers were treated with unspeakable cruelty: hidden away from society, drugged during childbirth, denied pain relief, coerced to sign adoption papers, and their babies snatched away from them immediately after birth.

The initial detachment trauma ruptured the primal mother-baby bond – a wound so profound it reverberated across generations, a silent scream encoded in cellular memory.

Some relinquishing mothers were raped, sent home without their babies, forever silenced, their grief and shame buried deep within. They were told to forget their children – unfit mothers, declared a system that prized social appearances over compassion.

These were more than institutional practices – they were barbaric systemic violences, a collective social pathology of the times that transformed human vulnerability into bureaucratic procedure.

Standing in those hallways decades later, I walked as both student and archaeologist – each step a delicate excavation of my own fragmented history, each breath a potential revelation. The building that had once cradled me in my most vulnerable state now stood as a silent testament to countless stolen and broken childhoods, to the profound violence of institutional 'care.'

In this mansionette, I hadn't been a high school student passing through corridors, but a living artefact – a survivor of a system that believed it could erase identity as easily as changing a birth certificate.

The walls of Geoghegan College had witnessed my earliest days, held my first breaths, processed my first separation. And now, they whispered back to me – not with words, but with the weight of unacknowledged histories, with the silent testimony of broken bonds and institutional secrets...

I looked back down at the documents and kept reading.

The document confirmed that I was 'illegitimate' and noted I was admitted to St Joseph's on 3 August 1964, nine days after being born at the old Royal Women's Hospital in Carlton.

Reading these clinical words about my earliest days, questions flooded my mind:

Why had I spent nine days in hospital?

Was my Mother with me during that time?

Did she hold me?

Did she nurse me?

In this clinical and sterile setting, who tended to my newborn needs during those first, formative days? Who, if anyone, became the temporary vessel for a mother's love? Who fed me? Who changed my soiled nappy? Who bathed me? Who held me during this precious first month alone? Did anyone comfort me when I cried out in hunger, or pain, or discomfort? Did my little body store away this profound rupturing?

Along with the other illegitimates, we were unwanted or forcibly relinquished, and then conveniently discarded. Shunned by society. Hidden away from our mothers' dirty, sinful shame. Shame that began in the womb. After birth, we would be cleansed by the Churches, the upholders of purity, and other adoption organisations. We would become reborn, christened with a new name, and given a new clean and wholesome false identity.

We would be permanently and forever – legally severed – from our biological, ethnic, and cultural roots...

The documents continued, describing my adoptive parents. Michelina, who couldn't speak English well, and Sebastiano, a labourer at Federal Springs. Each had only four years of schooling. A written assessment from Rev. Fr. Mulligan of Hadfield stated they were 'not well known but has seen them several times at Mass. Gave regularly to sacrificial giving fund at

Glenroy when in the parish. Appear to be good Italian Catholics.'

The home visit notes were equally terse: 'Two bedrooms, but bare and furnished in typical Italian style. Brother-in-law interpreted... Language difficulty made it hard to give a true assessment. However, they appear united in their love of children. May need later supervision.'

A follow-up note from 14 February 1965, described me as a 'nice, happy little girl' weighing 17 pounds, who 'eats everything, even spaghetti' and had 'the inevitable earrings.' The casual cultural stereotype revealed in that last comment made me wince – a reminder of how differently Italian families were viewed.

With my birth certificate and adoption documents in hand, I was at a crossroads. *Would I continue searching, or let the past remain the past?*

The name ▮▮▮ Zunica beckoned.

Could I find her? Should I?

I had read stories of reunions gone wrong – mothers who refused contact, who had never told their families about their relinquished children, who reacted with anger or fear rather than joy. The potential for renewed rejection loomed large.

But the need to know – to see a face that might resemble mine, to hear a voice that might explain mysteries of my own nature – was too powerful to ignore. Despite shaking with uncertainty, I decided to continue my search.

I headed to the Births, Deaths, and Marriages building, which was then located near the Vic Market to find my birth mother's marriage certificate. Inside the beautiful old bluestone structure, I was directed to a room filled with massive, dusty leather-bound volumes. As I climbed the wooden steps, my footfalls echoed through the hollowed chamber with each landing. Finding the one labelled 'Z' and flipped to the end, dust particles dancing in the afternoon sunlight. I searched for Zunica, then for my birth mother's name.

It didn't take long to find my birth mother's marriage certificate. She had married in 1965, at the Immaculate Conception in Hawthorn, almost 10 months after I was born. The irony of the church's name wasn't lost on me – there had been nothing immaculate about my conception. Her father was listed as being born in Eboli, Naples. Other details matched those on my birth certificate.

I obtained a copy of the marriage certificate and then searched polling records for an address. Finally, I checked the White Pages. Only a few entries with her married name, Schifforo, appeared – just one in an outer eastern suburb of Melbourne. Back then, it was a simple and straightforward sleuthing process – one that would be almost impossible today under stricter privacy laws.

As I stared at the phone number, my heart raced. After years of not knowing, I was now one phone call away from potential contact. The thought paralysed me. *What would I say? 'Hello, I'm the daughter you gave away?' How would she react? Would she hang up? Deny everything? Break down?*

Too afraid to make the call myself, I enlisted my friend, Bee. On a quiet evening at her home while her parents were at work, we devised a simple cover story: she would pose as a university student conducting a survey and ask for Ursula by name. If the right person answered, we would have confirmation.

My friend dialled the number. A woman's voice answered. My friend launched into her rehearsed survey questions. The woman responded normally, unaware of the true purpose behind the call. After the call, we stared at each other in silent amazement.

The next day, with renewed determination, I called Community Services Victoria and asked them to contact Ursula on my behalf. After a few days of agonising waiting, I received their call: she had agreed to meet me.

I was still working at Cabrini Hospital in Malvern as a medical microbiologist. During my lunch break, I stood anxiously at the side of the main road outside the hospital, scanning passing cars for a white sedan with a female driver. A car made a U-turn, pulled up alongside me, and stopped. A woman opened the door. I quickly scanned her features: light, sandy straight hair; large brown eyes – my eyes – and an oval face with pale complexion. At 44 years old, she looked remarkably youthful – a feature she had passed onto me.

'Hallo, Mirella?'

My heart pounding, I stepped into the car, feeling as though I were entering another dimension. 'Hello,' I said.

'I'm Ursula,' she said, in a softly spoken voice, just like mine.

She drove us to a local café in Camberwell, not far from where she lived. She was thin like me, about five feet tall, slightly shorter than me.

As we sat down at the café, the aroma of sugar, coffee, and cakes filled my nostrils.

She scrutinised my facial features, and then said, 'You look like your father.'

The words hung in the air between us – an acknowledgment of my paternity that simultaneously raised more questions. *Who was this man whose features I apparently carried?*

'*What was his name?*' I carefully ventured.

'Giuseppe. He lived in Carlton,' she replied simply.

At that time, I wanted to know about her and her family. 'Do you have any children?' I asked, keen to know if I had siblings.

'I have a daughter, 24, married and she has a baby, who is one and a half years old. I also have a son, 23. He is a musician and goes to music college. My youngest son is 8 years old.'

I noted the 18-year gap between myself and her youngest child, a curious coincidence. She told me that her Father, my maternal Grandfather, was still alive, but her Mother, my Grandmother, a homemaker, had died a few years earlier. Ursula confirmed what I'd read about her many siblings.

Although she was from Eboli, near Naples, and I was brought up Sicilian, we shared a southern Italian heritage. She revealed that her husband knew about me – 'the bastard baby' she'd had before marrying him. After their wedding, he had forbidden her to ever mention me again. He didn't know she was meeting me today. Our meeting was shrouded in secrecy, something I couldn't seem to shake off.

Sitting across from this woman – my birth mother, the woman who had carried and nourished me for nine months – I searched for some sense of deep connection, some feeling of recognition. But there was nothing beyond the physical resemblance. She was a stranger who happened to have given birth to me.

'Was I married? Did I have any children? How did I find her?' She asked the expected questions.

I asked a few more of my own. She said that over the years, she had thought about me. 'But what could I do? The decision had been made,' she lamented. 'I had no choice. My parents made me give you away. Having a baby while unmarried was too shameful.'

'I've always thought about you. You are, after all, my firstborn child,' she said, with a forlorn look on her face.

I discerned little of her personality during our brief meeting. *Was she caring enough to meet me, or merely curious?* Perhaps she felt guilt for having abandoned her firstborn.

Our meeting lasted about an hour before I had to return to work. As we parted, she said she wouldn't mind seeing me again. I left it for her to contact me, thinking it would be more convenient for her. I didn't feel an instant bond. There was no real connection. No tears of happiness. No warm embraces.

I waited, but the call never came.

In the days, months, and years that followed, I felt cursed –

trapped in limbo, waiting for what I couldn't have, burdened by what I didn't want. A lonely, family-less existence, save for my Mother and a few cousins who I only saw occasionally.

Eventually, the tears I'd suppressed for over a decade broke through the dam I'd carefully constructed – hot, mournful tears of primal grief. Tears of rejection, sorrow, loss, and deep longing. I had been abandoned again.

For years, I had avoided facing the pain – the deep wound of being severed from my mother at birth. Instead, I'd intellectualised it. It was the 1960s. She was young, unmarried, and Italian – three facts that, at the time, spelled catastrophe. Falling pregnant out of wedlock was taboo. She couldn't have kept me. I had been taught to suppress my own emotions – to prioritise the feelings of others over mine.

Acknowledging the primal wound would have unleashed everything else I'd kept buried. I had become skilled at concealing and suppressing emotion. The trauma, grief, and loss I carried felt too vast to face. I lacked the psychological tools – and the support – to hold them.

Adoption's deeper effects were rarely spoken about. I was expected to be eternally grateful – saved from a life of ruin by a respectable, married, Catholic couple who gave me their home, their name, their version of love.

My fragmented self had become a kind of map – jagged, uncertain – and I was following its broken lines, hoping they might eventually lead me home.

Some days, it suspended me in quiet questioning; other days, it thinned into sharp clarity – collapsing decades into a single moment.

The bus revelation still felt as vivid as the morning's coffee and toast.

I began to understand that for adoptees, time folds differently – our lives split into parallel timelines: the one we live, and the one we might have lived – creating a complexity those with unbroken histories never even have to imagine.

My search for identity wasn't a movement through space, but a slow excavation through layered time – an attempt to reconcile timelines that had split before memory itself began. Perhaps that's why birthdays, graduations, and anniversaries always carried a second shadow – each celebration illuminating the present while quietly mourning what was lost.

And somewhere, Giuseppe remained –
part myth, part man, stitched into the seams of my existence, a missing piece I was not yet ready to touch.

Mum and me – baptism (1964)

10

Final Rejection: Ursula's Farewell
(1991–1993)

Silences echoing across generations

Early 1991. The morning after a cocktail party with hockey mates. With a throbbing head and blurry eyes, I collected the empty hard liquor bottles and counted more empty bottles than there had been people present.

Frozen, I stared at the evidence of our excess. A truth I could no longer avoid.

I can't keep doing this.

I decided to cut back on drinking, which meant leaving behind my hockey companions. Instead, I channelled my energy into renovating my Californian Bungalow.

I kept drifting between part-time jobs. I was now working at the former Preston and Northcote Community Hospital, known as PANCH, doing shift work, in the biochemistry and blood banking departments, processing blood samples.

I had left Cabrini after a back injury sustained during a hockey game, when I was 26 years old. I kept playing hockey, even though I should have given my back a chance to heal. I still had a need to run. I was young and thought that I was indestructible.

I soon had another brief relationship – less secret than the last. We were out to some friends, but not to our families. The internalised homophobia was constant, invisible, crushing – a weight that never left my chest. I couldn't bring myself to tell my conservative Italian Mother. I told a few cousins; they were kind, accepting. But the larger silence – around who I was, what I carried – remained unbroken.

The silence didn't still the questions. It fed them.

The scraps Ursula had offered – Giuseppe, Carlton, a family business – weren't enough. I needed the full story. I wanted to hear the truth from the woman who had carried me and then let me go. I pictured her walking through her days, her grandson in tow, while I remained frozen in the moment she relinquished me.

The anxiety from our first meeting never fully left me. For three years I told myself I was waiting for her convenience. But silence doesn't need translation – it speaks. Hers said rejection. The absence was the message.

Still, eventually, the need to know outweighed the fear of hearing no.

My hand trembled as I reached for the phone, my heartbeat a thundering reminder of what was at stake.

Before I could reconsider, I dialled her number, and she answered, 'Hallo.'

'Hello,' I replied.

'Hallo, Lyre.'

'No. This is Mirella, your other daughter.'

The word 'other' hung in the air between us – an acknowledgment of my displacement, my secondary status in her life.

Did we sound alike on the phone? Did I sound like my sister?

I asked if I could see her again. She willingly obliged. We met again in Camberwell at a different café.

As I waited for her to arrive, I tried to imagine what her life had been like after giving me up. *Had she gone home from the hospital empty-armed and grieving? Had she wondered about me on my birthdays? Or had she sealed off that part of herself, walling away the memory of the daughter who could have ruined her chances of the life she ultimately built?* I would never know, because to ask those questions required a vulnerability neither of us seemed capable of in each other's presence.

This time she was more flamboyantly adorned. High heels and an abundance of jewellery – large gleaming rings on her stubby fingers, tipped with sharp painted nails. Bejewelled bracelets encircled her wrists; gold necklaces layered her neck. Light-coloured lipstick. Blackened eyelashes. Thick blue eye shadow.

In stark contrast, I wore no cosmetics. She still looked remarkably youthful for her 48 years – and she still remained a stranger.

We sat down at the small square timber table in the crowded café and ordered cappuccinos. White walls surrounded us. The aroma of cream-filled cakes, cheese and ham toasties hung in the air, along with the stench of cigarettes. Behind us, the milk frother hissed. Thud, thud on the counter.

Shortly after we sat down, she lit up a white menthol cigarette. She blew out the smoke up into the air and harshly asked, 'Why do you want to see me?'

The question sliced through the café noise like a blade.

Direct. Unadorned. Demanding.

The question struck me as both reasonable and impossible to answer fully. *How could I explain the chasm in my identity that her absence had created? The confusion of growing up sensing I was different without understanding why?*

It was difficult articulating my longing. Perhaps because I didn't feel the profound connection, I believed I should have with my biological mother. Yet there remained an urgent need to simply know her. And through her, know myself. She was my flesh and blood, the carrier of my DNA. Fashioned from her substance. Certain qualities I'd inherited from her remained mysteries I yearned to solve. Beneath all this lay a deeper yearning to forge some bond with her, simply because she was my biological mother. My fractured self craved family and connection. I wanted to mend the broken vessel I had become, gather its fragments and restore them. Then infuse it with love, belonging, history, and shared memories.

But instead of voicing these tangled yearnings, I sat mute – the words embedded somewhere between my heart and my tongue.

I could see the tension in her face – the way she held her cigarette a little too tightly. *Was she afraid I would make demands? That I would disrupt the life she'd built after giving me away?*

Perhaps in her mind, reopening this chapter threatened everything she'd constructed in the decades since – her marriage, her other children, her identity as a respectable Italian mother rather than a woman who'd had a child out of wedlock.

Yet here she was, with the child she had given away 29 years earlier.

As we sat in that noisy crowded café, I recounted to her what my disturbing childhood was like. Growing up with an abusive alcoholic Father. I tried to explain to her the scars that it had left in its wake.

She sucked on her cigarette, exhaling dismissively with the smoke.

'Forget about it and just get on with your life.'

The words landed like stones, each one cold and heavy, building a wall between us.

Her face remained impassive as she spoke, but I caught a flicker behind her eyes – her unprocessed trauma, her need to 'forget about it and get on with life.'

Was she told the same thing when she signed the papers giving me away? When she went home from the hospital without her baby? When she later married and had other children, never mentioning the firstborn she'd relinquished? Forget about your baby.

Her dismissal was a map of generational trauma – each syllable mapping the intricate topography of maternal rejection, tracing fault lines of silence that had separated us since my birth.

Is this how she had dealt with her past? Pretend it didn't happen – that it hadn't left a permanent scarring? A longing burning into the flesh.

She looked away. 'You can't be a part of my family,' she kept reiterating, ashing her cigarette with a sharp flick.

'I don't want to be a part of your family,' I replied, struggling to keep my voice steady.

'*What do you want from me?*' tapping ash from her cigarette in sharp, defensive flicks.

The question hung between us – clearer now, its meaning unavoidable. No longer chaotic noise, but cold precision.

The mother I had imagined for decades – warm, regretful, yearning – vanished like a mirage, replaced by a brittle, harsh, insensitive woman exhaling menthol smoke, her fingers flashing with rings.

Her question wasn't truly a question but a declaration: I was an inconvenience, a past she had interred until I materialised uninvited.

'I just want to know things about you. Your parents – my grandparents. Your brothers and sisters – my uncles and aunties,' I hesitated, then added softly, 'and about my father.'

She stiffened at the mention of Giuseppe, a barely perceptible tightening around her eyes and mouth.

What memories was I stirring? Was there still pain there, or anger, or something else entirely? Had he meant something to her, or was he just one of life's mistakes she preferred not to revisit?

She divulged little about Giuseppe, and what she shared wasn't flattering. I sensed she harboured deep resentment towards him.

'I can't remember his surname.'

The lie, transparent, hanging in the air like her cigarette smoke. *How could she forget the surname of a man who had changed the course of her life so dramatically?*

'He offered me the Earth and then dropped me like a hot potato when he found out that I was pregnant. He didn't offer or want to marry me,' she spat out.

'He warned me to never contact him again.'

The bitterness in her voice suggested a wound that had never properly healed – the rejection by Giuseppe, the humiliation within her community, the judgment from family members, the shame of being a fallen woman in a traditional Catholic Italian family. I wondered if her current husband really knew about me, or if I was a secret she had buried so deeply that even mentioning me induced shame.

She asked me again if I was married or had a boyfriend. I said no. Then, she gave me a quizzical look that pierced through my gay shame and told me that two of her brothers were gay.

This casual revelation stunned me – a genetic thread connecting me to people I'd never met. Something inherited beyond my eyes or the shape of my hands. A lineage of difference.

Plucking up the courage, I asked, 'Why haven't you called me?'

She replied, 'Because I don't want you to become too attached to me.'

The words seemed carefully chosen, crafted over the three years since our first meeting. *Had she anticipated this question? Had she wrestled with it herself, perhaps feeling guilty for not reaching out, perhaps even picking up the phone and putting it down again?*

Had she feared her own attachment rather than mine? Had seeing me stirred emotions she had spent decades carefully stuffing away?
Had she been unable to sever the maternal bond?
'Sometimes we make mistakes, but there isn't anything we can do about them but to go on with your life,' she offered, her voice hinting at regret.
I wasn't sure what she meant; I didn't ask. My mood was sinking.
'I've always thought about you. I wondered: What happened to you? I wondered, if you were happy and having a good life. You are, after all, my first-born child. I always told myself I had four children, not three,' she said.
This was an interesting comment as decades later I discovered a death certificate for a deceased daughter, Rosalia Zunica. She had five children, not four. *Two first daughters lost, two empty spaces at the beginning of her maternal story – was this too much truth for one heart to carry?*
Each word was a small gift – tentative, but precious, despite her defensive posture. Though she had kept me from her life, she hadn't erased me. I had lived quietly in her mind all these years, counted in secret.
It wasn't connection, but it was something. A fragile thread of acknowledgment in the face of absence.
She told me her Father had recently died. I would never meet him. She mentioned they had lived in Hawthorn, but when I later checked, I realised she had lied about the exact address. I couldn't help but wonder why.
To my growing irritation, she kept repeating, 'What do you want from me?'
'I'd like to see you occasionally,' I said.
Was that too much to ask?
I wanted to ask if she had mourned me. If she'd held me, even once, before they took me away. If anyone had comforted her, or if her natural grief had been buried beneath shame. But the distance between us was too vast. She had spent decades

bricking over this part of her life, and it was clear – those walls weren't coming down any time soon.

Still, she said she didn't mind seeing me again. We arranged to meet in two weeks. She even offered to drive to my place in Coburg. She said she had to leave quickly to babysit her grandson – my nephew – but that otherwise she would have stayed longer.

I walked her to her car. Before she got in, she kissed me goodbye – Italian style, a kiss on both cheeks.

That kiss – formal, cultural, expected – held none of the maternal warmth I'd quietly yearned for. It was the kind of kiss exchanged between acquaintances, not the reunion of a mother and her lost child. Still, it was something – a gesture, however restrained, that acknowledged a connection – however tenuous. In some ways, Ursula embodied the kind of mother I had always longed for: younger than the woman who raised me, Australian-raised, schooled locally, fluent in English. Someone I could talk to – really talk to – without the barriers of language or generational distance.

After we parted, the questions came flooding in:

Why should her husband care about me?

Why would my brothers and sister care about me?

Why would Ursula's siblings want anything to do with me?

As I drove home, I tried to see the situation from her perspective. She had been almost 19 when I was born – trapped in the vice grip of 1960s morality and family expectations. She had done what was expected, what she was told was best for her illegitimate baby – what may have seemed like the only choice. And now, decades later, a grown woman had appeared at her door – the living trace of a chapter she'd been instructed to forget. How destabilising that must have felt to the life she had carefully built.

I had always been exceptional at pushing away real emotion. Rationalising was easy – understanding her position was simple math. But beneath that tidy logic, a child's pain still stirred – irrational, unhealed, immune to reason.

I was, after all, a stranger. An illegitimate child who could bring shame to her respectable family. Between us lay a chasm carved by silence and secrecy. A mother who gave up her child, never expecting to see her again. Relinquished, but never forgotten. Her secret – premarital sex, pregnancy, surrender – carried like contraband through the years. That secret child was me.

I never saw Ursula again, except in photos – glimpses found decades later on Facebook or Instagram pages. Despite being her first-born child, it was clear I had no place in her world. That realisation settled like sediment, leaving me with a persistent sense of incompleteness I couldn't shake.

Ursula had offered me fragments – a name, a scattering of details – but not enough to complete the picture. Meeting her had been the slow climb of a rollercoaster, cresting with hope, only to plummet into silence and ambiguity.

My biological father, Giuseppe, remained a shadow – a name, a few faint outlines, and no clear path forward. I didn't know if I'd ever find him. Still, a quiet hope persisted.

Walking away from our final meeting, I realised I had been seeking something impossible – information about my origins, a retroactive belonging, a place at a table where a chair had never been set. I had secretly hoped Ursula would recognise in me what I could not yet recognise in myself: that biological connection creates not just curiosity, but obligations – of information, of inclusion. But the seating had been finalised decades earlier, soon after my birth. The painful truth was this: sometimes there is no chair. Sometimes, belonging cannot be retroactively granted.

More difficult than learning I was adopted was accepting that knowing this truth changed nothing in Ursula's life. I existed – perhaps in her heart, maybe in her mind – but I remained in the margins of her story, a footnote rather than a chapter.

This recognition – that truth does not guarantee connection, and that knowledge does not automatically confer belonging – forced me to confront a harder truth: that integration requires more than shared blood. It demands invitation. It demands acceptance. Neither had come.

Years collapsed into single moments whenever I glimpsed a woman with her distinctive walk – past and present briefly superimposed before reality snapped back into place. I imagined her, living just across town, carrying on as if I didn't exist, while I remained suspended in the quiet aftermath of her rejection.

What shape did her days take? Did she ever look at her other children and see flickers of me? Did she ever drive through Coburg and wonder if she might pass me on the street? These questions would never be answered – but they lingered, whispering at the edges of my awareness, quiet and relentless.

A few days later, I called my other Mother.

'You need to apologise to me for not telling me that I was adopted,' I said, my voice firm.

As always with uncomfortable truths, she deflected – gaslighting, making excuses, trying to change the subject.

But I held my ground.

'No! You need to apologise.

You should have told me!' I cried.

The words erupted from somewhere primal – not just a demand for an apology, but for recognition. For the truth she'd withheld. For the life I might have lived, had I known who I really was.

Reluctantly, she relented – and finally, said 'sorry.'

In that moment, the tension seemed to dissolve.

I couldn't have articulated it then, but what I longed for from both mothers was simple, yet profound: acknowledgment.

From my adoptive Mother, I needed her to see how the silence – her choice to keep the truth from me – had shaped and wounded me.

From my birth mother, I needed her to see *me* – to affirm that I existed, that I mattered.

I received one acknowledgment, but not the other. And that imbalance left me standing on uneven ground, always slightly off-kilter, trying to find my centre.

In 1993, my partner cheated on me – another rupture, another abandonment.

We split up soon after. It was becoming a pattern – grief layered upon grief.

The core wound reopened – this time, the descent into depression was deeper, darker.

Each episode felt worse than the last.

I didn't manage separations with the ease others seemed to – they left me ripped apart, hollowed out, worthless, unlovable.

Each departure awakened the infant within me – the one severed from her first bond,

who had learned – before she even had language –

that love could vanish,

that connection was conditional,

that safety was a temporary illusion.

Each breakup seemed to echo that first, primal abandonment when as a newborn I was torn away from my birth mother.

Though I had no conscious memory of that rupture, my body remembered.

Every ending reawakened the ancient wound, the original betrayal of trust, the unspoken message: I was not worth keeping.

In the midst of this latest heartbreak, I understood something had to change.

I needed direction – a focus beyond relationships that kept collapsing under the weight of unhealed grief.

Apart from taking up smoking again, I finally went to counselling.

Once the sessions began, the containment cracked.

I spent most sessions over the next six months crying.

For the first time, I had a calm, safe space where I could express, without judgment or interruption, the grief I had buried for years.

The loss. The pain. The shame.

It was cathartic, but not curative. There were too many wounds, and my counsellor lacked the expertise to address the complexities of repeated trauma and abandonment.

During this period, I also began spending more time with my Mother.

Soon after the breakup, I found myself in Mum's kitchen. A bright orange Bessemer Nylex Melmac ashtray sat on the now-round kitchen table. I was tapping ash into it, tears slipping down my face. I rarely cried in front of anyone – least of all my Mother – but that day, I couldn't hold it in.

She kept asking what was wrong, and I couldn't bring myself to tell her I was heartbroken again.

But she persisted.

Finally, I blurted out, 'I'm upset because I split up with my girlfriend.'

She didn't understand. I lacked the Sicilian vocabulary to explain that I was attracted to women. So I tried, haltingly, with the few words I knew.

'Jinka was my girlfriend.'

'*Girla-frienda?*' she repeated, puzzled.

The language gap gave us a brief moment of grace – a second where the truth hovered between us but hadn't fully landed.

She had met Jinka many times. I'd brought her over for lunches, dinners. But I had never introduced her as my partner.

Mum said little. Then I quietly left.

I braced for an explosion that never came. In our house, big emotions were usually followed by bigger reactions – my Father's rages, my Mother's outbursts.

But this time, there was only silence.

Unfamiliar.

Unsettling.

Maybe she needed time.

Maybe she didn't fully understand.

Or maybe, she did – and simply didn't know what to say.

A few days later, she called – and the scathing, homophobic, blinding rage began.

Her voice rose with each accusation, each rhetorical question slicing through me with brutal familiarity.

'What's wrong with you?'

'*Si anormali?*' (Are you abnormal?)

Each word landed like a hammer on the same brittle spot, shattering any fragile hope that I might one day be fully seen – and accepted – by the woman who had raised me.

The interrogation dragged on, her rage blinding, unrelenting. I was already raw from heartbreak – and now, here was my Mother, berating me for being gay.

The weight of her rejection pressed hard on an already cracked surface.

Then, from the background, I heard my stepfather's voice:

'*Lassa stari a piccirida.*' (Leave the child alone.)

I froze. His words, so gentle and unexpected, caught me off guard.

Here was compassion from the man I had spent years resenting – the one I'd blamed for drawing my Mother's attention away from me. His defence was brief, almost a whisper, but it pierced the noise.

It reminded me that even the most flawed people can still surprise us – that kindness can emerge from unlikely places.

Despite the cruelty of my Mother's words, I felt a small sense of relief: I had told her the truth. After all these years of silence, a part of me was no longer hidden.

I had taken on yet another part-time, shift-work job at the Repatriation Hospital in Heidelberg. After another brief fling, I met someone else.

In the years since leaving home and splitting with my boyfriend, my relationship with my Mother had softened. We were more like close friends than parent and child. The tension of my teenage years had faded into a quieter companionship.

One day, I asked if I could move back home.

She didn't hesitate. 'No. We get along better now.'

It wasn't cruel – just clear. A door not slammed, but gently closed.

Her answer stunned me at first. Then it made perfect sense. I had been yearning for safety, for uncomplicated belonging. But she saw what I hadn't yet realised – that our relationship thrived with distance, with boundaries, with the independence I had fought so hard to claim. Sometimes, the refuge we seek isn't behind us, but ahead – made not by returning, but by understanding.

As I entered this new chapter, the imprint of both mothers – one who raised me, and one who relinquished me – still shaped my fears, choices, and longings. But more and more, I was building something independent of them both: an identity patched together from fragments, drawn not from any single source but from the full range of experience.

Like a mosaic artist, I was learning that beauty lives in the broken edges – that wholeness doesn't require perfection or symmetry. The rejections that once shattered me had started to become something else: not acceptance, exactly, but a kind of hard-won peace.

If I would never be fully welcomed by either mother, then perhaps it was time I learned how to welcome myself.

11

The Second Orphaning
(1994–1995)

A second rebirthing of sorrow

Late in 1993, I stood at the precipice of reinvention, surrounded by lab equipment and sterile test tubes. The cold, gleaming surfaces mirrored my internal fragmentation.

I realised I couldn't spend my future processing samples and pressing buttons, trapped in the monotony of scientific routine.

Each repetitive task became a metaphor for my splintered self – endless motion without meaning, motion without direction.

The same restless spirit that had once propelled me across oceans in search of origin stirred again, drawing me inward toward a deeper kind of exploration – one that demanded presence, reflection, and the courage to face myself.

Like a wounded archaeologist excavating the ruins of self, I applied to study psychology – a return to the intellectual terrain that had first stirred my imagination during my high school days at Mercy College.

This was more than a career move; it was a deliberate act of psychological restoration.

Psychology became my sanctuary of reconstruction – a laboratory of the soul where fractured identities could be carefully examined, understood, and reassembled.

The systematic deconstruction of psychological theories became my ritual of healing – each concept was a glint from the surface of self – refracting parts of me I'd never fully seen.

I buried myself in study,

and pushed my body through training to keep grief at bay.
Sleep was broken – my dreams, restless and chaotic.

I was still running.

During the day, I dissected trauma.
At night, I tried not to feel it.

I told myself I was building a new self –
but I was only dragging the old one forward, fast enough to blur its outline.

I didn't know it then – only decades later, when I could no longer run.

I would use knowledge as my golden lacquer – filling the cracks of my fragmented self with understanding, transforming brokenness into a luminous map of resilience.

Each research module was a sacred act of self-archaeology.

My aptitude for mathematics made statistics courses more than numerical exercises – they became mathematical metaphors for rebuilding identity, each equation a potential bridge between disconnected fragments.

The reading, research, and writing components were not mere academic requirements, but instruments of gentle excavation – revealing the possibility of regrowth beneath accumulated trauma.

I was excavating the geological layers of my identity, exposing the intricate cross-sections of a self long buried.

Psychology became my cartography for mapping the internal landscapes of pain, resilience, and transformation – territories previously navigated blindly in the dark.

Earning a high distinction in my first-year psychology unit steadied my fragile sense of self.

Each achievement was another golden seam, another method of reassembling the shattered vessel of my identity.

I carried the stone of my own becoming up the Sisyphean hill of grief – not to conquer, but to continue.

Where once my fractured self had felt like a weakness, my scholarly pursuit became an alchemical process – transmuting personal pain into professional understanding.

Privately, university became my workshop of reconstruction.

Each lecture hall was an atelier where I examined the fragments of my experience under the scrutiny of new theoretical lenses – holding each shard to the light, tracing its texture, and potential for reconnection.

My academic journey became more than a scholarly pursuit – it was an interior cartography, mapping the terrain of loss, discovery, and integration.

My newly reinvented life found a tentative structure: a home that was more than walls, part-time jobs that were more than income, a relationship woven from shared emotional landscapes.

I continued playing hockey – maintaining a thread of physical continuity in a life quietly rebuilt from within.

The academic path offered a framework for shaping meaning from life's shattered remnants – assembling a mosaic out of what once felt senseless.

For a brief moment, life felt certain – a calm between storms, a quiet plateau before the next emotional tsunami crashed against the shores of my fragile, reconstructed self.

The Last Conversation 26 July 1994

One day after my thirtieth birthday.

'How could they do this to me?' my Mother ranted as I stood quietly beside her in the family kitchen.

These walls had absorbed decades of similar complaints – a soundtrack as familiar as my own heartbeat.

Her face contorted with that intense expression that reminded me of my Father, though without the cigarettes, alcohol, or menace – rage distilled to its essence rather than fuelled by external substances.

The veins at her temples pulsed visibly as she recounted her grievance.

Her tirade about being slighted at her Italian social club – where the vibrant cacophony of Italian voices usually provided her rare moments of belonging – was the latest in her pattern of emotional outbursts, her sense of injustice always disproportionate to the trigger.

This would be our last meaningful conversation, though neither of us could have known that the ordinary complaints of that afternoon would become precious in their mundanity, final notes in a complicated song.

She had arrived early at the club to secure a seat near the Bingo caller. After settling at a table with some people already seated, a woman told her to move, claiming the seat was reserved.

My Mother, who rarely confronted people directly, moved without protest but internalised the slight. Her anger festered until she returned home, where it erupted in familiar fashion.

This was a pattern I'd witnessed countless times – her hypersensitivity to perceived insults, her inability to express her feelings in the moment, and the subsequent explosion once safely home.

My Mother had learned conflict avoidance from her own Mother, a trait she passed to me like an invisible inheritance – one of many psychological heirlooms that shaped me more profoundly than shared genetics ever could – the architecture of behaviour transmitted across generations despite our severed biological connection.

After about 30 minutes of her venting, she finally calmed.

'Happy birthday,' she said, belatedly.

'My birthday was yesterday,' I replied.

'How old are you?' she asked.

'*Trenta, mamma.*' (30, Mum).

She shook her head, her expression conveying what went unspoken: *You're over the hill now. Too old for marriage. Too old to have children.*

I resisted my habitual urge to respond with indignation or slam doors in frustration. Instead, I accepted the immutability of her perspective – one of the few times I left the family home without storming out in anger.

The Moment Between – 8 August 1994

I drove to Bendigo, the car heater struggling against the bone-deep Victorian winter.

I, oblivious to what was unfolding near my family home, existed in that peculiar limbo of not-yet-knowing that precedes catastrophe, believing it was just another winter university day with its rhythm of lectures, readings, and discussions – soon to dissolve into the undifferentiated past.

As I drove down the Calder Highway in darkness around 6 pm, the headlights capturing brief territories of road before surrendering them back to night, I felt an inexplicable urge to scream, releasing primal sounds that rang through the car without explanation or context.

I arrived home in Coburg around 8 pm and went to bed shortly after, the memory of my inexplicable scream already fading into the background noise of ordinary existence.

Early the next morning, the cream-coloured push-button phone in the hallway rang. It was 7:30 am. My former neighbour, who still lived at home with her mother, was calling.

'Hi Mirella, it's Rugg. How are you?'

I never received calls from Rugg after moving out a decade ago. Instantly, I knew something was seriously wrong with my Mother. That strange animal intuition that had made me scream on the highway now crystallised into certainty.

'Hi Rugg, what's happened?'

'There's been an accident. Can you come over?'

'OK.'

Stunned, I hurriedly dressed and rushed to my Mother's house – a ten-minute drive that elongated into a purgatory of anticipation.

I unlocked the front door with my key and entered. The house felt eerily still, as if the air itself had thickened in anticipation of what I was about to learn.

My Mother's familiar scent – a complex bouquet of tomato sauce, Nivea cream, and that indefinable maternal essence – was already fading. Unwashed dishes and two water glasses sat in the sink.

Her brown hand-knitted cardigan was draped over a chair. A solitary chopping board rested on the table beside a fruit bowl.

Silky, our spirited 14-year-old Australian terrier, was nowhere to be found.

I crossed Middle Street to Rugg's home, directly opposite. She and her mother, *Signora* (Mrs) Felicia, greeted me with solemn faces.

'What's going on?' I asked, still unable to process what their expressions conveyed.

'There was an accident last night. Your mum and Rosario were hit by a car while crossing West Street.'

'Where are they?' I asked, assuming they were injured in a hospital somewhere.

They exchanged glances, their lower lips trembling as tears welled in their eyes.

The walls around me began to crumble, the solid ground of reality giving way beneath my feet – a terrible echo of that day on the bus 14 years earlier: another casual devastation, another unexpected collapse of the known world.

'They didn't make it.'

The words sent a seismic shockwave through my being, imploding in my heart.

I turned away without a word, walked outside, and kicked the brick wall in a sudden burst of rage.

The world had dissolved into senselessness once again, reality shattering into incomprehensible fragments.

First, I had lost my identity to a stranger's casual revelation – now I had lost my Mother to random chance.

Why?

When is enough, enough?

The Second Orphaning

I returned to my Mother's empty house – once my home, my sanctuary – but she was now gone forever. My emotions were scorched like bushland after fire – the surface still, but the roots still smouldering underground. This unexpected shock overwhelmed me.

The devastating reality would remain buried in ice for years to come. Grief moved through me not as a flood, but as Woolf described time – like waves lapping at the edges of consciousness, always returning.

I mechanically called my cousin, then my stepbrother. They already knew. Soon my Cousin Francesca and her husband, Frank, arrived. In collective shock, we began cleaning in silence, our minds too numb for conversation.

Shortly afterward, relatives, friends, and neighbours arrived with condolences. The mourning procession had begun.

My Calabrian neighbour, Signora Caterina, came over, tears flowing freely.

'Your mother was a good, kind person,' she sobbed. My Mother had ironed their clothes. Caterina didn't elaborate further, simply embracing me before leaving a packet of Italian biscuits and a *moka* pot of coffee on the kitchen table. This is what Italians do – they bring food and shared grief.

The day passed in a blur of visitors and arrangements. That night, I found a half-empty bottle of brandy hidden in a kitchen cupboard. The numbing shock was beginning to crack, like earth during a drought, allowing raw pain to seep through the fissures.

I carried the bottle into the darkened living room and drank directly from it, despite hating brandy. I needed to force these feelings back down as deeply as possible.

I couldn't believe life could be so utterly cruel. Just as I was finding peace and establishing stability, destiny had once again upended everything. My psychological resources were too depleted for this new trauma. The impact would profoundly affect the rest of my life – a permanent severing of my tenuous connection to family and belonging.

The Accident

The accident details emerged gradually. My Mother and stepfather had visited a widowed friend who lived around the corner on Glenroy Road. The friend had needed to leave to visit her son, so they returned home early.

On that cold, wet winter night, they attempted to cross West Street and stepped in front of a car driven by a middle-aged man who lived nearby. Silky, our family dog, somehow survived the impact. Along with the driver, he was the sole witness to their deaths.

I can't recall who first shared these details, but they seeped into my consciousness like a bloodstain spreading through fabric – impossible to remove.

For years afterward, I would visualise them crossing the road, being struck, my Mother dying instantly without comprehending what had happened. I imagined Silky moving frantically between their motionless bodies in the rain-slicked street.

This mental image became so deeply embedded that years later, when a similar scene appeared in a Traffic Accident Commission television advertisement – two elderly pedestrians hit by a car while crossing a road with their dog – I was certain it had been based on my Mother's death. The screeching tyres, the dull impact, bodies launched into the air, then bouncing off the windshield onto the pavement – these sounds and images would trigger visceral nausea whenever the commercial aired.

If others were present, I'd maintain composure, sometimes leaving the room or closing my eyes before the impact scene.

Even 30 years later, this sequence remains vividly imprinted in that part of my brain where trauma resides permanently. Shortly after that night, I visited the accident scene on West Street.

Walking around the intersection, I sensed my Mother's soul wandering aimlessly across the street – confused and unaware of what had happened. A ghost caught in the moment of transition, neither here nor there, much like I had felt throughout my fractured existence.

The brandy quickly penetrated my bloodstream, dissolving my carefully constructed restraint.

Disinhibited, I could no longer suppress my raw grief.

Rocking back and forth on the leather sofa, I hugged my chest, my body folding inward like a wounded animal, sobs rising from deep within my gut – *uncharted, unstoppable*:

Not my Mum.

Not my Mum.

Not my Mum.

Not my Mum.

No!

Not my Mum, I sobbed, the words torn from somewhere deeper than language.

The pain was so immense, I thought I would die of *Takotsubo* – another Japanese word describing the heartbreak that can kill. Torrential tears streamed down my face, carrying years of accumulated sorrow.

No, not my Mum.

She had been my only remaining family.

In an instant – unexpectedly – my entire family was gone. After 30 years, I was orphaned again. The word felt both familiar and foreign. Orphaned – something that had always been true but now carried a double weight.

I had lost my Mother twice: once at birth and now forever. In the days before my Mother was killed, I had dreamed of my Father for the first time since his death. In the dream, he held me while I sobbed uncontrollably. His comfort, even in sleep, seemed prescient now.

The Funeral Preparations

The following day, my cousins returned to help arrange the funeral. We'd spoken with my Aunts and Uncle in New York. My Mother's younger sister, Zia Giovanna, and one of my cousins were flying to Australia for the service.

My Cousin Francesca and I went shopping for burial clothes – a light mauve dress and matching shoes for my Mother. The experience was surreal and morbid, selecting fabric and style as if she were preparing for a gala rather than her eternal rest.

I found myself wondering if she would approve of our choices, then remembering with a fresh wave of grief that she would never voice an opinion again.

I had to identify my Mother and stepfather's bodies at the coroner's court. My stepbrother – too cowardly to perform this duty himself – was nonetheless eager to access my Mother's will. This would become a vexing legal battle in the coming year – an unnecessary struggle while I was still processing my Mother's death.

My cousins accompanied me to the coroner's court. The days blurred together in a foggy haze as shock insulated me from the full emotional impact.

I entered a quiet room where two curtains were drawn, the whiff of antiseptic mingling with something else – that unmistakable absence of life.

Behind glass windows lay two separate bodies on stainless steel tables, covered with white sheets – except for their heads. They rested motionless, eyes closed, expressions blank.

My Mother had a clear plastic breathing tube protruding from her mouth. My mind struggled to process what I was seeing. My heart sank as my legs weakened. Someone supported my arms to prevent me from collapsing.

I turned away and whispered, *Yes, that's my Mother and my stepfather.*

We left the building in silence and returned to my Mother's house. Sitting in the car on that cold winter's day, I stared blankly into space while a single tear escaped unnoticed.

The Funeral

The funeral preparations continued. I wrote an eulogy and selected W.H. Auden's *'Funeral Blues'* to be read at the service. My stepbrother remained absent from these arrangements, leaving my cousins to support me through the process.

Before the funeral, friends and family continued to visit and pay their respects. I received many cards in the mail – some from friends and neighbours I hadn't seen in years. Work colleagues sent flowers. These gestures softened the sharp edges of grief, though my appetite had vanished entirely.

Zia Giovanna, and a cousin arrived from New York days later.

On the funeral day, hearses and cars gathered at the house. The immediate family entered the vehicles and we made our sombre journey to the church.

The double funeral resembled a macabre wedding – the strange symmetry of two lives joined in death as they had been in life. Large bouquets of red and white roses adorned the two brown coffins, standing side by side before the altar of St Thomas More's Church – the same church that had held my Father's and Nonna's funerals, where I'd received my Holy Communion and Confirmation, where I'd sat countless Sundays as a child, wondering if God was real and, if so, why He seemed so cruel and unforgiving.

The church overflowed with relatives, friends from both families, neighbours, my friends, hockey teammates, and work colleagues.

I couldn't speak at the funeral – my grief was too overwhelming, the shock still too profound. The priest read my prepared eulogy. I sat in the front pew beside Zia and my Cousin Francesca as tears flowed freely. Physically present but emotionally detached,

I watched this nightmare unfold as if observing someone else's tragedy.

After the service, a seemingly endless procession of mourners filed past the immediate family, offering kisses, hugs, and condolences – a blur of faces expressing variations of the same sympathy, words washing over me like waves, meaningful yet indistinguishable in their repetition.

Then we made the short drive to Fawkner Cemetery along North, East, and South Streets, though my internal compass lay shattered.

My Mother and stepfather were buried together. As their coffins lowered into the crypt, some family members began wailing in cathartic release. I joined them, but my cry contained layers they couldn't hear – grief for the Mother I'd known, for all the mothers I'd never had: the biological mother who had given me away, the mother my adoptive Mother might have been had she told me the truth, the mother I had imagined during my search.

I was orphaned again, but the echo contained all my previous orphanings.

As her coffin found its final resting place, the present moment shattered, fragments of memory surfacing unbidden – her hands kneading dough, her voice calling me inside for dinner, her face illuminated by New York streetlights during our first trip together.

At the conclusion of the burial ceremony, each person passed the grave and tossed in a flower. I stood at the end of this procession. Alone amid the winter cold and dreariness, I peered into the grave.

From deep within me, I removed the chamber that had contained all my pain and misery – the accumulated weight of abandonment, secrets, and broken identity – and tossed it onto my Mother's flower-strewn brown coffin like a final offering, both burden and tribute. It would be buried with her for years to come.

With this second orphaning, another door to my origins had closed forever, leaving me even more adrift, without anchors to either my adoptive or biological roots.

Aftermath

After the funeral, we returned to my Mother's house for the wake, joined by many relatives, neighbours, and friends. I reconnected with neighbours I hadn't seen in years – some now married with children. We shared happier stories of our misspent youth in Middle Street and the neighbourhood adventures we'd had.

How could this have happened?

How could two people have been killed?

How could the driver not have seen two elderly pedestrians and a dog crossing the road?

How could two people not see an approaching car?

These questions would repeat endlessly in my mind in the coming years – a torturous litany of impossible hypotheticals that offered no resolution, only the hollow comfort of familiar pain.

Fuck! Fuck! Fuck!

So many times, my Mother had warned me to 'be *carefulla, fidya*', every time I ventured out of home. And yet she had managed to get herself killed through her own inattention.

I don't believe in accidents – most can be prevented. The coroner concluded that the driver was neither intoxicated nor speeding.

I was unforgivingly angry with her and would remain angry for at least another decade.

And I would miss her every single day.

I would miss going home to her home-cooked Italian meals, the fragrance of sweet *ragu* cooking on the stove filling the house with warm aromas of tomato, garlic, and herbs; our philosophical conversations about life; hearing her stories of her hometown that transported me to a place I knew only through her words.

Those same unanswerable questions haunted me daily.

I will never know precisely what transpired that night – only that it did happen. My poor Mother, who had suffered so much in life, met such a tragic end. She wasn't old – only 65. As I write this approaching 61, I realise 65 isn't old at all. However much I was – and still am – saddened by her sudden and unexpected death, I'm grateful she didn't endure a prolonged illness like her older sister, Concettina. Both my parents died young, suddenly, and unexpectedly. I never knew them in their old age.

These early experiences with death profoundly affected my outlook on life, creating conflicting responses. I either seized every day with passionate intensity – aware of life's precarious nature, or lamented the ultimate meaninglessness of existence, seeing how quickly a life can be erased.

Our individual human lives represent barely an eye-blink in the vast concept we call time. At 30, my existential crisis had begun.

What is the meaning of life?

What is the meaning of my life?

What is the worth of a life defined by suffering?

It would take decades to begin answering these timeless questions.

I'm grateful I was adopted by Michelina and Sebastiano. Despite their demons and the wounds they inflicted, I was, for whatever reason, destined to be part of their complex lives – as they were to be part of mine.

Shortly after my Mother died, I sensed her soul was confused, wandering aimlessly around West Street, but it soon moved on. By contrast, I've always felt my Father's soul has remained with me, watching over and protecting me throughout my life.

I know they both loved me and wanted me. I'm grateful for the home they provided, the opportunities for education, and the practical life lessons they taught me. In their way, they nurtured me and kept me safe. Though flawed, they didn't abandon me physically.

My Mother's death, though untimely, freed me to pursue my life without guilt, remorse, or obligation – a terrible liberation I neither sought nor celebrated, but which nonetheless altered my trajectory irrevocably.

Though finally unencumbered, I immediately plunged back into aimlessness. I had lost not only my Mother but my best friend, my comfort, my stability. I also lost my connection to the neighbourhood where I had grown up, to my Italian community, and largely to her family in New York.

I began to feel completely estranged from everything familiar. Again, I felt utterly isolated – a tiny piece of driftwood adrift in a vast ocean.

This feeling would persist for decades despite having friends, partners, and distant relatives.

If I had felt lost, disconnected, and aimless before, now I was completely bereft of purpose or direction. I was grateful to be in a relationship – I doubt I would have survived that period alone.

Briefly, I considered whether there might be a God, whether the Bible's stories were true, whether illegitimate children truly were cursed, or whether I was paying for sins from a past life through this lifetime's karma.

Did the Universe have a personal vendetta against me, or was this simply the random cruelty of existence – that indifferent chaos that both creates and destroys without intent or malice?

In the wreckage left behind, staying felt unbearable. Grief infected every room, every familiar smell. I needed to move – any movement – to survive.

Flight from Grief

In the months before my Mother's tragic death, I had planned an overseas trip with my partner. I decided to proceed with this journey and deferred my university studies, knowing that continuing would be futile in my current state.

The trip wasn't an escape – it was a necessary exile, a pilgrimage of grief across foreign landscapes where memories couldn't ambush me at every corner.

The house in Coburg, my neighbourhood, the entire city of Melbourne had become relentless reminders of absence. Every street corner, shop, and landmark was haunted by memories of my parents.

The ghosts were too numerous to outrun locally; I needed distance – foreign landscapes, the anonymous comfort of being a stranger among strangers.

Just before Christmas, we flew to the USA. My first stop was San Francisco. This wasn't a holiday – it was a desperate attempt to outpace my grief, a delusion that changing my geographical coordinates might somehow alter my emotional reality.

Reality struck when I realised I had no close family member to send postcards to, no one to call while travelling, no one to come home to.

No one who understood or acknowledged my profound aloneness in this vast world.

My childhood anxieties resurfaced with new intensity. Our tiny family tree of three had been reduced to one. Losing my adoptive Mother was another sickening lurch on the rollercoaster of my life – leaving me grasping for stability in a world turned upside down.

Partners and friends might come and go, but even my more distant family members, though present, didn't include me in their inner circles.

I was alone again, as I had been that night when my terrified Mother climbed into my bed. As a child, I had feared my Father killing my Mother. After his sudden death, I feared her dying too.

Now that fear had materialised.

With both anchoring figures gone – problematic as they were – the question of my origins took on new urgency, no longer an intellectual curiosity but an existential imperative. *Who was I if not Michelina and Sebastiano's daughter?*

The question that had haunted me since that bus ride 14 years earlier now demanded an answer with greater intensity.

I travelled to New York for my first Christmas there with my extended family since my Mother's death. Though not the snowy Christmas I remembered from childhood, it provided both sadness and comfort.

Outwardly engaged, I inwardly longed to sink into my grief, to drown in alcohol and oblivion, but circumstances prevented this escape.

Searching for a New Beginning

After my Mother's death, I sought constant motion, covering thousands of miles across the southern United States.

The endless highways and changing landscapes distracted me temporarily, the rhythm of travel creating a suspended animation where grief could neither advance nor recede but existed in a strange limbo of postponement.

But this motion couldn't fill the new emptiness inside. I was an orphan twice over now, with no home to return to, no parents waiting for my travel stories.

This realisation struck me somewhere between the Grand Canyon's vastness and New Orleans' humid streets – I was truly alone in the world.

Though there were fleeting moments of happiness and joy, mostly I carried hidden grief beneath a veneer of adventure.

From America, I flew to London, then embarked on a 7-day drive around England, visiting historic towns and coastal landscapes. This was followed by a month-long Contiki tour through Europe – Amsterdam, Paris, Rome, and a blur of other cities, castles, and coastlines – where new sights and sensations helped distract me from grief as I began to develop strategies for navigating the world as an adult orphan.

The world-tour distraction dissolved mid-flight. I returned home where reality awaited me with full force: my Mother was dead, my refuge gone, and utter despair engulfed me – intensifying the isolation I'd felt my entire life.

Meeting Ursula had given me pieces of my identity puzzle but not wholeness. The fragments remained disconnected, like puzzle pieces from different sets, forced together awkwardly.

I still believed there was a 'real me' waiting to be uncovered, rather than understanding that identity itself is something we construct from the materials life provides – a tapestry woven from threads both given and chosen.

This lesson would come only after more loss, more searching, more letting go.

Orphaned twice over, I faced a stark choice: remain fixated on the missing pieces of my past or begin deliberately weaving a future from the threads available to me.

The mosaic of my origins remained incomplete, but perhaps a tapestry didn't require every original element to create something whole and meaningful. Perhaps the gaps themselves were part of the pattern – the negative space didn't weaken the tapestry; it completed it.

Perhaps wholeness was never the goal. Perhaps stitching together what remains – gaps and all – was always the point.

12

Life After Loss (1996 – 2017)

Rising from scattered ashes

The Second Orphaning's Impact (1996)

After my Mother's death, I found myself in an unprecedented position – I was now an orphan twice over. First by birth, then by death.

This double severing created a peculiar kind of freedom – one that was simultaneously terrifying and transformative.

Without parents' expectations to fulfil or defy, I was answerable only to myself – yet also completely untethered from the anchors that, imperfect as they were, once held my life in place.

Inheriting the family home provided financial stability, but it couldn't replace the emotional stability I'd lost.

I stood now at the intersection of multiple identities – adopted daughter, orphan, independent woman – with no roadmap for integration.

The quest that began on that bus in 1980 had entered a new phase: *searching for wholeness without the defining presence of either set of parents.*

Building a Professional Self (1999)

The psychology studies that had once been merely an intellectual interest became my framework for understanding my fractured history. In the absence of family continuity, I built coherence through understanding human behaviour – including my own.

Following a two-year absence, I returned to university to resume my studies. Each academic achievement felt like placing another solid piece in the unstable foundation of my identity. If I couldn't know fully who I was by birth, I could at least define myself through accomplishment.

My academic and career successes were brief ascents on the rollercoaster, moments of hard-won progress that never quite overrode the constant undercurrent of my broken origins.

One crisp summer morning in 1999, I stood before the La Trobe University graduation stage, the ceremonial weight of academic regalia hanging from my shoulders like ancestral armour.

As I awaited my name, my eyes instinctively scanned the audience – searching for faces that weren't there and never could be. The empty seats where family should have sat formed negative spaces in the crowd, absences as tangible as presences.

'Mirella Di Benedetto,' the dean announced.

I stepped forward, my footsteps heavy in that brief silence before polite applause.

The 16-year-old on the bus, reeling from revelation, walked beside me invisibly across that stage – still searching, still asking: *Who am I?*

Each footfall reclaimed scattered pieces, arranged now to bear weight and purpose, spanning the chasm between past and future.

As I accepted my second degree, time seemed to fold in on itself – I was simultaneously the confused 16-year-old on that fateful bus, the grief-stricken 30-year-old at my Mother's funeral, the 9-

year-old at my Father's funeral, and this emerging professional creating identity through accomplishment rather than inheritance.

The certificate in my hand was more than academic validation – it was evidence that something whole could emerge from fragments.

And yet something fundamental was missing. Its realisation created a tension around my heart and tightened in my chest as I fought the rising swell.

My parents were not here to witness this proud moment or any other future achievements. Each had vanished with such finality, leaving a silence no applause could fill.

I had lost my real parents. Not my 'adoptive' parents – a qualifier I had unconsciously used for years as if it somehow made their role less authentic – but my parents in every meaningful sense of the word.

Initially, before finding Ursula, I had naively believed she was my 'real' mother simply because we shared DNA. I had imagined that biological connection automatically conferred some deeper truth to the relationship.

But Ursula's rejection, and now my parents' permanent absence, Michelina's in particular, had clarified what parenthood truly meant.

It wasn't carried in blood but built through thousands of meals prepared, tears wiped away, boundaries enforced, and sacrifices made.

It existed in presence, not in genetic connection.

Michelina, with all her flaws and complexities, had been my real mother all along – not because any document declared it, but because she had lived it, day after day, year after year. Ursula had given me life.

But Michelina had given me *a* life.

Only in losing her – and my Father – did I fully understand what I had possessed.

2000 – A New Millennium

The millennium's turn in 2000 mirrored my own threshold crossing. I entered a doctoral programme, grasping its rigours with a fierce, disciplined determination – a lifeline thrown across the abyss.

The first day as a doctoral student remains etched in my memory – stepping into the postgraduate research room with its institutional beige walls and identical brown desks, arranged like artefacts in a museum of academic aspiration.

I ran my fingers along the wooden surface of my assigned workspace, wondering if this too might become another fragment of identity to add to my collection.

My supervisor's invitation to become a tutor confronted me with my deepest anxieties – public speaking and social interaction had always triggered the hypervigilance I'd developed as a child witnessing my Father's outbursts.

Me? With the intense fear of public speaking and social anxiety? I questioned myself – even as I recognised this as an opportunity to rebuild aspects of myself that trauma had damaged.

Just as a kintsugi master carefully reassembles ceramic fragments, filling the cracks with lustrous gold, my doctoral journey became a deliberate process of reconstructing my fractured identity.

The morning of my first tutorial session, I stood frozen outside the classroom door, my meticulously prepared notes trembling in my hands like autumn leaves.

Within waited 25 undergraduate students expecting guidance from someone who still felt like an interloper in academic spaces.

The familiar nausea of anxiety rose in my throat, as if every past moment of exposure, vulnerability, and scrutiny were collapsing into this one.

This is different, I whispered to myself – a mantra against panic. *They only know the tutor. The academic.*

Taking a deep breath, I pushed open the door. Twenty-five pairs of eyes turned toward me – expecting certainty, knowledge, authority.

The fragmented self I carried inside remained invisible to them; they perceived only the cohesive professional persona I'd constructed.

'Good morning,' I said, my voice steadier than I felt. 'Today we'll be discussing theories of attachment.'

The irony pierced me – teaching attachment theory from my position as someone whose earliest attachment had been severed at birth.

I was simultaneously the professional analysing human behaviour and the subject being analysed.

Each theory I taught offered another lens through which to view my own disrupted beginnings.

Perhaps this was why psychology had called to me – a career and a map to navigate my own internal terrain.

Oscillating Between Extremes

Late one night in my office, surrounded by stacks of research papers, I confronted a truth about myself I'd long evaded: I lived at the edges, forever swinging between total immersion and utter withdrawal – between the fierce order of monastic discipline and the seductive pull of self-annihilation.

This pendulum swing wasn't merely a personality quirk but a direct response to my splintered foundations – without a solid centre, I careened between attempts to create perfect order and surrenders to utter chaos.

My desk told the story: meticulously organised research materials on one side, a chaotic tangle of personal items on the other.

My calendar revealed the same pattern: weeks of punishing work schedules followed by periods of aimless drifting.

The fragments of my identity weren't just separate; they were at war with each other, pulling me in contradictory directions with exhausting intensity.

My entire existence was defined by asymmetry, by the uneven distribution of knowledge and ignorance about my own origins.

My relationship with alcohol exemplified this pattern – a temporary analgesic for the persistent anxiety of not belonging anywhere, a momentary silencing of the voice that had accompanied me since that moment on the bus, endlessly asking, *Who are you really?*

During stressful teaching periods, I drank not for pleasure but for numbness – for temporary reprieve from the discomfort of existing in fragments and being discovered.

Evolving Social Identity (2002)

One warm November evening in 2002, I stood amid thousands of LGBTQIA+ athletes at the Sydney Gay Games opening ceremony. Aussie Stadium pulsed with an energy I'd never experienced – a celebration of sport, authenticity, and the refusal to deny oneself to meet social expectations.

As k.d. lang performed *'You'll Never Walk Alone,'* tears sprang unexpectedly to my eyes.

Looking around at the sea of faces – people who had struggled with different kinds of fragmentation, who had fought to integrate parts of themselves that society had tried to suppress – I felt a profound recognition.

The lyrics promised something I'd sought my entire life: that I wouldn't have to walk alone, that belonging was possible even outside conventional family structures.

For those two weeks – competing with my hockey team, sharing meals and laughter with athletes from around the world – I experienced a different kind of wholeness.

It was a wholeness built not on biological connection but on shared values and experiences.

This community had created family from choice rather than blood, assembling belonging from fragments society had once deemed incompatible.

Perhaps integration was possible after all – just not in the way I'd been searching for it.

Western society was becoming more accepting of diversity, creating space for parts of my identity that had previously remained hidden.

These moments of connection and community offered glimpses of what wholeness might feel like – belonging based not on shared DNA but on shared experiences and authentic self-expression.

They suggested an alternative path to integration: *perhaps identity wasn't something to be discovered in my origins but created through my choices and connections.*

More travel – (early 2006)

At the start of 2006, I journeyed to Sri Lanka for a wedding and climbed Sri Pada, the holy mountain. Upon my return, my friend, Bee, announced her pregnancy. I was genuinely happy for her and her partner.

Months later, their son was born on the eighth of August – the exact date my Mother had been killed on West Street a decade earlier.

It was only recently that I had stopped thinking about her every day, riding the waves of constant grief. My body still tensed at the thought of her carelessness crossing the road.

The heart-sinking feeling when a whiff reminded me of her meatballs in tomato sauce – a recipe I could never quite emulate. The moments of raucous laughter we would never share again at her kitchen table on my random, unexpected visits.

Wishing the phone would ring and I could hear her voice one last time.

I returned to the present moment. *How could the Universe have slapped me in the face yet again?*

The coincidence felt like a cosmic jest – new life arriving on the anniversary of death, my friend's joy beginning precisely where mine had ended.

The curse of the bastard child continued.

Later that year in Borneo, I climbed Mount Kinabalu – Southeast Asia's tallest climbable peak.

The thin air made each step more difficult, my muscles screaming in protest, yet something primal drove me forward.

When I finally reached the summit in the dawn light, the world opened beneath me. My heart hammered against my ribs, from exertion and a profound, elemental connection to the ancient rock beneath my feet and the infinite space above.

The rain washed away tears from my eyes and carried away the weight I'd been carrying for months.

These were moments of pure joy – where pain and ecstasy merged, where my small human struggles dissolved into something vast and timeless.

During these journeys, I found myself repeatedly drawn to mountains.

The act of climbing – of striving upward against gravity and exhaustion, seemed to mirror my internal struggle to rise above the circumstances of my birth and abandonment. From each summit, the patterns of my fractured life seemed momentarily comprehensible.

One night in my Borneo accommodation, unable to sleep, I retreated to the bathroom, sat on the hard, cold, red-wine-coloured floor tiles, and sobbed alone in darkness.

I couldn't identify which grief had surfaced. It didn't matter.

Sorrow recognises no neat boundaries – it flows across experiences, blending disparate losses until they become indistinguishable.

Was I mourning the Mother I'd lost, the father I'd never known, the siblings who kept me at arm's length, the children I might never have?

All of it, perhaps. The drips held every shard of my broken narrative.

I'd grown accustomed to these solitary outpourings.

I would sit and cry, often in darkness, then pick myself up and carry on, always believing that tomorrow offered something new.

Despite the emotional turbulence, life remained exciting, exhilarating, challenging. I had loyal friends who carried me through the peaks and valleys.

Forging Continuity from Fragments (end of 2006)

By the end of 2006, I submitted my thesis and earned my doctoral degree. I was now officially Dr M.

This achievement represented something purely my own – not inherited, not bestowed or withdrawn by others, but forged through persistence, intellect, and sheer will.

Whatever Ursula or my siblings thought of me, whatever Giuseppe might never know about me, this accomplishment was irrefutably mine.

My final graduation ceremony carried the same bittersweet quality as previous milestones.

No parents, siblings, or family members witnessed this crowning moment – only my loyal friend, Nic.

The daughter of non-English speaking migrants had earned a PhD – a feat my Father would have celebrated with immeasurable pride, while my Mother might not have fully comprehended its magnitude.

I wore the red silken doctoral robe with its light-blue velvet panels and ceremonial black Beefeater cap with pride – pride tempered by absence.

As I accepted my testamur from the Vice Chancellor amidst hundreds of fellow graduates, the positive feelings could not entirely drown the persistent undercurrent of loss and disconnection.

The empty seats where family should have sat underscored the absence at the centre of my life.

Yet standing there in academic regalia, I felt a strange completion – as if the professional identity I'd constructed was filling spaces left by the biological connections I still lacked.

Perhaps integration would happen not through finding every missing piece, but through creating new ones that fit the unique shape of my life.

At year's end, I applied for a lecturing position at the University of Ballarat. The interview day remains vivid – I wore my Mother's pendant as a talisman, my hands trembling slightly as I articulated my teaching philosophy to a panel whose faces have since blurred in memory.

When the offer call came days later, I experienced that familiar collision of emotions: exhilaration intertwined with trepidation.

After years of academic nomadism – punctuated by hospitalisations and grief – I was being invited to claim professional legitimacy.

The position represented stability I'd never known, which made it both compelling and frightening.

I accepted the full-time position as a psychology lecturer at this regional university, set amid rolling hills and eucalyptus forests.

As I arranged my books and credentials in my new office, positioning my doctoral diploma on the wall, I felt a sense of arrival that had eluded me throughout my previous attempts at building a life.

Standing at the lectern for my first full lecture as Dr Di Benedetto, I noticed my hands trembling slightly – the same tremor that had haunted me since childhood, hiding from my Father's rages, as a teenager on that bus, and as a daughter at my Mother's funeral.

But this time, the trembling carried a different meaning.

My voice, steady despite my racing heart, filled the lecture hall as I spoke about resilience and post-traumatic growth.

Mid-sentence, I caught sight of my reflection in the darkened window – professional attire and confident posture belying the internal complexity beneath.

For a fleeting moment, all my selves converged: the abandoned infant, the shattered teenager, the grieving daughter, and now this emerging academic.

The pieces didn't disappear, but in that moment, they aligned into something resembling wholeness.

My professional identity wasn't a mask covering my fractured self, but an architecture built upon its foundation, incorporating rather than concealing the breaks.

Each lecture I delivered on attachment theory or trauma response was simultaneously academic discourse and personal testimony, each concept explained both through research literature and lived experience.

The trembling in my hands connected these seemingly disparate selves across time – the frightened child and the accomplished professional existing not as sequential identities but as simultaneous facets of a complex whole.

Perhaps this was what integration truly meant: not the disappearance of fragments but their incorporation into a self whose coherence came not despite complexity but because of it.

'Dr Mirella Di Benedetto,' the nameplate on my door announced – a small but significant marker of identity.

This name – not my birth name of Zunica, not some future married name, but the name I had carried through my ruptured childhood into my professional adulthood – had become mine through lived experience rather than biological inheritance.

Teaching became my dedicated lifestyle. My mind was constantly engaged with preparing lectures, marking assignments, reading research papers, applying for grants, supervising students, or attending conferences.

The work was varied, stimulating, and rewarding compared to the repetitive lab work I'd previously done. It kept my overactive mind from drifting into melancholy rumination.

I had less time for hockey and running.

Some of my demons had departed.

I had confronted the figure in my dreams who chased me – I decided to stop, turn, and face it, telling it to go away. And, it did.

This confrontation with my nightmare figure paralleled my real-life journey – I was learning to face rather than flee from difficult truths.

The running that had defined so much of my life – both literally and metaphorically – was gradually being replaced by standing my ground, facing painful realities, and building something meaningful despite them.

By 2017, as I approached my mid-fifties, I had constructed a life that accommodated my fragmented history without being defined solely by it.

My professional identity as an academic, my connections with chosen family and friends, my pursuits and passions – all formed a mosaic that acknowledged breaks without being reduced to them.

The questions about my origins remained, but they no longer threatened to consume me entirely.

My search for biological roots continued alongside these professional developments, but with less desperate intensity.

I had built enough of an identity to sustain me through the uncertainty.

In quiet moments – sitting alone in my garden as twilight descended, waking in the stillness before dawn – the desire to know still surfaced.

Not with the raw urgency of earlier years, but with a steady, patient persistence.

The patching up of my identity had progressed remarkably.

The gaps shimmered like lost tiles in an ancient mosaic – insects forever trapped in the thickened amber of memory.

Fragments missing, their absence visible in the incomplete patterns of my assembled self.

Me at the Melbourne Pride March (2013)

State Veterans Hockey Tournament Darwin (2014)

13

Meeting Siblings

(2003–2018)

Blood memory stirring, refusing to be still.

Search Rekindled (2003)
Back in 2003, I found myself at a crossroads. The biological clock I'd long ignored was now ticking loudly, inescapably. I decided that I wanted to have children, so I started an IVF journey.
As part of a same-sex couple, I was discriminated against at the time, as IVF was not available to single women or lesbians in Victoria. So, I had to travel over to the northern border into Albury for treatment.
A decade after my last encounter with Ursula, the yearning to connect with my biological family returned with a force that took my breath away.
The void widened – with my Mother's death, with every failed relationship – becoming more unbearable with each holiday season where I sat as the singular outsider at gatherings of people who had chosen me but didn't share my blood.
The ache evolved – from a dull throb to urgent howl.
This wasn't mere curiosity anymore. It was survival.
I needed to find my half-siblings – the only people on earth who shared my maternal DNA. Absence grew sharp, like a wound

refusing to heal. *Tangible blood over echoing nothingness. Surely even pain was better than this.*
The memory of Ursula's rejection still stung, but there was a stubborn resilience in me now – a determination not to let her coldness deny me potential connections with siblings who might be more welcoming.
I knew I had at least three half-siblings and a nephew plus countless uncles, aunts, and cousins out there, somewhere. I wanted to make contact.
Back then, we still had the White Pages, so I looked up A. Schifforo, who was born the same month as I, July, but two years later.
Fortune smiled: only a couple of entries in the phone book.
I called and lied. I told him that I was an old school friend of his sister, who was also born in July, and I said that I was trying to track her down – which, technically wasn't a lie.
He believed me and told me her married name and where she lived.

The Letter
With this information in hand, I sat in my study, staring at the blank computer screen, crafting the letter that would potentially change everything.
My fingers hovered above the keyboard as dread and anticipation warred within me.
How does one introduce oneself to siblings who don't know you exist?
What tone conveys both urgency and respect? Too casual might trivialise the gravity of our connection; too formal might create distance before we'd even begun; too apologetic might suggest I regretted disrupting their lives, when in truth, I regretted only the decades of separation.
I drafted and deleted a dozen openings, each attempt falling short of the momentous reality.

In the end, I opted for simple honesty – explaining who I was, how I'd found them, and my desire to know them without expectation or demand.

The letter was neither poetry nor legal document, but something in between – a bridge built of careful words, extending from my solitude toward their unknown shore.

I had written a letter to Alessandro six years earlier, but at the time I hadn't sent it. I was too paralysed by the prospect of more rejection.

I didn't want to involve my younger half-brother, Nathan, as he was still living at home with his parents, and I didn't want to cause any tension.

It was an odd coincidence that we were all born around my birthdate, in July.

As I dropped the letters in the mailbox, I felt a familiar tightness in my chest – that same breathless anticipation I'd experienced when meeting Ursula years before.

Would they respond? Would they welcome me, or would they, like our mother, push me away?

The days that followed were excruciating. Each ring of the phone, each trip to the mailbox charged with possibility.

The Call

A week passed. Then two. Every day without response added weight to my shoulders. *Had they received the letters? Were they discussing how to respond, or had they simply discarded this unwelcome intrusion from a stranger claiming blood connection?*

When Alessandro finally called, his voice was guarded, curious. 'I thought it was a prank at first,' he admitted. They hadn't known I existed. Ursula had never mentioned me. This revelation alone pierced me anew – even in my absence, I had been made invisible.

First Meeting

We arranged to meet, and on the morning of our meeting, I stood paralysed before my open wardrobe, a ridiculous yet profound dilemma confronting me.

What does one wear to meet siblings for the first time at nearly 40?

Each garment seemed to project a different message – too casual might suggest I didn't appreciate the gravity of the moment; too formal might create unnecessary distance.

I finally settled on something neat but approachable – not trying too hard yet signalling respect for what the day represented.

It was an odd and nervous meeting.

These strangers were my siblings, my blood. We shared DNA.

I arrived at the house, walked up to the door, and nervously knocked.

There was no instant connection.

The faces before me were pleasant, polite, but unfamiliar.

We shared genetic material but no history, no childhood memories, no family jokes, or traditions. The weight of those missed decades hung between us like an invisible wall – all the milestones we hadn't shared.

We sat in their living room – three strangers connected by blood but separated by lifetimes of experiences.

The awkward, halting conversation felt like a dance where no one knew the steps.

We resembled each other in subtle ways – the same arch of eyebrow, similar gestures when speaking – yet remained fundamentally unknown to one another.

Mother's Shadow

'I showed your letter to our mother,' Lyre said, her eyes watching carefully for my reaction. 'She said you were a lying troublemaker.'

The words struck with surgical precision.

Even now, Ursula was working to erase me, to deny the inconvenient truth of my existence.

I had expected this, had prepared for it, yet the confirmation still landed like a physical blow.

I learned some years later that Ursula eventually admitted or acknowledged to them that I was indeed her daughter.

I had approached this meeting with carefully managed expectations – yet still harboured a secret hope.

That some spark of recognition would ignite.

That some invisible thread of connection would pull taut between us.

I had imagined a moment like those reunion TV shows – where separated siblings embrace with immediate, instinctive recognition.

DNA ≠ Belonging

Reality proved far more subdued.

We had our mother's features distributed differently among us – my chin on Alessandro's face, Lyre's eyes mirroring mine – but there was no emotional resonance.

We shared blood but little else – not interests, not mannerisms, not worldviews.

The DNA that linked us had failed to create the bond I'd yearned for.

This was the cruel reality of adoption reunions I hadn't fully anticipated – that biology alone does not create meaningful relationships.

The siblings sitting across from me had been shaped by their shared upbringing, their family dynamics, their collective history.

I was an outsider to all of that – a biological footnote, perhaps, but not truly family in any way that mattered to them.
I maintained contact with my siblings but remained excluded from the larger family gatherings, possibly their father's insecurity or need for control.
I would always be an unwanted and unwelcome outsider.
I did not – and could not – attend my youngest brother's wedding, or birthdays, christenings, Christmas gatherings, or any other family celebrations.
I still didn't fully belong anywhere.
I shared genetic material with my siblings, but no other family history. No growing up together stories. No sibling rivalry.
Connected, but disconnected.
To be acknowledged, but never truly welcomed, hurt more than outright rejection would have.
Each encounter with my biological family was another unexpected turn on the rollercoaster – simultaneously thrilling and disorienting, offering answers but also new questions.
I was acknowledged but kept at arm's length, invited to individual coffee meetings but never to the gatherings where real family bonds were expressed and reinforced.
It was like standing outside a brightly lit house on a bitter winter night, able to see the warmth and connection inside but forever barred from crossing the threshold.

2004
Throughout 2004, I methodically worked my way through the Zunica listings in the White Pages, calling uncles whose voices I'd never heard, whose faces I'd never seen.
Each call followed the same pattern – my carefully rehearsed introduction, followed by uncomfortable silence, then either feigned ignorance or awkward admission.
'I don't know anything about that,' most said, their voices tight with discomfort or genuine ignorance.

'I didn't know you existed,' others admitted, their surprise sounded authentic.

There was one Uncle – later revealed to be gay – who made a sincere effort at kindness.

'I've met him,' he said of my birth father, 'but I can't remember his name,' he lied.

Hope flared briefly, only to be extinguished when he called back a week later, his voice subdued.

'I spoke to my sister about you,' he explained reluctantly. 'She gave me an earful. Told me never to mention you again or she'd disown me.'

'Sorry, I can't help you. She's my sister.'

The message was clear – I was a secret to be kept, a potential disturbance to be contained.

Even those who might have wanted to help were bound by loyalty to Ursula.

My existence was subordinate to her comfort, just as it had been when I was given up for adoption. The pattern continued, decades later.

I spoke to Ursula for the last time soon after these phone calls. She was furious that I had contacted my siblings and her brothers, and told them about my existence.

Her dirty little secret – me – was out.

She screamed down the phone at me: 'How dare you talk to my family! You keep away from my family!' – with an emphasis on *my*, somehow forgetting – or overlooking– that this was also my biological family.

As if she could magically sever the biological bonds between us. She couldn't and wouldn't control who I could or couldn't contact.

I was hurt, but undeterred by her nasty, selfish, bitter words. Her rage erupted through the phone with such force I had to hold the receiver away from my ear.

The primal fury in her voice matched the fire that had been building in me through decades of exclusion and denial.

Her emphasis on '*my family*' cut deeper than any knife – reinforcing that I was forever outside, never included, never acknowledged as rightfully belonging.

Yet the pain of this second rejection differed profoundly from the first.

At 26, her rejection had devastated me, leaving me broken and adrift.

Now, at 40, I felt a cold, clear anger crystallising within me.

I recognised her words for what they were – the desperate attempts of a woman still imprisoned by immense secrets and shame, still operating under outdated notions of family honour and propriety.

I had survived without her for 40 years; her continued rejection could no longer define me.

As the years passed, I began to increasingly despair that I would never be able to find this elusive Italian, Giuseppe, with brown hair and hazel eyes, born around 1938, who had once lived in Carlton and whose father had a business.

The man who was my biological father.

Life is complicated at times, but I firmly believe that all children have a fundamental right to know the truth about their birth histories, their unique story, and above all else, who their biological parents are.

Anyone who withholds this information is being incredibly selfish, heartless, and only looking after their own needs and interests.

My blood is my family, my heritage, my DNA, my continuous life story, of which I was deprived.

I felt incredibly frustrated and annoyed.

I had waited long enough to reach out to other family members. While processing these complex feelings about my maternal family, I sought solace in travel – a way of connecting with my heritage while escaping the immediate pain of rejection.

November 2003

To celebrate our anniversary, my partner and I went overseas to Paris for a few days. Then we hired a car, and I drove to Lyon, Avignon, Carcassonne, Nice, and then into Italy, where the previously chilled-out and serene driving turned into a symphony of horn blasts, impatient arm waving, and would-be Grand Prix drivers.

I soon adjusted to the faster, more aggressive, less patient style of driving required on Italian roads.

It came easily.

To my astonishment, I found the chaotic Italian driving strangely instinctive – as if some dormant cellular memory recognised and adapted to this rhythm that should have been foreign to me. It was in my blood.

This unexpected aptitude for navigational chaos revealed something profound about inheritance that goes beyond conscious knowledge or direct instruction.

No one had taught me to drive like this – to anticipate the seemingly erratic movements of other vehicles, to communicate through subtle adjustments of speed and position, to participate in this elaborate dance of mechanical bodies moving at velocity. Yet my neurons fired in patterns laid down long before my birth, my reflexes responding to stimuli my conscious mind hadn't yet processed.

This unconscious competence in a foreign context demonstrated how deeply inheritance penetrates – beyond physical features, beyond conscious memory into the realm of instinctive response and embodied knowledge.

The Italian road became a metaphor for my journey of self-discovery: I was navigating by instincts I hadn't known I possessed, responding to signals I hadn't been taught to recognise, finding my way through patterns established long before my conscious existence began.

Perhaps identity itself operated similarly – less a matter of conscious construction than of recognising and trusting these inherited patterns of response, these ways of moving through the world that existed before language could name them.

We travelled to Venice, Ravenna, Florence, Tuscany, along the Amalfi Coast, Assisi, and Pompeii.

We hadn't planned to do so, but spontaneously took the ferry to Messina, Sicily from Naples.

Away from the crazy Italian drivers on the boat, I felt calm for the first time while travelling in Italy.

The gentle rocking of the ferry, the salt-tinged Mediterranean air, the distant view of the land where my adoptive parents had been born – all combined to create a feeling of homecoming I couldn't explain rationally.

This wasn't my birth country, not my heritage as far as I knew then, yet something in me responded to this place with recognition.

After arriving in Sicily, we drove to Taormina, Cefalù, and briefly through my parents' old village Vizzini.

There I sat on an ancient stone wall overlooking the centuries-old church where they were married, feeling the strange doubling of identity that had become my constant companion – I was both stranger and native here, both connection and disconnection embodied.

As church bells rang across the ancient hillside village, I wondered about the generations of my adoptive family who had walked these streets, and how their decision to adopt me had irrevocably altered my path.

From there we continued to Agrigento, Siracusa, and finally back to Messina.

I felt a deep affinity to the landscape and surroundings when I was in Agrigento at the Valley of the Temples.

I had long been drawn to the old and ancient relics that had been left behind by many generations that went before us.

Did I carry any of their DNA?

Standing among ruins that had witnessed thousands of years of human history, my own 40 years of searching seemed simultaneously momentous and trivial.

These stones had seen empires rise and fall, generations come and go.

My quest was just one thread in an endless tapestry of human longing for connection and belonging.

In Messina, we caught the ferry back to the mainland and ate hot, greasy, cheese-filled arancini on the way to Reggio Calabria and drove through Calabria, staying overnight in a town further north.

I had no desire to stay in Calabria, as I didn't know much about it.

It wasn't famous for anything that I was aware of other than the Mafia.

I had avoided Palermo for the same reason.

The Mafia frightened me.

Violence frightened me.

Little did I know then that my biological roots were deeply embedded in this very region I was passing through so quickly.

The Calabrian soil beneath my rental car's wheels held secrets about my origins I couldn't yet imagine.

Had I known, would I have lingered in those sun-drenched villages?

Would I have pressed my palms against ancient stone walls, searching for some ancestral resonance?

Would I have recognised something of myself in those rocky hills and azure coastal views?

The cosmic irony of nearly touching my biological homeland without knowing it – of being drawn to Italy yet choosing the wrong region to explore deeply – would only become apparent decades later.

I had been a mere visitor to the land that had shaped the DNA flowing through my veins, passing through my ancestral home like a tourist, taking photos of a heritage I couldn't yet claim.

I had mapped a journey from Naples to Vizzini and through Calabria, not knowing that those three regions would be the intimate triangle that shaped me.

2006

Back in Australia, the IVF journey continued alongside my search for identity.

It was now 2006.

My unsuccessful IVF journey came to an end.

More heartache.

Each failed attempt felt like another rejection – my body now betraying me as thoroughly as Ursula had.

The maternal identity I had hoped might help anchor me was slipping away alongside my tentative connections to biological family.

It was difficult to process these ongoing losses.

Mostly I grieved alone or in silence.

Yet again, the Universe chose to be cruel and unfair.

At least I had tried – and failed – better than to have not tried at all and lived with regret.

I threw myself into my new career.

It conveniently distracted me from the heartache of not being able to have my own family.

The years between 2006 and 2010 unfolded in a paradoxical rhythm – while one hand reached perpetually backward, searching for biological connections, the other built a life rich with chosen experiences and relationships.

It was as if I needed to prove to myself that identity wasn't solely determined by DNA, that I could construct meaning from materials other than biological inheritance.

I experimented with identities like trying on costumes – basketball player, cricket bowler, volleyball server, tennis partner, even lacrosse midfielder – my *'Naughtiest Girl in the School'* dreams finally realised in adult form.

I plunged from heights while abseiling, pitched tents under starstrewn skies, cultivated vegetable gardens that bloomed with colours I'd chosen myself.

My kitchen became an alchemist's laboratory where I transformed raw ingredients into elaborate dinner parties, my dining table a haven where friends became the family, I created, not inherited.

Each new activity, each relationship carefully cultivated, each skill mastered added another tile to the mosaic I was constructing in place of the biological narrative I'd been denied. If I couldn't have roots, I would have branches – extending in all directions, creating my own ecosystem of belonging.

Mid–late 2000s

I had gained a new perspective through my second year at university.

I was in this world and given this precious life and I wasn't going to waste a minute of it feeling too sad or too morose – even though in the pit of my being, I did often feel sad and sorry for myself.

My overseas travels continued.

At the beginning of 2008, I travelled through Thailand. While I was in Chiang Mai, I was scrolling through Facebook, and I came across Prime Minister Kevin Rudd's National Apology to the Stolen Generations.

As I listened to his thoughtful speech, I was reminded that I was a member of the White Stolen Generations.

Medical Interlude – A Wee Stroke (2009)

On 9 February 2009, I was at an outdoor Boot Camp session at the lush green gardens surrounding the Melbourne Museum, next to the grand old Royal Exhibition Building, home to Australia's first parliament, in Carlton, just north of the CBD. Carlton – the familiar territory of my elusive Giuseppe.

The irony of standing on ground that might have been familiar to him, while still having no idea who he was, would only become apparent years later.

It was a warm summer's evening, and I was doing a fitness assessment.

Boot Camp is an intense and demanding workout.

The instructor pushes you to capacity for about 50 minutes. During every session, my muscles would be screaming in fatigue and pain, my lungs would feel like they might burst.

I thought I might collapse in exhaustion, but at the end of every session, as the sweat poured off my body, enlivened by the warm blood pulsing through my veins, I felt a great sense of accomplishment and satisfaction.

I had survived another gruelling fitness session.

On this night, after the assessment that involved doing as many sprints as possible, step-ups, push-ups, burpees, or sit-ups you could do in a minute, I had a quick dinner on Lygon Street. A few slices of pizza, from a casual-looking Italian fast-food place.

Then I drove home.

After I'd showered, feeling exhausted, I went to bed and promptly fell asleep.

My life was about to take another unexpected turn – not through discovering a new fragment of my identity this time, but through confronting my own mortality.

An hour or so later, I was violently wrenched from sleep by a sharp, jabbing pain in the right side of my neck – as if someone had driven an ice pick into my flesh and given it a cruel twist.

My eyes flew open to the cream-coloured walls of my bedroom, which had begun to revolve around me with sickening speed, reminiscent of that memorable Fourth of July in New York, 1983.

The same sudden rising nausea clutched at my throat.

I attempted to stand, but my sense of balance had vanished completely.

The floor tilted beneath me like the deck of the Spirit of Tassie across Bass Strait.

I collapsed and found myself crawling across the light sky-blue carpet, my cheek pressed against its rough fibres as I inched toward the small toilet room adjoining the bathroom.

Once again, I found myself in the humiliating position of hugging a toilet bowl as my dinner violently vacated my body.

Unlike my marijuana misadventure in New York, I had eaten this time – pizza slices reappearing in a grotesque reversal of consumption.

My head felt woozy, detached, as if I were experiencing my own suffering from a slight distance.

This couldn't be mere food poisoning – the drunken disconnection, the persistent spinning of the world suggested something far more sinister.

Had they drugged my pizza? I thought.

I vomited for what seemed like hours.

There was a numbness in my left arm, but I put that down to grasping on to that toilet bowl too tightly with each chunder.

The nausea and vomiting subsided and I managed to crawl back to bed, blue bucket close by.

The next morning was a workday.

I had to get up and get ready for my hour-long drive to Ballarat. Sitting on the downstairs couch, my head was still woozy. I felt like I had a mild hangover.

The nausea returned.

This time, I was dry retching.

I thought, *This doesn't feel like just a common bout of food poisoning.*

I got dressed and had the good sense to take myself to a local GP. I told my tale to the female doctor attending to me.

She said, 'I think it's just gastro, but just to be sure I want you to have a CT scan.'

I didn't think to ask why she thought gastro was related to something amiss with my brain.

I was only 45 years old.
I had given up smoking 16 years earlier, I didn't have high blood pressure, high cholesterol, or diabetes.
I was perfectly fit, although a little overweight.
Then came the dreaded question.
She asked me about medical family history.
'I don't know,' I answered with the same rehearsed neutrality I'd perfected over decades.
'I'm adopted.'
As I spoke those familiar words yet again, the irony struck me anew.
In this moment of medical crisis, my lifelong search for identity had direct, practical consequences. Without a medical history, I was a blank slate to the doctor – my genetic risks unknown, my inherited tendencies a mystery.
This wasn't just about feeling incomplete emotionally anymore; it could have life-or-death implications.
These medical events would be a constant reminder that my family medical history was unknown to me.
After the scan, I went home to bed.
When I awoke there was a voice mail on my phone – now a very basic white Nokia mobile phone, with a sliding lid.
I heard the GP's voice as I played the message.
'You have to go to the emergency department at the Austin Hospital immediately,' she said in an urgent but calm fashion.
My heart lurched as I heard these words.
In an instant, all my existential questions about identity seemed to recede against the more immediate question of whether I would live to continue my search.
Would my story end here, with so many questions still unanswered?
I headed to the hospital along Camp Road.
Along the way the nausea resurfaced, and I had to stop a few times to throw up and wondered whether a brain tumour had shown up on the CT scan.

Upon arrival at the Austin Hospital in Heidelberg, I approached the Triage nurse.
I told her my name and my condition, and I was immediately whisked into the ER department and given a bed. I was told to put on a hospital gown.
Bloods were taken and I had an ECG and another CT ultrasound on my brain.
At one point, I recall lying on my side and not knowing which way the earth was pointing.
My proprioception was momentarily out of whack.
Lying on the cold hospital trolley bed, I recalled a story my Mother had told me.
The first time I had been to hospital was as a 2- or 3-year-old when I had my tonsils taken out.
I don't have any recollection of it, but Mum told me I kept pleading '*Scarpi, scarpi, Mamma,*' when they came to visit me, because I wanted my shoes so I could leave.
Mum wasn't here now, as I lay frightened in this hospital bed. Another journey I had to navigate without immediate family, another moment when my solitude was thrown into stark relief.
A few doctors came along, and I was asked to repeat my story. Then the head neurologist, stood at the end of the bed.
'Any family history of stroke or cardiovascular disease?' she asked.
'I don't know. I'm adopted.'
My unknown medical history, suddenly critical in this sterile hospital room.
Without access to this knowledge, doctors were forced to make decisions without the context most patients take for granted.
How many adoptees face medical crises with this same handicap, I wondered – their biology a mystery to be solved rather than a roadmap to be followed?
'You've had a TIA, a mini-stroke,' she said in her very efficient, but blunt expert doctor voice.

'It was probably caused by a dissection in your vertebral artery. The blood clot from the tear has travelled up to your right cerebellum.'

I was grateful for my strong grasp of medical terminology.

I had studied anatomy and physiology, had taught biological psychology – without that background, her words would have been nothing but a mumbo jumbo of incomprehensible medical word salad.

Later, I thought, there must be special classes in med school that teach doctors to deliver serious medical information in the least caring, uncompassionate, and insensitive way possible.

This contrasted with the careful, considered, and empathic psychologist speak that I had been trained to use.

Blunt doctor-speak was truly an art form – and a perfect way to add trauma to an already traumatising and frightening experience for anyone.

'We will have to do an MRI to confirm the diagnosis.'

'What caused it?' I enquired.

'We don't know,' she replied adding anxiety to trauma, and walked away.

I was taken up to the stroke ward. I was in a room with very sick-looking and much older patients.

Most lay motionless.

A nurse came in every hour or so to give me a stroke assessment. Another sudden and surreal moment.

As I lay there in that hospital bed, facing mortality at a relatively young age, I couldn't help but wonder:

If I died, who would mourn me as family?

My adoptive parents were gone.

My birth mother wanted nothing to do with me.

My biological father remained unknown.

Who would carry my memory forward? Who would tell my story?

The thought was profoundly isolating.

Word of my hospitalisation travelled quickly through my social network.

In the following days, friends and cousins came to visit, their presence breaking the sterile monotony of hospital routine. Their visits highlighted the family I had built rather than inherited – people who had chosen to love me despite the absence of biological connection.

After four days of tests and monitoring, I underwent an MRI. Hours later, the head neurologist appeared at my bedside, her crisp white coat and clinical demeanour unchanged.

'The diagnosis is confirmed,' she stated, pointing to images of my brain displayed on a tablet.

'There's a small scar on your right vertebral artery, confirming the dissection hypothesis, and clear signs of a cerebral infarct – a stroke in your right cerebellum. This explains the balance issues you experienced.'

She delivered this information about my compromised brain with the same emotional investment one might use to describe minor car repairs.

I stared at the glowing images – my brain, my damaged cerebellum – trying to reconcile this medical reality with my subjective experience.

The scan showed the physical manifestation of what I'd felt that night: the world literally shifting beneath me as blood flow to my brain was compromised.

'You can go home now. See me in six weeks.'

I did some 'Dr Googling' upon returning home but quickly stopped.

The statistics I found were terrifying – I'd been fortunate that the blood clot from the dissection had travelled to my cerebellum and not my brainstem, the area of the brain that controls breathing and heartbeat.

What had felt like a bizarre episode of vertigo could easily have been fatal.

Grateful yet shaken, I faced a stark revelation: I might have died without ever knowing my biological origins, without finding the missing pieces that had defined my quest for so long.
The fragility of my mortality lent new urgency to my search.
Six weeks of mandatory rest stretched before me – time to contemplate what mattered most.
Surprisingly, I wasn't deeply psychologically affected by the experience.
Perhaps because I had a stronger social support network looking out for me.
Some of the loneliness I had felt had dissipated.
But the experience had reinforced something I'd learned through my search for biological family – that human connection was not a luxury but a necessity, especially in moments of crisis.
I would spend the next few months contemplating my near-death experience.
Again, I was seeing the world through different eyes. I was grateful to be alive.
Since my Father's death, I hadn't taken life for granted.
After my Mother's death, this outlook was reinforced.
Now, facing my own mortality had further clarified what mattered most – connection, truth, identity.
The search I had put aside for years suddenly felt more urgent than ever.
I'd become more acutely aware of time's precarious nature – more determined than ever to find Giuseppe before it was too late for either of us.
The possibility of dying without knowing my origins had become an unacceptable risk.
My motto was now firmly: *Carpe Diem. Seize the day.*

Meeting My Youngest Sibling (2009)
Soon after this event, in a development that felt like the Universe responding to my renewed commitment to finding answers, I got a Facebook message from my youngest half-brother, Nathan.

I was by this stage Facebook friends with Alessandro.
He asked me how I knew him – his way of introducing himself to me.
We met in Lygon Street, Carlton, and had dinner with his girlfriend.
The aroma of pizza, garlic, and coffee hung in the night air. He was somewhat shy and quiet, like me.
He played drums.
We shared a love of music.
The inevitable question came, as he ashed his cigarette – *reminiscent of Ursula's quick flick of the wrist* – and the same question I'd heard from his sister years before: 'What do you want?'
I was tired of explaining. 'Nothing.'
This time, I meant it.
What would I have in common with a male, 18 years my junior?
The only things we had in common were a mother and a biological and DNA connection.
Yet, meeting Nathan brought a surprising sense of peace.
Unlike my earlier meetings with my half-siblings, which had been fraught with tension and expectation, this one felt simpler – less burdened.
Perhaps I had finally accepted that these biological connections might never develop into the deep family bonds I had once hoped for.
Or perhaps I was just grateful for any connection at all after my brush with mortality.
At least I had finally met my youngest maternal sibling.
The following year, at the start of 2010, I would meet him and his partner again in a hinterland region of Queensland, where Alessandro was living.
Alessandro and his wife had just had their first son – my nephew.
I felt a special connection to this young newly-born blood relative.

As I held my nephew, for the briefest moment, I felt a connection – a familial bond I had searched for across decades finally manifesting in this tiny new life that shared my DNA.

As I gazed at his tiny features, into his big, blue eyes, I wondered which of our shared genes he might have inherited, what invisible threads connected us across the generations.

The siblings had spoken to their father – a simple, hard-working man who had worked as a labourer – about me. Apparently, he had pleaded with them.

He cried and said, *'Don't have anything to do with this person. I know who her father is.'*

I thought this was strange.

Why didn't he want me to know who Giuseppe was?

Why was it such a big secret?

The ominous nature of his warning would only make sense years later, when I discovered the truth about Giuseppe and his connections.

At the time, it simply seemed like another cryptic obstacle in my path to understanding.

This man was technically my stepfather – another to add to my collection of mother and father figures.

His older brother had married Ursula's sister.

He warned his younger brother not to marry Ursula, claiming she was 'not a virgin,' and 'not to be trusted.' He used the language of shame – harlot, whore, fallen woman – as if her worth could be undone by rumour.

But he married her anyway.

Apparently, the two brothers – the only family they each had in Australia, had a strained relationship.

The families kept their distance.

As they shared these family secrets, I began to see a web of relationships far more complicated than I'd imagined. Behind my simple quest to know my origins lay intricate family dramas, old grudges, and possibly darker secrets.

My existence was just one thread in this complex pattern – and perhaps a particularly inconvenient one for some.

I began to wonder if the brother had had an affair with Ursula and maybe he was my father.

I couldn't understand why Giuseppe's identity was such a secret.

Was I the product of incest? Rape?

It was possible. It happens.

My yearning and questioning never abated.

As a person, my incomplete being was like a great forest of trees. I had the names of some trees and a few of their fruit on one half of the vast, fertile, verdant, and lush mountainous land.

The other half was barren, except for a tiny Italian male fruit, tiny genetic fragments, belonging to the elusive Giuseppe, with a couple of distinguishing bits of phenotypic Mendelian material – brown hair and hazel eyes.

I stared into this empty vastness that stretched back for centuries, possibly back to the first *Homo sapiens*. I stared into that emptiness with a deep longing, uncertainty, and despair.

How would I ever fill in the missing pieces that were my biological/genetic ancestors?

December 2010

Towards the end of 2010, I separated from my long-term partner, which was followed by a long acrimonious legal battle, emotional upheaval, and a rapid dive into suicidality.
What should have been simply the end of a relationship became another profound and complicated loss, another separation to process alongside all the others that had defined my life.
So battered was my mental health through this ordeal that I ended up in a psych unit.
I had the good sense to call 000, rather than attempt to end my life with the pills I had lined up on the kitchen bench.
It was a cold, dark April night.
The legal nightmare that was unfolding was becoming too much to bear alone, along with the re-emergent feelings of being utterly on my own, without close family to support me through this legal battle.
In that moment of crisis, the absence of family support was no longer just an emotional wound but a practical, urgent need.
The void created by my fractured origins now felt like a gaping chasm into which I might disappear entirely.
The ambulance arrived quickly.
As the paramedics assessed me – a stranger's hands checking my vital signs, a stranger's voice asking clinical questions – I felt the full weight of my isolation.
There was no mother to call, no father to rush to my side, no siblings to hold vigil at the hospital.
Just me and the professional kindness of medical staff, doing their job with efficiency and compassion, but unable to provide the comfort that only family can offer.
In the psychiatric unit, surrounded by others in various states of crisis, I had time to contemplate how thoroughly my fractured origins had shaped every aspect of my life – from my emotional resilience to the practical support systems available to me in moments of need.

I too had descended into the basement of the self – where memory, shame, and longing argued in the dark.
The journey that had begun on that bus with a stranger's casual revelation had led me here, to this sterile room where I was forced to rebuild myself once more from the fragments that remained.

I emerged from the hospital determined to survive, for myself, and for the answers I still sought. The quest for Giuseppe had become more than a search for identity – it was becoming my reason to continue, a thread of purpose when all other motivations had temporarily failed me.

Saying Sorry

Despite exciting adventures overseas, hockey events, or participating in music, being adopted and its effects were never too far from my conscious mind.

These were brought front and centre once more when I found myself listening to Australia's Prime Minister Julia Gillard on 21 March 2013.

She was giving the National Apology for Forced Adoptions.

As I heard her words, I felt a collective acknowledgment of what thousands of us had experienced – the first time my pain had been recognised at a national level.

The speech was delivered in the packed Great Hall of Parliament House, Canberra in front of hundreds of adoptees, relinquishing mothers and fathers, and others psychologically affected by the barbaric practices of forced adoption.

> 'Today, this Parliament ... takes responsibility and apologises for the policies and practices that forced the separation of mothers from their babies, which created a lifelong legacy of pain and suffering.'

Listening to her speech, an instant knot formed in my throat, and the swelling of tears in my eyes grew, as I sat with that old feeling that is hard to fully describe to those who are not adopted...

The personal became political in that moment.

My individual story was part of a national history – a systemic injustice that had affected thousands.

> '... the shameful practices that denied you, the mothers, your fundamental rights and responsibilities to love and care for your children. You were not legally or socially acknowledged as their mothers.'

Her words began to unleash decades of mental and emotional anguish.
After years of feeling my pain was invisible, unimportant, here was the most powerful person in the country acknowledging the wrong that had been done.

> 'To each of you who were adopted or removed, who were led to believe your mother had rejected you and who were denied the opportunity to grow up with your family and community of origin and to connect with your culture, we say sorry.'

Tears full of decades of grief gently cascaded down my face, as I listened to words that finally acknowledged my pain and suffering.

> 'We apologise to the sons and daughters who grew up not knowing how much you were wanted and loved. We acknowledge that many of you still experience a constant struggle with identity, uncertainty and loss, and feel a persistent tension between loyalty to one family and yearning for another.'

The words rang so true.

The yearning continued to grow with each passing year of not knowing.
Never had I heard such a perfect articulation of the adoptee experience – that 'persistent tension between loyalty to one family and yearning for another' had been the defining struggle of my life.

The tears continued to drip down my sodden cheeks.

> 'To you, the fathers, who were excluded from the lives of your children and deprived of the dignity of recognition on your

> children's birth records, we say sorry. We acknowledge your loss and grief. Many are still grieving. Some families will be lost to one another forever. To those of you who face the difficulties of reconnecting with family and establishing ongoing relationships, we say sorry.'

She was speaking directly to my plight.

I had disconnected from my birth mother due to her shame. I had little connection with my siblings.
I couldn't help but think of my unknown father – *was he one of those who had been excluded, or had he willingly walked away?* Either way, there was loss on all sides.

> 'We offer this apology ... to shine a light on a dark period of our nation's history. To those who have fought for the truth to be heard, we hear you now. We acknowledge that many of you have suffered in silence for far too long.'
> '... Our focus will be on protecting the fundamental rights of children and on the importance of the child's right to know and be cared for by his or her parents. With profound sadness and remorse, we offer you all our unreserved apology.'
>
> ... 'a wound that does not heal'

Words can never undo what was done – what has been lost, and can never be recovered – but validation is the first step towards healing, accepting, and letting go of the things that cannot be changed.

I felt something shift inside me during that speech – not healing exactly, but acknowledgment.

My experience was real. *My pain was legitimate. The systems that had separated me from my origins were flawed and harmful.*

The tears kept flowing, long after the speech had ended.

14

Fading Hope
(2018–2022)

Hope, vanishing, resurfacing, calcifying

As I entered my mid-fifties, the search for Giuseppe had become both more urgent and more hopeless. The possibility of finding him was gradually melting like frost on a spring dawn – nearly four decades had passed since that fateful bus ride, and almost 30 years since my brief, disappointing meeting with Ursula. Unbeknownst to me, the technological revolution was unfolding like a map finally revealing its secret trails. I had yet to discover its possibilities.

The years from 2018–2022 would become the final chapter of my decades-long search for my biological roots – though I didn't know it then – as resignation and determination battled within me, right up until the moment everything changed.

The paradox of my existence during these years was stark – outwardly successful as a psychologist and academic, inwardly navigating the landscape of an unfinished story. Each professional achievement felt both meaningful and hollow, like rooms in a house I could never fully occupy. When colleagues spoke casually of family resemblances or hereditary traits, I would smile and nod, the familiar ache rising in my throat – it was a quiet reminder of the chapters missing from my personal narrative.

2020–2021

During this period, I was quietly grateful that my Mother, Michelina, wasn't alive – potentially living in a nursing home ravaged by COVID-19. The elderly were hardest hit by the pandemic. Panic buying followed. Toilet paper became absurd currency – a symbol of fear and survival.

As Melbourne went into repeated lockdown, an eerie quietness fell around my suburb. The planes that once inhabited the sky were now a rare sight. The night's curfew brought with it a stillness that I found comforting. Brave kangaroos could be seen venturing through our street at night in search of food. The neighbourhood footpaths, once barren, were now teeming with life. People riding bicycles, walking their dogs, jogging in pairs. Groups huddled on corners chatting.

In 2021, as a clinical health psychologist working from home, I found myself delivering telehealth to clients who'd had their hearts surgically mended, but their minds broken. In a strange symmetry, I became a quiet kintsugi for others while my own fragments remained scattered. The enforced isolation brought an unexpected clarity to my search, as if the world's stillness had created space for long-buried truths to surface.

Living alone during these solitary COVID-19 years, I had ample time for reflection. The past still intruded, but now I could recognise these intrusions for what they were – memories, not present reality. 'That was then,' I would remind myself as images of my Father's rage surfaced. 'This is now.' The boundaries between timeframes began to settle into place, allowing me to contain what once threatened to overwhelm me. I embodied the strategies I suggested to my clients – cultivating a stiller mind, a slower way of being. My front garden became both meditation and metaphor, tending to vegetables while processing thoughts of roots and connection.

In the strange timelessness of pandemic days, I spread the artefacts of my search across my dining table – adoption papers, photographs, letters, DNA results. The quiet allowed me to see patterns I'd missed before, connections hidden in plain sight. Like a researcher finally able to focus on a complex dataset, I could see how each piece of my identity – the adopted daughter, the psychologist, the seeker – had shaped the others.

In these quiet moments of isolation, my thoughts inevitably returned to my elusive Giuseppe.

Was he alive? Was he married? Did he have children? Would I ever find him? How could I find him, without Ursula telling me his surname? Why won't she tell me who he is? Why is she being so selfish? Was it just revenge? Vindictiveness? Was there some dark shame about this man that compelled such secrecy? Some truth too painful to reveal?

The streets of Brunswick and Carlton drew me like a magnetic compass pointing north. Though the neighbourhoods had evolved since Giuseppe's time, their Italian essence remained unchanged – a palimpsest of old and new where past and present coexisted. The aroma of espresso from corner cafés, the melody of familiar dialects floating from doorways, the comforting fragrance of pizza and pasta, the tableau of elderly men playing cards outside social clubs – each sensory detail connected me to a world that might have been mine, might have been his. I would scan the faces of elderly Italian men, wondering if any could be him. Wondering if I had ever passed him unknowingly, some vital connection missed by mere centimetres on a crowded footpath.

Unlike my fixation on finding Giuseppe, I rarely contemplated the extended family I might have – the grandparents, aunts, uncles, or cousins whose blood I shared. Perhaps this selective focus was self-protection; the absence of one person was painful enough without multiplying it across generations of unknown relatives.

The mathematics of mortality became an obsession. With each new year, I would calculate Giuseppe's age, watching the odds diminish with each passing birthday. It was now 2022, and the statistics were merciless: only two per cent of men over 85 remained alive in Australia. Time itself had become my adversary, more relentless than Ursula's denials or societal indifference to adoption trauma.

A moment came when I had to extinguish the flame of finding him alive – a surrender more painful than I'd anticipated. Like a lone candle in a darkened church, hope flickered and died, leaving me in shadow. All I could reasonably wish for now was to discover who he had been. A name on a page. A photograph to search for my own features. Stories from those who had known him.

I had to accept the cruel probability that I might never know even these basics of my origins. This resignation brought a new heaviness, a physical ache that settled beneath my ribs and made each breath laboured, as though grief had materialised into something tangible lodged within my chest.

Yet something in me refused absolute surrender. Perhaps it was the stubborn familial blood pulsing through my veins – a quality I must have inherited from someone, possibly the very man I sought. Or perhaps it was simply that after 40 years of searching, giving up had become impossible. The quest for Giuseppe had become so fundamental to my identity that abandoning it would mean abandoning a part of myself.

Against my bathroom mirror stands a treasured photograph – my 26-year-old self with my puppy Joey. The age creates a perfect triangle of connection: I was 26 when I first met Ursula, Giuseppe was 26 when she got pregnant with me. 'You look like your father' – words that would repeat through decades of frustration and futility, both curse and clue.

Day after day, I would study this photograph, searching my younger face for clues, for the paternal features Ursula had recognised instantly. The ritual became almost devotional – each morning, examining my reflection beside this younger self, creating a temporal bridge to the age Giuseppe had been when I was conceived. In the soft morning light, I would study the particular arches of my eyebrows, the set of my jaw, the way my eyes crinkled at the corners when I smiled.

Genealogy became my quiet obsession. Each digital connection was a thread in an intricate tapestry I was weaving – part scientific mapping, part emotional archaeology. Social media platforms transformed into archaeological sites where genetic patterns emerged like ancient pottery shards. Uncles, cousins, siblings – each became a coordinate in the complex cartography of my biological inheritance. But the paternal half remained a void – a black hole in my genetic cosmos, pulling at me with invisible gravity. This wasn't merely missing information; it was a phantom limb of my identity. With each passing year, this absence grew more profound, evolving from curiosity to yearning to something approaching desperation.

Did I have his hazel eyes and wavy hair? Did I have his personality? Mannerisms? Was he kind and sensitive? Did he know that I existed? Had he ever thought about me? Had he ever tried to find me? Would any of his children or other family members want to meet me? Did they know that I even existed?

These questions haunted me like poltergeists, materialising in quiet moments – while washing dishes, during my morning walks, in the hazy territory between wakefulness and sleep – demanding attention. They were no longer just questions but companions, familiar presences that had accompanied me through most of my life.

Ursula steadfastly maintained her silence about Giuseppe's full identity. The secret she had guarded for nearly six decades would go with her to the grave – or so it seemed. I could not forgive her, though I would learn to let go of this rage. Some years later, I asked a sister-in-law for some further insight into Ursula's personality. What was she like? Among the list, my sister-in-law said that Ursula was fun, softly spoken, liked to garden, liked art, she was loyal, kind, and generous. She also suffered from depression and anxiety. I realised in that moment that I shared many of Ursula's qualities, including the hot temper and her mental health issues.

When I began my search in the 1980s, I carried an unexamined assumption about what 'finding my family' would mean. I imagined a moment of recognition; an instant biological connection that would fill the void I'd carried since learning of my adoption. The family I sought existed in my mind as a completed puzzle – with me as the missing piece that would slide perfectly into place once discovered.

By the time I met Ursula in 1990, this fantasy had already begun to dissipate. Ursula's rejection was my first lesson in biology's limitations. Blood could be as thin as water when diluted by decades of absence.

After my Mother's death in 1994, my understanding of family underwent another transformation. Standing at her grave, I realised that family wasn't simply who bore you, but who supported you through life's hardships. She had been imperfect – often frustratingly so – but she had been present, constant. This constancy, I was beginning to understand, might be more valuable than any genetic link.

The years of searching that followed each disappointment gradually reshaped my expectations. Each time I reached for connection and found emptiness instead, I was forced to redefine what I was truly seeking. *Was it merely information? Recognition? Belonging? Or something more fundamental – a continuity of self that extended beyond my singular existence?* Probably the latter.

By 2010, after meeting my siblings and experiencing the complex reality of these connections, I had developed a more nuanced understanding of family. These biological relations were neither the magical completion I'd first imagined nor entirely meaningless. They existed in a complex middle ground – connections with potential, but without the shared history that forms the bedrock of most family bonds.

The pandemic years brought a final evolution to my thinking. Isolated in my home, I found myself sustained not by biological connections but by chosen ones. Friends called daily. I shared food and casual conversations with neighbours. I met colleagues through Zoom meetings. Family, I realised, was not a static entity to be discovered, but a living network actively created through care and presence. This understanding didn't diminish my desire to know Giuseppe, but it changed what finding him would mean. It was no longer a completion, but another beginning – another piece in the mosaic I had been assembling all along.

In my darkest moments, during the teens and beyond (2010 onwards) I'd envision Giuseppe slipping away – dying without knowing I had searched for him, without me ever discovering his full name, my real surname. In these bleak imaginings, I saw an elderly man drawing his final breaths, unaware that somewhere in Melbourne, a daughter he'd never acknowledged was thinking of him, carrying his genetic legacy forward. His death occurred just beyond my reach, the possibility of connection extinguished permanently, the Universe's final cruel joke in a lifetime of missed connections.

These thoughts were most persistent at night, when daylight's distractions receded, and existence's fundamental aloneness pressed close. I would lie awake calculating diminishing odds, while Melbourne's night traffic created a soundtrack of distant possibility – each passing car might be carrying someone connected to the mystery of my origins, each set of headlights momentarily illuminating a street Giuseppe might once have walked.

In time, I would have to accept what I could not change – some questions might remain forever unanswered, some fragments forever missing from my mosaic. Hope didn't vanish – it calcified, hardening into something sharp and unmoving. Like frost on glass, it blurred the outlines of what I once believed I could reach. I wasn't losing faith. I was learning how to live without it. Yet each time I reached this point of surrender, something in me rebelled.

2022 – Hope and Resignation

The urgency had dissipated, replaced by a quiet, persistent attention to possibility. I had found a way to integrate the not-knowing into my sense of self, to carry it not as an unbearable burden but as one element of a complex identity.

In the waning days of 2022, I found myself in a strange emotional suspension – no longer searching, not yet resigned – hovering between hope and acceptance. This delicate equilibrium – an acceptance without resignation – fostered an almost mystical openness to possibility while protecting me from the crushing weight of expectation.

Reluctantly, I had begun to accept that I might never know more than fragments of his story. But sometimes, just when hope seems lost, when the mosaic of identity appears permanently incomplete, the Universe conspires in unexpected ways.

Interlude 2

Inheritance

More than blood,
memory, dreams.

Ursula. Giuseppe.

Names,
whose fragments I carry –

eye colour, a face passed down.

Along with a whispering shame,
secrets and falsehoods,
a burning flame in irises.

I was given mothers who abandoned,
fathers who became absent.

Formed by what I was withheld.
Haunted by what remains hidden.

Sacred, intertwined threads,
pulling me to their origin.
Blood memory screaming –

And that is mine alone.

Part III

The Sinful Fathers

15

DNA Detective

(2022–2023)

Unearthing golden threads through a labyrinth

In the quiet twilight of my search, when hope had calcified into a resigned acceptance, in late 2022 – just as I was making peace with never finding my biological father alive, accepting that statistics and actuarial tables were against me – a seemingly inconsequential decision changed everything. I bought a friend a DNA test kit as a Christmas gift – a small box containing vials and swabs that promised to reveal ancient migrations and ethnic percentages. Trivial knowledge, I thought, compared to the vast unknown that had haunted me for decades. That small gift became a catalyst – a pebble that would start an avalanche.
By January 2023, guided by an unseen but trusted inner compass, I had enrolled in a professional development course on the psychological effects of forced adoption practices. The clinical course description mentioned nothing about personal revelation, yet this academic pursuit – chosen ostensibly for professional reasons – would unexpectedly reignite my search, just as its embers were cooling to ash.
The Forced Adoption Era negatively affected everyone involved: mothers forced to relinquish their babies, fathers who often had no say or didn't know they were fathers, and adoptees like me – separated from their biological families. The ripple effects

extended to grandparents, aunts, uncles, and siblings – a heartbreaking legacy affecting an estimated 250,000 Australians, and millions in the United States. Children torn from their biological families by those who wrongly believed they'd be better with strangers.

Completing the course stirred emotions I had deeply buried. The old feelings resurfaced like bodies rising from a billabong – the yearning, the incompleteness, the sense of existing in fragments. The desire to find my elusive Giuseppe, dormant for years, awakened with a renewed urgency and desperation. I decided to resume my ever-hopeful, yet seemingly futile, search.

I Googled *adoption*, as I had done a hundred times before. Again, I joined various adoption online search groups. None were fruitful.

How would I ever find him? I continued to lament.

A few months later, in mid-March, while scrolling through Facebook late one night, I discovered a group called *DNA Detectives*. The name alone quickened my pulse. Posted on their webpage were stories like mine – adoptees searching for mothers, fathers, grandparents, or siblings, or stories of people who had found members of their biological families.

I read through many posts – happy and not-so-happy reunions, warm embraces or sad stories of rejection, blocking, and ghosting. Joyful photos of adoptees with parents, siblings, grandparents, and other family members. Some horrific stories – mothers who had been raped or assaulted, adoptees discovering parents who had committed crimes, ended up in jail, were addicted to drugs, had serious mental health issues, or had taken their own lives. Some had simply died. As I read each story, I cried – sometimes happy tears, sometimes sad, sometimes angry, sometimes frustrated. Their stories were fragments of my own adoption mosaic, echoes of my uncertain journey.

People posted their DNA matches and *search angels* helped them find their biological families. Unlike my previous searches – conducted through bureaucracy and paperwork – this approach seemed almost magical. Scientific yet intimate. It combined the precision of genetics with the mystery of family. Group members suggested uploading DNA results to all available genealogy sites. Ancestry.com for Americans, MyHeritage for Europeans and Australians, and others – GEDmatch, 23andMe, Living DNA, FamilyTreeDNA, and Genomelink. With renewed hope, I promptly did so.

The technical side was straightforward enough – upload genetic data, compare matches, trace connections – but behind each clinical percentage lay potential heartbreak or revelation. Each centimorgan (cM) shared with an unknown cousin might lead to the biological father I'd sought for decades.

In the family trees listed on sites such as MyHeritage or Ancestry.com, living members are listed as *private*, by convention. To find their names, members of the *DNA Detectives* group suggested that if we found distant DNA matches or deceased potential great grandparents or grandparents, we should then search for that person's obituary – or any other information – online. *I hadn't thought to do that.* Luckily, we now lived in the age of the internet and social media – and the internet is a font of information. I don't think people realise how much information is out there about individuals and their families.

The members also warned – in big bold red letters – *if you find anything, STOP! Screenshot everything before making any contact with anyone.*

I had suddenly entered the world of DNA-family history sleuthing.

On Saturday, 18 March 2023, I posted my adoption search story on Facebook. I had mentioned Ursula's name in the post. I was asked to take it down. I was told it would embarrass our mother – shame her. *As if truth could be shameful.* After 33 years of having first met her back in 1990, I no longer cared about her feelings or needs. I had been patient and considerate for long enough.

Time was now precious.

'I'm warning you! Or else I'll take legal action. I'll sue you for defamation.'

I resisted the urge to tell them to look up the meaning of defamation.

Around this time, I ordered another DNA test – this time with Ancestry.com. With nervous excitement, I swabbed the inside of my cheek, sealed the sample, and sent it off – another small piece of myself dispatched into the world in search of connections. While waiting for those results to process, I immersed myself in the mechanics of genetic genealogy – learning about centimorgans, haplogroups, and the Leeds method for sorting matches.

Tuesday, 21 March 2023

It was an ordinary night – coincidentally, exactly 10 years after Australian former Prime Minister Gillard had given the National Apology for Forced Adoptions, 20 years after that horribly nasty last phone call with Ursula, 43 years after the bus ride that had changed my life – and it was the last year of my 50s.

Late into that night, I was lying on my bed with my mobile phone, casually discussing a friend's DNA results. We were discussing DNA and families and what had been found. DNA results can often unearth skeletons in firmly closed family closets. I was also on my iPad as we chatted.

At midnight, I methodically navigated through my MyHeritage DNA matches. I had a strategy now – separate maternal connections from paternal ones. Any DNA match that didn't appear in my half-brother Nathan's results could potentially lead to Giuseppe. The science was straightforward – we share approximately 50% of our DNA with each biological parent (approximately 3,400 cM). The more DNA you share, the more recent and closer your common ancestor likely is. Somewhere in these digital strands lay the map to my biological father.

I studied the first match carefully – a potential second or third cousin from France. We shared only 129 cM of DNA. A scientific measurement of the invisible threads that connected us across continents despite decades of institutional separation – not a huge amount, but significant enough to indicate a common ancestor within the past few generations – possibly a great-grandfather. When I clicked *'Review DNA Match'* and scrolled through our shared connections, I noticed something crucial: Nathan, my half-brother, wasn't listed among them. This could only mean one thing – this connection came through my paternal line.

Heart pounding, I clicked to view this person's family tree. There, among the branches of unknown names, one jumped out at me: *Giuseppe Verduci*. He was listed as the grandfather, but the birth year – 1929 – made him a decade too old to be my Giuseppe.

I dismissed this match and went back to my DNA matches. The next paternal match was a female third cousin from France. We shared only 115 cM. I clicked on, *'View Profile'*. She had only joined MyHeritage 10 months earlier. I looked at the possible relationships – there was a 41% probability that we had the same great grandparents. I went back a page and clicked on *'View in Tree'*.

Her father and grandfather were listed as <Private> Verduci – the same surname as in the previous family tree. Her great grandfather was an *Andrea Verduci*. There was a sepia photo of a very dashing young man with dark eyes, short wavy hair centrally parted, and sporting a very fancy cupid's bow moustache twirled at the ends to fine points. He was wearing a suit jacket, tie, and a white shirt. Expressive big puppy-dog eyes, large ears, and a strong chin – features I recognised in myself. I clicked on his photo, and then, *'Research this person'*. I clicked on the first entry. He was born in Montebello Jonico, Reggio Calabria, Italy on 1 September 1878, and he died on the 17

September 1961 in Anna di Melito di Porto Salvo. These places were completely foreign to me.

He had been married twice. His first wife, Filomena Iamonte, was born 1886 and she died 12 April 1916, in Saline Ioniche. She was only 30 years old – a life cut violently short while her children were still young.

A fleeting thought crossed my mind, sending a shiver of recognition through my body. *Could these people be my Bisnonno and Bisnonna?* (Great-grandfather and Great-grandmother).

A minuscule heart flutter grew into a pounding sensation against my ribs. Curiosity and anticipation swelled within me. *After decades of searching, could I really be this close?*

Would I be able to find my very elusive Giuseppe – my biological father – with a miniscule DNA match?

I studied each entry methodically, assembling the pieces with newfound clarity. Each name represented another connection, another branch of a tree I was meticulously reconstructing: Margherita, Carmela, Giuseppe, Bruna, Vincenzo, Giovanni, Filomena. The terrified 16-year-old on the bus could never have imagined this moment – this deliberate excavation of truth, this controlled reassembly of what had been abruptly severed at birth.

This was the same Giuseppe as in the previous DNA match I had examined. This Giuseppe could not be *my* Giuseppe. One detail was especially jarring, he was '*Reported to have killed someone.*' He had migrated to France, and I deduced that he was the father or uncle of VV.

12:14 am – Carlton and the Italian Connection

The house was silent except for my fingers on the screen and my shallow breathing.

I clicked again and found that Andrea had another son, Bartolomeo, who was born in 1908 – the same year the great Messina earthquake had wiped out much of Reggio, buildings collapsing and thousands dead while this new life was taking form. Birth amid catastrophe – a beginning threaded through ending.

I switched to Ancestry.com, the glow of the screen illuminating my face in the darkened room and searched through historical documents with increasing urgency. I typed in Andrea Verduci and found a public family tree, which contained close to 600 people – an entire constellation of lives connected by invisible threads of DNA and circumstance. I searched the site owner, Rosemary's grandfather, Bartolomeo. He was born on 5 June 1908 in Montebello Jonico and had died, at 97, in Melbourne, on 13 December 2005. He had lived in Melbourne – perhaps passing me unknowingly on streets we both walked, our blood-ties invisible yet binding – and had married a Giuseppina Raco, who was born in Motticella, Reggio Calabria, in 1912 and had died at 92, on 18 September 2004, also in Melbourne.

Another tiny heart flutter, like a feather caressing my cheek. I was suddenly captivated by this sleuthing process – this archaeological excavation of my own history – digging through digital layers to unearth bones of truth buried beneath decades of silence.

I clicked on Bartolo's name and was led to a *Facts* page, where I found a migration passenger list. I clicked on it. Bartolo migrated to Australia on 21 February 1952, and he arrived in Australia in March 1952 – on the same boat that my parents had sailed to Australia on.

I sat up straight, my breath catching. The coincidence seemed too perfect to be random – Bartolo Verduci and my parents sharing the same migration journey, crossing oceans on the same vessel, their lives intersecting without their knowledge. *Had they passed each other on deck? Had they spoken?*

I clicked on the electoral roll that listed Bartolo as living in Donald Street, Brunswick in 1980 – Brunswick, a Melbourne suburb that neighbours Carlton. *Another heart flutter.*

Bartolo was listed as having four daughters and five sons. Two were named in a family tree, Bruna, 1949–2009 and Giovanni, 1947–1969. I noted that he was only 22 when he died. I wondered what had caused his death. *An illness? An accident? So young*, I thought.

I clicked on the magnifying glass search button and kept searching and reading. Listed were other electoral roll entries: Carlton North, Melbourne, 1967 and 1968. One of the scant pieces of information I had about my elusive Giuseppe matched. One of my seven pieces fell into place. *He had lived in Carlton at the time of my birth.* My heart skipped a beat.

12:22 am – 'Giuseppe'
I then went to Google and typed in *'Bartolo Verduci obituary'*. I clicked on the first link *VERDUCI, Bartolo | Death Notices | Melbourne. mytributes, Herald Sun*, 14/12/2005. I read the obituary notice *'VERDUCI Bartolo Passed away peacefully on Dec. 13, 2005, Age 97 years. Beloved husband of Giuseppina (dec.). ... loving father and father-in-law of Andrea ... Giuseppe and Alice (dec) ...'*

Suddenly, the room seemed to tilt around me. My chest tightened as if gripped by a vice. Blood rushed to my head, making me dizzy with the implications of what I'd just read. There it was – *Giuseppe* – nestled among names in an obituary, connected to Bartolo, connected to Carlton.

Giuseppe Verduci. I repeated the names several times over to myself. *Ver-du-chi* – the soft Italian *'ci'* pronounced like *'chee'* – foreign on my tongue, yet somehow familiar.

Suddenly my heart started thumping against my chest. That familiar *Ba-boom. Ba-boom*, only this time not reaction to fear – but excitement. My eyes widened. Incredulously, sceptically I dared to muse, *Could this possibly be my elusive biological father, my Giuseppe?!*

My heart thudded faster as I entered a hyper-alert state – sharply focused, with steadfast concentration. As if my nervous system recognised him before my mind could – the fragments aligning, forming the outline of my father. My mind was racing. Trying to keep up with this information trail.

Three shards of my seven-piece puzzle now gleamed with clarity – the name, the place, the date – each one a filament drawing me closer: Giuseppe, born in Italy and he had lived in Carlton around the time of my conception.

I read the rest of the list of Bartolo's nine children and their partners. I assumed that they were listed in birth order as would be customary. John (Giovanni) was the second youngest. I read the names of the 21 grandchildren and 15 great-grandchildren. *'Will be greatly missed by all.'*

The words from the DNA Detectives group suddenly leapt into my mind: *'Screenshot everything!'*

At this point, I wasn't absolutely sure this was my Giuseppe's family that I was reading about – but just in case it was, I went back and started to screenshot everything.

My First Screenshot – 12:14 am.

Time warped – speeding and collapsing all at once. Instead of slow painful decades, now I was excavating information within mere hours – minutes. My mind struggled to keep up with all of these revelations.

In less than an hour of online searching, my life was about to change irrevocably. What had begun as a casual conversation about DNA had led me to evidence that might connect me to my biological father – perhaps even suggest he was still alive, a possibility I had all but abandoned. Now I had names, connections, and a path forward – but I still needed to confirm what I'd found and, if possible, make contact with a man who might not even know I existed.

The methodical researcher in me demanded more evidence – more connections to verify this wasn't just another false lead. My hands trembled slightly – a tremor born not of terror but of anticipation, the kind that comes when you're standing at the threshold of a door you've been trying to open for most of your life.

12:56 am
I searched, 'Giuseppe Verduci', on Ancestry.com and found him on a passenger list from Italy to Australia. He was 16 years old when he travelled alone from Messina, Sicily. His arrival date: January 1954, Fremantle, Western Australia. His birth year was listed as *about 1938*. The fourth piece snapped into the puzzle. The contours of Giuseppe became clearer with each new detail. *1938. Just as Ursula said – 26 when I was conceived.*
Thoughts repeatedly swirling through my mind with each new discovery.
Was he the elusive biological father I had wanted to find since I was 26?
Adrenaline surged. My hands shook as I clicked through records. I was fully awake – every sense heightened, every detail crystalline. I went downstairs and outside to my garage, sat smoking, disbelieving, scrolling, screenshotting. It was now the wee early hours of Wednesday.
My head spun.
Disbelief spiralled. I kept clicking, scrolling – frantic.

12:57 am – A Family Business
I found a Giuseppe Verduci on an electoral roll – 1972, ACT and then 1967, Carlton North.
I clicked the image: *Verduci, Lygon Street, Carlton North, Bartolo, shopkeeper, Bruna, student, Giuseppe, director, Giuseppina, home duties.*
Each fragment was part of a constellation – stars slowly forming into a recognisable face.
A fifth fragment – a family business.
Another vital edge found, another border defined. The mosaic of Giuseppe was taking shape – piece by piece, the outline of the man I had never met began to emerge with startling clarity.

I Googled the street address and found an image. A red brick Edwardian home with a bay window. I'd passed it, unaware, more times than I could count.

1:05 am
I found another electoral roll. Giuseppe had lived in Canberra in 1977 and again in 1980.
In less than an hour's sleuthing, I had a rough map where my possible biological father and his family had lived during the 60s, 70s, and 80s.

1:09 am – An Unexpected Revelation
I opened a new browser tab and Googled, 'Giuseppe Verduci'.
The first entry...
National Library of Australia
'Verducci (sic) *will be murdered one day, says former detective.*'
A Canberra Times article by Diego Campbell.
'*The Calabrian Honoured Society would murder police informant Giuseppe "Joe" Verducci (sic) one day,' a former Australian Federal Police detective told the Winchester inquest yesterday.*'
I skimmed the article... '*the society*'... '*Winchester's murder*'... '*National Crime Authority*'... '*killing*'... '*Donald McKay*'... '*Bungendore, cannabis plantations*'...' *Queanbeyan.*' I froze – cigarette burning, forgotten. The words wouldn't settle into sense.
Winchester
Killing
Donald McKay
Cannabis?
Giuseppe – a police informant?
Mafia connections?
Had he killed someone?
Black-and-white images from the McKay story flashed in my mind – Griffith, 1977, Mafia-style shooting.

Had Giuseppe also been murdered?
Was this my Giuseppe?
This couldn't be my father, I told myself.
I scrolled through more articles. Giuseppe Verduci – police informant. Cannabis cultivator in Bungendore. Supervised by Assistant Commissioner of the Australian Federal Police, Colin Winchester.
I wasn't reading about Giuseppe anymore – I had tumbled down a rabbit hole into Australia's underworld. *Mafia. Bungendore. McKay. Griffith. Winchester. Operation Seville.*
Two parallel universes formed:
– the elderly Calabrian father tending vegetables
– the younger man: a gun-wielding informant, potential killer.
I couldn't reconcile them.
It was too surreal.
The man I had imagined was a fantasy.
An idea. A figment built from fragments.
I had pictured a typical Italian migrant – married after I was born, maybe had an affair, more children, grandchildren. A quiet life in suburban Melbourne. A businessman. Tending veggie patches, making *passata* (tomato sauce), sausages. An Italian father like others in my childhood neighbourhood.
Never – never – had I imagined *Mafia*.
The possibility felt like a cruel joke. That after decades of searching, I might find my father – only to discover *this*.
Perhaps it wasn't him, I told myself. *Perhaps this was just another Giuseppe.*
My heart kept pumping faster and faster, as I kept smoking and reading, while sitting on my small red fold-up camping chair in my garage, next to my Angel, who was lying in her outdoor bed, giving me quizzical looks that asked why she was out here with her human in the cold rather than snug and warm inside asleep in her upstairs bed.
Why was her human so excited?
I Googled the search terms, 'Giuseppe Verduci Mafia.'

It produced more newspaper articles about the Mafia, Operation Seville, Bungendore, and Winchester, who had been shot in his neighbour's Deakin, Canberra driveway, assassination style on the night of 10 January 1989. A story I only vaguely remembered hearing about. Giuseppe's name was linked to Winchester and one of Australia's most infamous unsolved murder cases.

Nothing existed but this moment – this pursuit, this unfolding revelation.

The ordinary world – my job, my home, my routines – seemed to recede into the background, temporarily irrelevant in the face of what I was discovering.

As I sat in a haze of cigarette smoke, the moonlight filtering in through the mist-covered window, I read news articles that dated back to the 1980s. Somewhere I read that this Giuseppe Verduci was born in 1937.

Was this a different Giuseppe?

I kept reading and searching. I read the word, "*Ndrangheta.*' I didn't know what that meant so I Googled it.

'One of Italy's oldest criminal organizations, forming in the 18th century in Calabria.'

Calabrian Mafia?

Growing up, Mafia was not ever something connected to my adopted family or my Italian-Australian life. The few things I knew about the Mafia came from reading and watching Marlon Brando and *The Godfather* series. I hadn't even watched *The Sopranos*. I wasn't a fan of violence or violent movies.

The few other loose connections I'd had to Mafia or gangsters was via the *Underbelly* series that depicted Melbourne's gangland killing spree – 36 gangsters killed each other between 1998 and 2010. I recalled the killings that occurred in places I had frequented or knew well.

A gangster had been shot near my former address at Queen Street, Coburg, in 2003.

Jason Moran, along with Pasquale 'Little Pat' Barbaro, was shot dead execution style in the car park of Cross Keys Reserve, North

Essendon, as his kids were playing Auskick – the same oval I used to walk past, on my nightly walks around my Coburg neighbourhood.

His father, Lewis Moran was shot dead at the Brunswick Club on Sydney Road in 2004.

The Morans used to drink at the Laurel Hotel, in Ascot Vale, which was once the pub the RMIT hockey club members drank at, and my former hairdresser's cousin was Mario Condello, a member of the Carlton Crew, who was shot dead in 2006.

This was the extent of my knowledge of gangsters.

1:53 am – Business Enterprises

I went back to searching the name Verduci.

I found a young bespectacled Joseph Verduci on LinkedIn. We had somewhat similar features.

Was this a cousin, a nephew?

I kept searching, the name Verduci: Verduci lawyers. Verduci Real Estate. Verduci Market Gardens. Verduci Enterprises. Then I started searching individual names that were listed in Bartolo's obituary.

3:22 am – The Eyes Staring Back at Me

As the search continued, I had little time to reflect. I was doing my best to take it all in, though my mind could barely keep pace with my heart. After much searching and scrolling, I had made my way back to Ancestry.com and was looking at a Verduci Family Tree. The owner was listed as Rosemary.

I scrolled through photos and found an old black and white photo of four young women. Two of Giuseppe's sisters, Angela and Joanne.

Sets of eyes staring back at me.

Then I found another black and white photo of another sister, Bruna. If this Giuseppe was indeed my father, then these women were my aunties.

As I looked more closely into the last photo of Bruna, as would Sherlock scrutinizing a vital piece of evidence with a magnifying glass, I saw – in a flash of recognition – parts of younger myself.
Similar smile.
Similar cheek bones.
Similar chin.
I didn't dare yet assume that this was indeed my paternal family staring back at me.
Stunned at the sudden and unexpected finding, I was engulfed – the moment reverberating like a mirror image of the blow that first struck me in 1980.
I still wasn't yet 100% certain that this Giuseppe Verduci was my biological father, although he was a good match to the person I was looking for – Southern Italian, born about 1938, had a business, and lived in Carlton.
I didn't know what that business was or where it had been located.

3:41 am
I searched for Bruna Verduci. I found an obituary listed in the Herald Sun, 1/2/2010. It read, 'VERDUCI-ROMANO. -- Bruna Motticella (RC) 18.11.1942 Canberra 27.12.2009. Always missed by husband ... children ... brothers and sisters Andrea, Joe ...'
Joe had another wife listed. I found another article ...info/lawyers/biogs... Bruna Romano, Barrister, Lawyer, and Solicitor. Bruna migrated to Australia with her family. She came to Australia as a 13-year-old in 1956. She completed her HSC in 1961, only five years after arriving in Australia. She was admitted as a solicitor and barrister of the Supreme Court of Victoria in 1968 – four years after I was born.
She became the first woman to establish a law practice in the ACT.
I read the rest of the bio. Bruna died after being diagnosed with an aggressive brain tumour. She was only 67.

She had been a high achiever. A ground breaker. Studious. Dedicated to her craft. Taken too soon.

4:42 am – Family Vengeance
I went back to MyHeritage – Bartolo. 'Family tragedy. After 1909. Following the attack on his sister, Bartolo was convinced by his other sister Bruna to move to Motticella, so he didn't try to seek vengeance. It was in Motticella that he met his future wife, Giuseppina Raco.'

4:49 am
I looked up Verduci Lawyers. Established in 1969. One of the partners was an Alfred Verduci.
Was this the same Alfred listed in Bartolo's obituary?

5:02 am – A Family Tragedy
I found Giovanni 'John' Verduci's death record. His birth was listed as circa 1947, age 22, death 1969, Carlton, Victoria, Australia. Father: Bartolo Verduci. Mother: Giuseppina Raco. Again, I wondered, *what did he die of?* He was so young. The more I searched, the more answers I found, the more questions came up about Giuseppe and his massive, well-educated, and business-venturing family.
How and why did Giuseppe get involved in the Mafia?

Verduci Bros Furniture Business, Brunswick
I stalked social media pages and found Alfred Verduci on a Facebook post. It mentioned the Verduci Bros furniture business, Sydney Road, Brunswick. He had been interviewed by 3AW. The Verduci Bros had advertised on the Melbourne radio station during the 1960s. This may have been the business that Giuseppe was involved in around the time I was conceived.
As I read my DNA results, I realised I was neither floating above my life nor drowning in it. I was simply present – fully embodied

and engaged in this search. The observer and the experiencer had finally become one person: me.

Every name, every record, every image was a shard of a greater truth. I had spent decades collecting these fragments in isolation. Now, they were not just facts – they were connective tissue, forming the outline of a man, a past, a heritage. As I pieced them together, I wasn't just building a profile of Giuseppe – I was constructing the missing half of myself.

Exhausted but not quite weary, I switched off the iPad. Plunged into darkness, I fell onto my bed.

Names, dates, eyes, scrolling eyes – all dissolved into a kaleidoscope of unsettled dreams.

The blue glow from the screen remained under my eyelids long after I had closed them.

Data had become a language of grief.

In the dark, something waited. Not hope. Not closure. Something else.

Around 10 am, I went downstairs for my morning coffee ritual. Although I had had little sleep, I was wide awake – still in a hypermanic-like state.

The sort of wide awake that is caused by shock and disbelief – often caused by trauma.

I switched on the electric kettle and then stood by the sink in a corner of the blue kitchen bench and waited for the water to boil. A cloud of steam was starting to emerge from its spout.

I found myself grasping onto the bench on either side of me. My legs failing me.

The gurgling, rumbling sound of water slowly reaching a boil.

Then suddenly, a rush of pent-up emotion came bursting out of me.

I began to sob frantically.

Huge, big guttural sobs.

Desperately gasping for air between each one.

Cross-armed, clutching my chest.

Protecting my heart.

It felt too much.
The enormity of the night's discovery revealing itself.
Years of pent-up frustration, gushing out of my eyes – dripping with tears of longing, sadness, and, finally, overwhelming relief. The emotions I had tried to quash and ignore for the past 20 years.
The detached, denialistic thoughts and feelings – I had convinced myself, *it didn't matter, if I never knew the identity of my father – the biggest lie, I had ever told myself.*

I took a sip of my coffee.
Reflecting on the night's discovery.
I was fairly certain that I had finally found my elusive Giuseppe. There was a faint possibility that he was still alive, as I had not come across his obituary.
He wasn't listed by name in any of the Verduci family trees that I had found.
I reminded myself that usually only the deceased are named in these online public family trees.
I drank my coffee, smoked more cigarettes, and like one possessed, continued searching on the internet and social media – gathering as much information as I could about this big family that shared my blood. My family DNA fields that had been empty were now being rapidly filled with names, people, dates, places, professions, and faces. I was finally finding my place in my genealogical, biological, and cultural history. My fragmented tree was no longer adrift.
It had found its familial forest roots.
The DNA technology offered more than just the missing mosaic pieces – it provided new threads I could actively weave into my life's tapestry. Each match, each new connection represented discovery and possibility: relationships I might choose to develop, stories I might incorporate into my own.
Around this time, I also conducted a deep dive into Ancestry.com and internet resources, searching for information about my

maternal Grandmother, Marianna – the woman I was likely named after, the invisible thread connecting me to a history I'd never known. My Grandmother's surname was Castiglia. She had been born in Eboli near Naples, Campania – a region whose very name resonated with ancient Rome – and raised in an orphanage. The records of her parentage were non-existent; her own origins as mysterious to her as mine had been to me.

The pattern of orphaned children, I realised with a start, extended backward through generations in my family like a genetic inheritance more persistent than eye colour or bone structure. This wasn't just my story but a recurring family theme children separated from parents, growing up without knowing their origins, identity itself becoming a question mark passed down through generations. What I had experienced was part of a much larger narrative that stretched back through time, suggesting that perhaps my search wasn't merely personal but the continuation of an ancestral quest spanning centuries.

With each new discovery, renewed hope, a seismic shift began. The great darkness that had long consumed me was moving, breaking, loosening its hold. I had not yet contemplated the possibility that Giuseppe was still alive. In my mind, he had been long dead. I was not prepared to be that hopeful.

Looking back, I can see how my understanding of identity was evolving – from something fixed and lost to something fluid and created. The language of my early journals reveals a desperate search for a single truth. Now, my thoughts had become more nuanced.

I was learning to navigate paradox: I was both Di Benedetto and Verduci, both orphan and child, both lost and found. The DNA revolution ahead would not simply add new information – it would transform how I understood information itself.

My Bisnonni – Filomena Iamonte and Andrea Verduci

Aunty Bruna Verduci Romano

Giuseppe

My Nonni - Giuseppina and Bartolomeo Verduci

16

Dr Rosemary: The Historian
(March 2023)

Archival puzzles holding ghosts

Later that day, following my night of discovery, I took a break from my internet detective work. I had lunch with a former work colleague and now good friend. Over lunch in her sunlit kitchen, I could barely contain myself.

'I think I may have found my birth father,' I told her, my voice catching. I watched her eyes widen as I shared the incredible night of research I'd just experienced.

She asked, 'Mirella, after all these years. How do you feel?'

The question was simple but profound.

How did I feel?

Stunned. Hopeful. Terrified.

The possibility that Giuseppe might still be alive felt almost mythic.

For years, I'd been preparing myself to find only a grave, a death certificate, a collection of memories from those who'd known him. Now, as sunlight streamed through the back window, illuminating dust motes suspended in air – much like the fragments of identity gathered over decades – I faced a possibility I'd hardly dared imagine.

As I sat in what I thought would be just another ordinary day, my hands wrapped around the soup bowl to stop them from shaking.

I was facing the extraordinary possibility that my father could still be alive and that I might be able to meet him in the flesh rather than read his name on a tombstone.

As soon as I returned home, I resumed my mission – resolute, electric with possibility. I texted my friend, Bee, who had called Ursula back in 1990 and told her, 'I might have found my birth father.' We arranged to meet that Sunday. I was 99% sure I had found Giuseppe, but I had to be 100% sure before I made contact with anyone. To confirm that I was on the right track, I needed more information.

On Wednesday, 22 March – just one day after my late-night research breakthrough – I decided to contact my youngest maternal Uncle Bru. Though we'd never met, we were Facebook friends. We had texted each other over the previous few years. I sent him a text about my recent discovery. He was happy to talk by phone. He hadn't known about me when Ursula was pregnant with me. He was only 14 at the time and just thought that she was getting fat – then she went away and came back skinnier. The innocence of youth.

I told him that I had possibly found my biological father, but I needed to be sure and needed some corroborating information.

'Where did Ursula work when she was about 18?' I asked.

'Pelaco. A shirt factory in Richmond. She used to go out alone.'

Uncle Bru said he'd speak with his sisters. He also told me that a younger brother, Claudio, had died in infancy and two other babies were stillborn. So, Ursula was one of 15 children. He then told me about his parents, my grandparents, himself and all of his siblings and their children's and grandchildren's names. The maternal branch of my biological family tree was now replete with names and family history. Seven uncles, five aunts, and a few busloads of cousins. He also gave me some medical history. Two days later, on Friday, 24 March, Uncle Bru called me back. He had spoken to an older sister, Valda. She had told him that Giuseppe had a furniture shop on Sydney Road, Brunswick. She mentioned the surname Verduci. This now confirmed what I had found.

The confirmation struck me like an electric current – these were not merely digital records but living memories. The shop on Sydney Road wasn't just a data point, but a physical place where my father had once worked and breathed. Another mosaic piece of my identity snapping into place – its edges no longer quite so jagged.

I was grateful that Uncle Bru was able to get this information for me, but also livid that family members had known who Giuseppe was – where he lived, where he worked, and what his surname was. Yet, they thought it was appropriate to keep this information from me. Emotions cascaded through me like a flooding river, carrying grief and anger. Emotions that would take me months to process. I later wrote in my journal, 18 April 2023:

> Uncle Bru helped me with some information. His sisters knew it was a furniture shop and that the surname was Verduci. They all kept this from me for 33 years!

The betrayal burned deep, but I couldn't afford to let anger completely derail me now. Not when I was so close. The situation was still very surreal. I didn't know if Giuseppe was still alive or how to contact him. I needed more information, and that meant taking a deep breath and taking a giant leap into the unknown – reaching out to complete strangers who could be blood relatives. And again, facing the prospect of rejection, denial, or stonewalling. However, the momentum kept me steadfastly moving forward. I would not let the fear of rejection interfere with my quest to find my father.

I assumed that Giuseppe had children, but I didn't know who they were. I thought the names in the obituary were listed in chronological order, so initially I thought that he had two daughters and a son. I set out to track them down – once more by stalking social media pages and Ancestry.com.

On Sunday, 26 March, I met my friends for lunch. I told them what I had found and how I had found my information. I showed them photos of the Verduci family, and they agreed it wasn't just my hopeful imagination – there was a family resemblance. The detective work was done; now came the delicate dance of making contact.

Over the next few days, I carefully crafted messages to send to potential relatives through Facebook Messenger. My approach had to be cautious – I'd learned from my experience with Ursula that too much revelation too quickly could cause people to withdraw. I was about to drop a potential bombshell into these people's lives, and I needed to do it with care. I created a systematic outreach plan, starting with the person most likely to have information, but least likely to be emotionally overwhelmed by my sudden appearance – someone who managed the family tree I'd found, who might have a researcher's objectivity.

The messages I sent progressed from vague to more specific as I gauged responses:

Wednesday 22 March – *'Hi, are you related to Giuseppe Verduci and his father Bartolo Verduci?'*

Thursday, 23 March – *'Hi, are you related to Giuseppe Verduci son of Bartolo by any chance?'*

Saturday 25 March – *'Hi, I'm doing a family tree, and I'm connected to the Verduci family. Is your dad Giuseppe by any chance? His father Bartolo had a shop on Sydney Road in the 60s. I think we may be related.'*

Sunday, 26 March – *'Hi Rosemary, I'm doing a family search. Is your father Giuseppe Verduci who lived in Lygon Street, Carlton. His father Bartolo had a furniture shop. We might be closely related.'*

Monday, 27 March, 7:11 am. A response finally came.

I saw the notification on my phone and my heart leapt to my throat.

I opened Facebook Messenger with trembling fingers.

Rosemary: *'Hi Mirella, Giuseppe is my uncle. He is my father's older brother.'*

I was digging for more information about the identity of any siblings and had to tread carefully – so as not to scare Rosemary away.

Monday, 27 March, 8:08 am
Me: '*Oh. Ok. My internet search has indicated that he may have three children to Alice. I need to be sure I'm on the right track. Everything I have so far leads to this Giuseppe. Are you the Historian who has a PhD and compiled the extensive family tree?*'
I waited patiently and eagerly for a response.
I'm not sure how I managed to work during this time, as my mind was elsewhere. Every spare minute was taken up with my ongoing searching, reading, and stalking social media pages. It was characteristic of my all or none approach to life, interests, and people.
In the evening, the reply came.
As I stared at the words on my screen, they confirmed what I'd suspected – this was the right family, the right Giuseppe.
My hands shook as I read:
Rosemary: '*Yes, I am a historian. Giuseppe (Joseph) has five children.*'
Five children, not three!
This Giuseppe had more children than I'd realised – meaning more potential family connections, more complex relationships to navigate, more people who might be affected by my appearance in their lives.
Wow. I have five more siblings.
The revelation struck me with the force of mathematical certainty – $5 + 3 = 8$. Eight siblings.
After decades of being an only child, I suddenly possessed a battalion of brothers and sisters, along with all of the other family members. The lone fig tree of my life had exploded into an orchard, each sibling a different variety of the same fruit. I stared at my reflection in the darkened computer screen, wondering if

they would see themselves in my face as I was beginning to see them in mine.

Since Rosemary was not a sibling, it was safer to reveal the reason for my search. Siblings can act in unpredictable ways. Some are welcoming and some are not.

Me: *'Hi Rosemary, Is Joseph still alive? I was adopted just after I was born. I have lots of evidence to Joseph being my father.'*

I continued, my heart pounding as I typed the words that would change everything:

'My birth mother told me my birth father's name was Giuseppe.'

Rosemary: *'Wow! Yes, he is still alive.'*

He – is – still – alive!

For a moment, the world stopped turning. My vision blurred. The words struck me like a physical blow.

My breath caught.

I had to read the line three times to make sure I wasn't imagining it.

After decades of searching, after years of believing I might be too late, *my father was alive!*

The possibility I'd barely allowed myself to hope for was suddenly, incredibly real.

Overwhelmed, my mind now splitting again.

In that moment of revelation, the fracturing I had experienced on that bus in 1980 was bizarrely mirrored – but this time, instead of identity shattering into painful fragments, it was splitting between disbelief and ecstasy, between the observer and the experienced. The vessel wasn't breaking further – it was beginning its transformation into something new.

The emotional brain was merely observing the week's scene unfold – as if casually watching a Netflix series, while munching on popcorn. I wasn't living it. I wasn't feeling it. It was all too surreal.

The enormity of this reality would awaken well over a year later, as I lay down these words.

The rational brain was thinking, OMFG! I have finally found my biological father AND he is still alive!!!

Despite the disconnect, my heart was thumping out of my chest.

Ka-boom, Ka-boom, Ka-boom.

The blood rushing so quickly through my vessels I was becoming lightheaded.

It was impossible to remain calm. A different kind of adrenaline coursed through. Instead of horror and fear, this represented excitement and anticipation. I could now discern the difference between these heightened states.

Thoughts charging through my mind, like the Spanish running of the bulls – part of me was eager trampling over stray, irrelevant thoughts.

I really should get ready for work. I need to have a shower.

Would he acknowledge me as his child?

Would he want to meet me?

Would he care?

Part of me was eager – and the other, terrified.

Again, I would have to steel myself against the possibility of rejection or denial.

Fear of rejection surfaced again.

What if he didn't want to see me?

I sent my new cousin Rosemary another message.

Me: 'That's all I have known about him until last week when my DNA search linked me to the Verduci family tree.'

My mind splintered in two.

Rosemary: 'That's a bit of a blindside I have to admit. Not sure how you continue with your search tbh. Can you leave this with me overnight?'

Me: 'Sure.'

I sent her some background about my adopted family.

Rosemary: '*I would want to find out more if I was in your shoes. I need to think about the best means of getting you in touch with the right family member to continue your search. If you are correct, it will be a difficult process.*'
What did she mean, a difficult process?
Me: '*Ok. I very much appreciate your help. Thank you.*'
I sent a few photos of myself at various ages: 26, 16, 2 months old, and a photo of my adopted Dad and Mum. After decades of not knowing much about my biological father, within just a few days I knew so much about his notorious past, his large Verduci family, and – best of all – he was still alive at 85! I felt like it was a miracle and that the timing was right to meet him, and possibly the rest of the family. I had learnt over time that people's attitudes can change and mellow as they get older.

Tuesday, 28 March: 10:59 am arrived, and with it, more news that would propel me toward an actual meeting. Dr Rosemary's response seemed cautiously positive.
Rosemary: '*Hi Mirella, I forwarded the details to my Father. I'm not brushing you off. I just want to take this slowly.*'

12:55 pm, I replied, '*Hi Rosemary, yes, I understand perfectly. I wouldn't mind talking to your dad, if he wouldn't mind so I can hear about the early days of the family.*'
That evening, my phone rang. The caller ID showed an unknown number. With a trembling hand, I answered, but the call had already gone to voicemail. When I played the message, a male's voice with a slight Italian accent filled the room:
> '*Hello Mirella, this is Alfred Verduci, Rosemary's father. I hope you're well. I'd be happy to talk to you about my brother and pass on any messages to him that you want to. It's nice to hear from you.*'

The voicemail resonated in my quiet house like an artefact unearthed from ancient soil – this voice with its gentle Italian inflections was a stranger's – my father's brother, my Uncle. For decades I had existed between identities – two distant worlds divided by silence. Now, those boundaries were softening, their edges becoming porous where once they had been sealed shut. That was the first time I would hear a paternal family member's voice. Relief washed over me. I couldn't stop smiling. After decades of searching, of hitting walls and dead ends, suddenly doors were opening.

In the span of just one week, my world had completely transformed. I had gone from not knowing my father's surname to having contact with a cousin and an uncle, confirming my father was alive, and discovering I had five more siblings than I'd ever known existed. The speed of these developments left me reeling. It was all overwhelming. Looking back, over a year later as I write, I know I was in shock. Emotionally numb. In disbelief. The same emotional experience as grief but mixed in with euphoria and gratitude. From orphan at 30, to discovering that I had a massive blood family. All this information swirled around in my head. I was dazed. Everything was moving too quickly for me to process. I hung on and went with it.

I found more information. Photos.

Digital archives became my archaeological site, each algorithmic search a delicate excavation revealing fragments of an identity previously sealed behind secrets. Photographs emerged like artefacts, each pixel a potential connection to a history deliberately fragmented.

Birthdays, weddings, Christmases. Looking at faces that looked back at me, and me looking at parts of myself. I found photos of my siblings, their partners, and their children. It was like filling in the blank fragments of my past. Filling it up with as much as I could. Making obscure connections via photos to my blood family. Yet as I gathered these digital fragments, I still hadn't met these people face to face. The transition from virtual discovery to real-world connection would prove far more challenging than clicking through online photos.

Wednesday, 29 March: Just eight days after my late-night discovery of the Verduci family – it would become one of the most important dates of my life. After a restless night with minimal sleep, my mind racing with possibilities, I called Uncle Alfred back. As we spoke, I felt an immediate connection to this gentle-voiced man who was offering to help bridge the gap between me and the father I'd never known.

I had initially decided I would drive into the city to the electoral office to try to find Giuseppe's address, in case I hit a dead end. I couldn't be sure that Uncle Alfred would pass on information to Giuseppe – nor whether Giuseppe would even want to meet me. These were the kind of precautions people in the DNA Detectives group had advised, and that experience had taught me.

Uncle Alfred claimed he hadn't known I existed. He said he was young at the time – 19 and studying. He now lived in Carlton, not far from the old family home. He confirmed that the family had indeed, once lived there.

Uncle Alfred sounded lovely, warm, and kind on the phone. He answered all my questions about the Verduci family business on Sydney Road, Brunswick. Giuseppe and his eldest brother Andrea were partners in a very successful furniture and electrical business during the late 1950s – 1960s. They were very well known in the Italian community. They had about 10 shops across Melbourne and a furniture factory in Werribee. The first furniture shop they had in Brunswick was at 163 Sydney Road, next to the Cornish Arms Hotel – where I used to rehearse with the ukulele group. A strange coincidence.

Most importantly, Uncle Alfred confirmed what Rosemary had already told me – Giuseppe was alive and well. He now lived in

Brunswick, and he even gave me his address. It was the home where my grandparents had once lived. They moved into the house in 1984, my first year at RMIT. All those years that I lived in Coburg, my paternal grandparents were a mere 2.3 kilometres away, a five-minute drive.

The geographical proximity was staggering – all those years, I had been orbiting their existence like a satellite, never quite making contact but held in their gravitational field, nonetheless. The Universe had arranged for us to live as neighbours, separated by mere minutes, yet wholly unknown to each other. The cosmic joke of it all wasn't lost on me – we had been close enough to pass each other on the street yet remained worlds apart.

Aunts and Uncles had various businesses on Sydney Road in Coburg and Brunswick. I used to shop in the area. I went there as a teenager. I must have passed my Auntie's shop a hundred times, not ever knowing that she was my Auntie.

Had I ever passed my grandparents on Sydney Road? Had I rubbed shoulders with them in a supermarket? Had I sat next to them on a tram or a bus? Had I spoken to any of them?

Uncle Alfred told me something that made my heart race: 'I'm going to see Giuseppe this Saturday to tell him about you.' The reality of what was happening suddenly hit me full force. In three days, my father would learn of my existence. After nearly 60 years of separation of mutual unknowing, he would discover he had a daughter who had been searching for him.

Would he be shocked? Angry? Curious? Would he refuse to see me? The possibilities were overwhelming.

Uncle Alfred asked me what I did for work, and I told him I was a psychologist. Then he said something that caught me entirely off guard: 'It would be nice to catch up for a coffee sometime.'

'Well, I have Wednesdays and Fridays off,' I replied, expecting he might suggest something in a few weeks' time.

'What about next week?' he asked. Not quite expecting it to be so soon, I readily said, 'OK.'

We agreed to meet the following Wednesday at 1 pm, at the Abruzzo Club, on Lygon Street, Carlton. Much to my surprise, everything happening so fast. My head barely having time to absorb what was going on. Just over a week earlier I hadn't known who my biological father was, and this coming week I was going to have a coffee with his brother, my Uncle.

After talking to Uncle Alfred, I called my bestie, Bee, and told her what happened, my voice breathless with excitement and disbelief.

'I can't believe how quickly this is moving,' I said. 'Alfred is going to tell Joseph about me this weekend, and next Wednesday, I'm meeting Uncle Alfred for lunch.'

I felt like I was on the set of some bizarre movie. With all sorts of plot twists. Now that I had Uncle Alfred's commitment to help, there was no need to go into the city to search electoral records. I drove to Brunswick instead and slowly passed Giuseppe's house.

It was one of those typical old Italian houses, with a great large vegetable patch in the front yard. Although his garden was more ramshackle, elaborate, and eccentric. Shrubbery was overgrown from the front yard to the nature strip. Ornaments and fairy lights hung from the shrubbery, which formed a thick canopy over the pavement.

As I drove past the house, my hands gripping the steering wheel so tightly, my knuckles whitened, I felt the strange doubling of perception that had become familiar since my adoption revelation. I was simultaneously the terrified teenager whose world had shattered on that bus and the composed professional woman investigating her roots. The abandoned infant seeking her father and the independent adult who had built a life without him. The house before me was both ordinary suburban residence and sacred archaeological site – each weathered brick potentially bearing invisible traces of the man whose DNA I carried.

The front garden was filled with odd and old bits and pieces, a bit reminiscent of Steptoe and Son's junkyard. Across from the house, in the middle of the road there was a median strip about a metre wide that had been cultivated with plants. These had to have been tended by Joseph. It was mostly filled with succulents, including a small prickly pear plant.

I was so eager to meet him. I couldn't believe that for most of my life, he and his family had been living so close by.

Wednesday, 29 March, 7:08 pm I sent a message to one of my newly found siblings: *'Hi, I'm doing a family tree search. Are you related to Giuseppe Verduci, Father Bartolo? They lived in Carlton during the 60s. They had a furniture shop.'* I never got a reply.

My online search continued. I got distracted and read about the Honoured Society, 'the *'Ndrangheta,'* the Calabrian Mafia in Australia. It was well entrenched in Griffith by the 1970s. Sergi, Barbaro, Romeo, Trimboli – all big players from the same Calabrian town.

I read in the Canberra Times, my father, Giuseppe, was cultivating marijuana near Canberra. At the time I was in Year 9 and blissfully unaware that I was adopted. In May of 1985, he was in remand for drug offences. Meanwhile I was in my second year at university, still living at home and playing hockey on the weekends. Perhaps I had smoked the pot he had been cultivating.

Later, I read more about Winchester and Giuseppe's alleged involvement in a book called *The Winchester Scandal* by Campbell, Tui, and Pinwell. An interesting read.

Each online revelation about Giuseppe's past created a peculiar cognitive dissonance – I was simultaneously drawn to and repelled by this man whose blood I carried. The criminal connections, the police informant role, the marijuana cultivation – these weren't abstractions but concrete historical facts about my father. The Giuseppe I was about to meet wasn't just any elderly Italian man but someone whose life had intersected with Australia's criminal history in ways I was only beginning to understand. The golden lacquer would need to join the fragments of my identity. Elements that seemed fundamentally incompatible.

As the days passed, I continued my online research, but now it was focused on preparing for my meeting with Uncle Alfred – and potentially, with Giuseppe himself. I wanted to be ready for any questions they might ask, to understand the family dynamics I might be walking into. The weekend arrived – the weekend Uncle Alfred had said he would speak to Joseph about me.

I found it nearly impossible to concentrate on anything else – wondering what was being said, how Joseph was reacting, whether my existence was being welcomed or rejected. By Sunday evening, my nerves were frayed with anticipation.

Staring into The Hazel Eyes

I kept stalking social media pages, searching for a photo of Giuseppe. I finally found one on 30 March, which I confirmed with Dr Rosemary. The photo may have been taken a few years earlier, when Joseph would have been about 82. I was looking at a very old man, with seemingly sad or perhaps just older eyes. I wondered what his life had been like. I shared the photo with my friends and my cousins. They said they saw a resemblance. I couldn't see too much of a resemblance. Perhaps that's what I will look like when I'm 82.

Friday, 31 March, 8:52 am

I sent Uncle Alfred a long message, trying to express the complex emotions I was feeling as the meeting drew closer:

> *This morning, I am feeling happy, sad, relieved, scared, grateful, and love. But above all, relief and gratitude that he is alive and well. Thank you for helping me with this search.*
>
> *My birth mother refused to tell me much about him and abused me when I asked her brothers and children. I gave up all hope of ever finding Giuseppe – born around 1938, who lived in Brunswick/Carlton, whose father owned a business, and who worked there in 1963. That was all I've ever known about him. As the years went by, my heart grew heavier and sad, believing I would never find him and that he might by now be dead.*
>
> *I'm still in shock that I've been able to find him. Alive and well.*
>
> *He has sad eyes. I hope he is well. I know that he may not want to have anything to do with me. I'm preparing myself for that.*
>
> *But I hope he does. See you next week.*

Saturday, 1 April – the day I knew Uncle Alfred would be meeting with Giuseppe to tell him about me. When my phone buzzed with Uncle Alfred's reply, my hands shook so badly, I could barely read the message:

> *'Hope you are well. I visited my brother today. He was very pleased to hear the news.*
>
> *He told me that over the past twelve months he has also been trying to find you.*
>
> *He is happy to come to lunch on Wednesday if you wish.'*

The words on my phone screen blurred as I read them. I had to sit down, overwhelmed.

Giuseppe was willing to meet me.

He even claimed that he had been looking for me!

The claim that he had been searching for me created a strange temporal vortex – while I had spent decades looking for him, apparently, he had been looking for me too. Our separate quests had been running parallel without intersection, like trains on adjacent tracks, until this moment when the tracks finally converged. The symmetry felt almost scripted – too perfect to be coincidental, too remarkable to be fabricated.

What had prompted his search after all these years?

What awakening of conscience or curiosity had led him to look for the daughter he had never known?

Holy crap! Two weeks ago, I didn't know who my biological father was, and now next week I was going to be having lunch with him!

I replied, 'Oh ok. That's better news than I expected.'

During the days that followed, I drifted between dreamlike disbelief and sharp bursts of panic.

I rehearsed what I might say to Giuseppe. I tried on outfits. I practised deep breathing exercises. I called friends to process what was unfolding.

What if we have nothing in common?
What if he doesn't like me?
What if I'm disappointed?

As I had done in 1990 when searching for my birth mother, I pushed the 'what ifs' aside.

The night before the meeting, I barely slept. Tossing and turning, I imagined a dozen different scenarios – warm embraces and cold rejections, awkward silences, and flowing conversation.

By morning, exhaustion had dulled my anxiety to a low hum. This was happening – ready or not.

I had a week to try to focus on work and reflect on the enormity of what had happened. It was still too early. The reality had not sunk in yet.

As Wednesday approached, I prepared myself for what would undoubtedly be the most significant meeting of my life – coming face to face with the man whose genetics I carried, yet whose life had been entirely separate from mine for nearly 60 years.

After decades of longing and hoping, I was now mere days away from meeting the man who had contributed half my DNA, then disappeared from my life.

Would I finally find answers to the questions that had driven my search?

I was about to find out.

As the day drew closer, I felt the seven enigmatic fragments of my identity beginning to realign – physical appearance, name, biological heritage, medical history, cultural origins, family history, and psychological self. The fragments that had scattered on that Melbourne bus were moving toward integration, not yet whole but no longer chaotically dispersed. The vessel was being prepared for its golden repair.

Uncle Andrea

17

Giuseppe: The Meeting
(April 2023)

Answers arriving in unsettled ambiguity

Excitement, relief, and joy surged through me – as changeable and intense as Melbourne's weather. My close friends shared my elation about finding Giuseppe, their messages and calls carrying genuine happiness for my discovery, though some expressed apprehension given his criminal past – the newspaper clippings, the court testimonies, the documented Mafia connections. I shared their caution – I even told friends where I was going, scribbled the meeting details and left them prominently on my desk, in case I mysteriously disappeared into some underworld narrative I was only beginning to comprehend.

Wednesday morning crawled. Minutes stretched to hours as I checked and rechecked the clock. After two weeks of intensive research and scrutinising photos, I felt like I already knew the elusive Giuseppe and Uncle Alfred – in that creepy way people feel they know celebrities they've never met, intimate with images but not reality.

I had memorised the contours of Giuseppe's face, noting how his once-youthful features had softened with time, searching for traces of myself in the familiar angles of his expressions.

I showered and dressed, selecting clothes with unusual care, nervous but composed – less anxious than when meeting Ursula decades earlier, when I'd still been searching for stable ground.

I'd grown into a more confident adult, tempered by loss and sustained searching. Outside, a bright, warm, sunny autumn day waited, Melbourne showing its gentle face, the air still and carrying that distinctive musty scent that precedes winter. In my car, I played '*Che sarà*' by Nicola di Bari, the Italian lyrics connecting me to a heritage I was still discovering. A calmness enveloped me with his words: What will be, will be. This surrender to the moment, this acceptance – of what I could not control, of whatever story awaited me.

The grey-blue clad Abruzzo Club came into sight at 12 pm, where Uncle Alfred had arranged for us to meet. I parked the car, crossed the busy road and waited. It was now 12:15 pm and no one was here.
Was I being stood up?
I checked inside with the receptionist. They weren't doing lunch today. So, I rang Uncle Alfred and told him.
'Oh, I should have checked.'
'Let's go to the Kent Hotel, in Carlton instead.'
'I'm sorry, I'm running late. I'll be there by 1 pm', he said.
'That's ok. I've waited decades. I can wait a little longer,' I replied.

I drove along Lygon Street to the Kent Hotel, which was a further 10-minute drive. I parked the car some distance away so that I could walk off the increasing butterflies I felt in my stomach. With each step, the ground felt more solid, as if the cracks beneath me were sealing shut. A clear blue autumnal sky wrapped itself around me. I felt the scrunching of large, autumn leaves beneath my feet. I could barely contain the mixture of excitement and trepidation. I forced myself to breathe long, slow, deep breaths.

At almost 86, my father was miraculously still alive – and I was finally about to meet.

I couldn't really believe that this moment was real. I sat outside the Kent at a small wooden table. The air was still and warm. To distract myself from my restlessness, I spoke to a friend on my mobile phone while I waited. After a little while, I saw Uncle Alfred arrive. A slightly pudgy elderly man with grey-white wavy hair. He walked with an air of sophistication and quiet confidence. He wore a white shirt and had black-rimmed glasses on.

'I've got to go!'

'Ok, good luck!'

I went into the Kent, which sat on a corner, and I walked up to Uncle Alfred.

I smiled. 'Hi, I'm Mirella'

He was warm, friendly, and spoke gently. 'Hello Mirella, I'm Alfred. It's nice to meet you.' He had a slight Italian accent.

We kissed hello. Italian style. A kiss on each cheek. We stepped outside and made small talk while we waited for Joseph to arrive.

I saw a small grey beaten-up sedan pull up across the road. My heart began to race; the moment I'd imagined for decades was finally arriving. An elderly man wearing black pants and a black jacket slowly stepped out of the driver's seat. He had a head of short cropped thinning white hair. His younger partner stepped out of the passenger side. Together they walked towards me. The elderly man shuffling slowly and delicately in my direction.

As they approached, I catalogued every detail of this man who had contributed half my DNA yet remained a stranger for six decades. His gait was slow and measured – a careful shuffle that spoke of age and fragility, so different from the vigorous young man who must have existed when I was conceived. His partner hovered protectively at his side, leaning to whisper in Italian,

'*Joe, a ti assomiglia*' (She looks like you.). The words floated across the space between us, gentle yet seismic.

He wore a somewhat crumpled black shirt against black trousers – clothing I would later learn had significance beyond mere fashion. The black shirts, I would discover, were a nod to Mussolini's fascist movement, one of many unexpected political leanings I would uncover in the months ahead. When a shaft of sunlight caught the silver-white of his closely cropped hair, I searched for signs of my own appearance in his features.

Would I age like him?
Did his hands gesture as mine did?
Was that familiar crease between his eyebrows something I'd inherited or merely coincidence?

When he stopped before me, I saw my own eyes looking back – the same questioning gaze. His face was a roadmap of deep lines, each crease a story I hadn't been present to witness. He smiled and extended his hand.

I took it, expecting fragility, but found unexpected strength. His skin was paper-thin, blue veins visible beneath the surface, yet his grip remained surprisingly firm – as though something essential had remained unchanged through decades of separation. The scent of him – earth, mustiness, slightly medicinal – triggered nothing familiar in my memory, yet felt somehow like finally being home.

'Hallo Mirella,' he said, his voice gravelly with age, his thick Italian accent transforming my name into something both foreign and deeply familiar – a melody I'd never heard, yet somehow recognised in my bones. His eyes – my eyes – crinkled at the corners as he studied my face with naked curiosity, perhaps seeing his own reflection as clearly as I was seeking mine in him.

'*Benvenuta nella famiglia Verduci.*' (Welcome to the Verduci family).

My throat constricted as 60 years of absence, wondering, and searching collapsed into this single, unrepeatable moment. The weight of it pressed against my chest – all those birthdays, Christmases, milestones that had passed without him, all the questions I'd accumulated that now seemed simultaneously crucial and irrelevant.
'Hello,' I managed, surprised by the steadiness in my voice that belied the earthquake happening within. 'It's good to finally meet you.'
These simple words – utterly inadequate for the moment – somehow bridged an impossible gap between strangers who should never have been strangers.
In that moment, my father's identity and my cultural origins suddenly aligned. His voice sang of a homeland I'd never visited but somehow knew, connecting me to generations of Calabrians whose DNA flowed through my veins. This elderly man in black wasn't just Giuseppe (Joseph), the abstract figure I'd sought for decades – he was the living embodiment of lineage, of heritage, of a cultural tradition that had shaped me from a distance.
We all went into the restaurant and sat at a square wooden table for four towards the back. We ordered our meals. The mingling of cutlery, glasses, and of other conversations surrounded us. Uncle Alfred ordered a pizza with prawns and zucchini for us to share for entree. Droplets of cooked garlic wafted in the air as it arrived. For main, I had the same meal as Joe – grilled Scotch fillet, caponata red wine jus with chips. He had his well done. The pinker juices of mine oozing onto my plate as I cut into my steak. The scene was dreamlike – one I had never dared to imagine.

It felt natural to think of him as Joe now – not the abstract Giuseppe I'd searched for all these years. Joe – the man across the table – was real, not a phantom. The name settled comfortably between us, acknowledging the present rather than the past.

Uncle Alfred ordered some white wine; Joe and I partook. With every sip, I felt more relaxed and at ease.

Joe asked me what I did. I told him I was a psychologist.

He said, 'You can fix my head.'

I asked him if he remembered Ursula.

'Oh yes, I remember Ursula very well. You were a very expensive baby. You cost me t'ousands of dollars,' he said, with a long emphasis on 't'ousands'.

I didn't know what he meant. Did he pay Ursula off to quietly disappear?

I didn't ask for clarification, though questions bubbled inside me. The philosopher, the historian, the astronomer, the physicist in Joe emerged as he spoke of existential matters – Quintiliano, the Big Bang, and photons – where I'd expected emotional conversations. I would learn this was his way – often processing life's pivotal moments through the lens of transaction rather than sentiment.

He said that at the time he had been engaged to someone else and couldn't marry Ursula. I didn't care. I was now finally sitting with my Giuseppe. The more we easily talked with one another, the more I felt like I had known him my whole life – this was just another family get-together. There was an instant easiness – a familiarity that I hadn't expected or experienced when I met Ursula or her children, my siblings or her siblings.

Joe went on to tell me that he had slept with *'t'ousands* of women,' again with that characteristic emphasis that I would come to recognise as uniquely his. Ursula, he explained almost dismissively, was only one among the many. Something in his casual recounting of past conquests struck me as both brazen and defensive – as though quantifying past relationships somehow diminished the significance of any single one, including the one that had created me.

'There are more like you,' he revealed.

More like me? Did he mean, bastard children? I had even more siblings. In later meetings I would ask for clarification. He confirmed how I had interpreted his comment, but he refused to reveal their identity. He did not want to disrupt their lives. One may have a Greek mother and the other a policewoman. He also mentioned a couple of children living in Perugia, Italy.

My father had been the male equivalent of *'puttana'* (loose woman) – but curiously, neither in Italian nor English does such a derogatory word exist. It is only reserved for women.

I spent most of that hour or so talking to Joe, but I tried to politely include Uncle Alfred.

Surreal is the only way I can describe those early days of connection.

I wanted to take a photo, but Joe said he was 'a suppressed man'. The phrase hung in the air, mysterious and loaded with implications I couldn't yet grasp. Only later would I understand he was referring to court-ordered suppression orders related to his testimony in high-profile criminal cases – another breadcrumb on the trail to understanding the complex man before me. Instead, I took a photo of his black tie, emblazoned with a flame in green, white, and red and one of Uncle Alfred and myself. His partner took a photo of the three of us at the table. Later I would be able to get a copy of that photo.

At the end of the meal, Joe ordered a Drambuie on ice.

Was he a drinker or was he anxious too? I wondered.

My 79-year-old Uncle said he had to go back to work, to his law firm in Footscray, which he started in 1969, just after qualifying as a lawyer. I told Joe that I was heading to Sydney that day. I would be there for two weeks.

Joe's family is a family of entrepreneurs, businesspeople, scholars, lawyers, and shopkeepers. He proudly told me

repeatedly that over 40 members of the family have been to university. And I proudly told him that I was the first with a PhD. In later encounters, he introduced me to his elderly paesani, as my daughter, *La Dottoressa* (the doctor)
'Could we meet again when I get back?' I asked.
'Of course,' he replied. 'Take my number.'
We exchanged phone numbers.
I warmly kissed and hugged Uncle Alfred and Joe's partner goodbye.
Uncle Alfred kindly paid for the meal. Joe tentatively shook my hand again.

After parting ways, I sat in my car for several long minutes, hands gripping the steering wheel, unable to drive as waves of elated emotion washed over me. Six decades of questions, of searching, of wondering – culminating in this ordinary lunch. My search was finally over. I had met my father. The simple sentence I'd yearned to say for so long could finally be spoken in the present tense, not the conditional.
As I drove away from the Kent Hotel, Melbourne's traffic continued its ordinary flow. A distant tram clanged its bell. Pedestrians walked past, unaware that the world had just shifted on its axis. I sat quietly, motionless between parked cars, feeling gravity slowly return.
I drove home in a daze, my mind replaying every moment, every gesture, every word exchanged. Part of me wanted to call everyone I knew, to shout from rooftops: 'I found him! He's real! He knows me!' Another part needed solitude to process what had just happened, to let the reality sink in that Giuseppe Verduci – no longer just a name or a concept, but a flesh-and-blood man – was now part of my life.

At home, I stepped into my garden and sank into my smoking chair, lighting a cigarette with trembling fingers. The familiar ritual calmed me as I stared out at my lush green garden against the bright blue sky beyond. I called a few friends, recounting details of the meeting, struggling to articulate the strangeness of seeing my own features reflected in this stranger's face, of feeling an immediate connection that transcended the absence of shared history.

For almost 60 years, I had orbited an absence. Now that absence had form, voice, and substance. I touched my own face, tracing features that suddenly had context – a nose with history, eyes with lineage. The ghost that had haunted me was flesh, and the mystery was no longer if I would find him, but who we might become to each other.

The golden seams were beginning to form, threads woven between fragments that had existed separately for six decades. Still fragile, still setting, but undeniably connecting what had been torn apart at birth and on that bus.

18

My Sinful Father: The Shadow Archive

Sinful legacies staining ancestral marrow

After the meeting, I drove eight hours to NSW to visit a friend. There, I momentarily diverted my online sleuthing, turning my attention to my maternal Grandmother, Marianna Castiglia. I had shared DNA with people with the surname Castiglia, living in the United States – all descendants of Gennaro (John or Gerry) Castiglia who was born around 1854. He migrated to New York in 1888 with his wife – coincidentally Marianna (Maria) Caputo.

At some point, Gennaro changed his surname to Costello. But since then, the family has changed their name back to Castiglia. This remains deeply mysterious to me. I failed to find any information about Gennaro's parents anywhere on the internet. His family remains a mystery. I had descended into the shadow archive – where names disappeared, documents blurred, and identity whispered through gaps. Soon after, I received an email from a distant cousin, who lives in the United States.

> 'Dear Mirella,
> Greetings from a 3rd cousin in the USA.
> According to the 'Cousin Calculator Chart' we should share a 2nd or 3rd Great-Grandparent ... might be the parents of my Great-Grandfather Gennaro Castiglia who came to New York in 1888 with his wife
> Marianna Caputo who came from Eboli.'

Her grandfather was Gennaro's son Pietro (Peter) Castiglia. We exchanged a few emails, and she shared very little concrete information about how we might be directly related. It was frustrating. I trawled through the internet, social media pages, Ancestry.com and MyHeritage and was able to piece together all the DNA matches I had with my distant American cousin. Then I plugged the names into an online tool called DNA Painter. Then she wrote something chilling:

> 'I do not want to put anyone's personal situation in jeopardy either. Our family is VERY discreet ... because Italians have long memories.'

These cryptic warnings resonated with something primal in me – a sense that the silences in my maternal history weren't just personal awkwardness but protective barriers against dangerous truths. The secrecy that had shaped my entire existence suddenly appeared not as individual choices but as cultural imperatives spanning generations and continents. My invisible heritage carried shadows I hadn't anticipated.

I then emailed the distant American cousin, with my latest hypotheses:

> 'I came across a DNA tool today in DNA Painter called 'What Are The Odds' (WATO). By putting in the family tree I created for your Great Grandfather Gennaro, his offspring, and my DNA matches and the cM amounts, the hypotheses created in WATO suggest that my Grandmother Marianna Castiglia's Father or Mother would be a descendant of a sibling of Gennaro. You said in an email that Gennaro had two sisters and no known siblings in Italy. Did these sisters have children and grandchildren? If yes, then one of their children or grandchildren is most likely to be my Grandmother's parent. I'm guessing perhaps a woman who went to Italy and gave up the child to the orphanage in Naples. Unless, of course, Gennaro had another sibling in Italy. As we know families have secrets. If you suspect that my ancestor could be a Caputo, then perhaps one of

> *Marianna Caputo's brother's sons or grandsons may have been the father.'*

I didn't hear from her again.

Genetic material connected all these fragments. A recurring pattern of separation and concealment. This wasn't just my personal tragedy but a family inheritance as powerful as any physical feature. Understanding this didn't heal the wounds of my adoption, but it placed them in a context that made them less isolating. My separation wasn't random misfortune but part of a multi-generational pattern I was now seeing clearly for the first time.

The silence was familiar – another door closed on my search for complete understanding of my origins. But by now, I had learned to continue forward, using whatever fragments I could gather to build my own understanding of who I was and where I had come from.

One evening, while having dinner with my friend, an episode of *Under Investigation* appeared on television. The title caught my attention: *Mafia Hit?* My casual interest turned to shock as I realised the subject matter – the assassination of Colin Winchester, the 'Jack in the Pack.' The year 1980 – the same year I discovered my adoption – was when Winchester had undertaken an undercover drug operation with a police informant named Joe Verduci.

My blood ran cold as the screen showed a handsome man in a well-tailored dark suit with thinning grey hair, walking outside the Queanbeyan courthouse. The narrator intoned, 'Winchester's Mafia middleman, Giuseppe Verduci.' Another shot showed Giuseppe in a cream-coloured suit with a blue tie, then again in a courtroom.

'That's him,' I whispered, my wine glass frozen halfway to my lips. 'That's my father.'

My friend stared in disbelief as I explained the connection. There on national television was the man I'd just had lunch with, being identified as a key figure in one of Australia's most notorious unsolved crimes. The calm, elderly man who had ordered scotch fillet and reminisced about Ursula was being described as a member of the 'Ndrangheta – the Calabrian Mafia – and a police informant whose testimony was central to a murder investigation.

Fragments of what I'd read during my research suddenly crystallized with sickening clarity. The marijuana plantations in Bungendore. The police protection. The Mafia connections. The 'business' that had taken him to Canberra. The 'suppression' he had mentioned. All of it now played out in documentary format, with archival footage and crime reporters discussing my father's role in Australian criminal history.

'My Goodness,' my friend whispered. 'Are you okay?'

I nodded slowly, unable to articulate the storm of emotions. This revelation transcended personal family drama – it situated my search within Australia's hidden criminal history. This wasn't merely discovering your father had a questionable past; confronted with the enormity of his crimes, I stood paralysed – caught between horror and an inexplicable, almost shameful relief. This personal reckoning; discovering that my search for identity had led directly to a key figure connected to organised crime, marijuana cultivation, and a high-profile political assassination – events that had shaped Australian national security policy.

The Giuseppe I'd just met – gentle, frail, reflective in his eighties – seemed irreconcilable with the figure being described on screen: a central operator in the Calabrian 'Ndrangheta's Australian operations during the 1970s and 80s. I grappled silently with the paradox of Giuseppe – my biological father, simultaneously my life's greatest yearning and most troubling discovery. His duality echoed the famous vision of the divided soul – half yearning for redemption, half seduced by shadows.

Could I accept him wholly without justifying the harm he'd done? Could I claim his heritage without inheriting his sins?
As I watched the documentary unfold, each revelation about the 'Ndrangheta's family-based structure – created a disturbing parallel to my own search for family. Here was the dark mirror of the biological connections I'd sought: clan loyalties that had twisted the very concept of family into something dangerous. That my DNA connected me to this history wasn't just shocking but philosophically disorienting – blood ties, which I had idealised for decades, suddenly revealed their potential shadow. The discovery of Giuseppe's criminal past added yet another layer to the family patterns I was uncovering. My father's history revealed how the rigid expectations of family honour had shaped lives across generations – sometimes driving men to self-destruction, sometimes pushing them toward dangerous paths outside society's boundaries. I couldn't yet know how deeply these patterns had affected my siblings, whose stories awaited me in the months ahead.

After searching so long for my biological roots, I now faced the complex reality that these roots extended into territories I'd never contemplated. The seven enigmatic fragments I'd been seeking to integrate now included dimensions I hadn't anticipated – the same blood that gave me my intellectual curiosity and hazel eyes had also flowed through a world of criminal enterprises and violence. This wasn't merely discovering a father with flaws; it was confronting how deeply identity is shaped by histories we neither choose nor control. The vessel of self I was reassembling now contained pieces that challenged my understanding of what family truly meant.

The Winchester assassination represented a critical juncture in this history – the moment when the 'Ndrangheta's activities became impossible for authorities to ignore, leading to Operation Seville and other major investigations. Giuseppe's role as informant placed him at the nexus of criminal organization and law enforcement – a dangerous position that explained much about his family's sudden relocations, his periods of absence, and the fear that seemed to permeate my siblings' childhood memories.

Discovering my father's criminal past would have devastated me years earlier, when I still believed perfect origins could explain an imperfect self – still operating under the naive assumption that biological connection would provide unambiguous belonging and clarity. But the woman watching the TV documentary now was fundamentally different, tempered by loss, seasoned by solitude, and finally secure enough to accept complexity without fragmentation.

I had spent decades imagining my father in various configurations, but never once had I imagined him as a member of the 'Ndrangheta. Yet strangely, I wasn't remotely shattered by this revelation. Perhaps because I had already integrated so many fragments, this new piece – however unexpected – could be acknowledged and incorporated without threatening the integrity of the whole I had carefully assembled.

The same resilience that had carried me through my adoptive Father's alcoholic rages, my Mother's death, and years of searching had prepared me to absorb this final irony: that my long-sought father came with his own complicated darkness. Besides, that was a past that I had not been part of. I did not see a potential criminal; I saw a caring, elderly man who would later hint at moments of remorse and regret.

A few days later Joe sent me a text.

'My dear child. Time as the only provider finally brought you to me. I want to wish you a happy Easter. Guardando il tuo viso mio.' (I looked at you and saw myself).

After I sent him photos of myself at various ages, he responded with another poetic message:

'Mi sembrava di averti conosciuta tutta la mia vita, per sé innanzi agli occhi miei solo per alcuni istanti lo sei stata nella famiglia Verduci ci sono altri come il tuo sia

> lieve la vita ovunque tu cammini.' (It seemed to me that
> I have known you all my life, even if you were before
> my eyes only for a few moments, in the Verduci family.
> There are others like you. Let your life be gentle
> wherever you walk).

I, too, felt like I had known him always, like he'd always lived inside me. His blood, my blood coursing through my veins. We kept exchanging texts and I sent him photos of my time in NSW.

> 'My dear Child, I hope that life is joyous for you and
> as bright as the light of the sun. Wishing you a good
> weekend from your old man.'

His messages revealed an unexpected side of Joe – poetic, reflective, capable of a tenderness I hadn't anticipated. This was the same man whose criminal exploits I'd just seen documented on television, yet here he was sending me messages of affection tinged with philosophical musings. The contradictions were dizzying. I found myself wondering which version was more authentic –

Was he the Mafia middleman?
The gentle elderly father?
Or the poet philosopher?
Maybe all three.

As I travelled through NSW, I found myself analysing landmarks with new awareness. *Was this town connected to the drug trade my father had participated in? Had he driven these same roads during his 'business' operations?* His criminal past now coloured my perception of ordinary Australian geography, revealing hidden histories in places I'd previously seen as simply scenic or mundane.

Joe, like me, was also a writer and a poet.

A few days later, on Easter Sunday, I got a call from Joe. I stepped outside into the warm, humid, and sunny day. I sat on a seat under a tree in the shade. He told me that he was happy to meet me and that we'd catch up when I was back in Melbourne. I grinned from ear to ear and had to remind myself that this was really happening.

On the drive home, I decided to take a historical detour – a pilgrimage of sorts to places connected to my newly discovered father. I drove through Queanbeyan and Bungendore, small towns that had featured in news reports about Giuseppe's marijuana operations. Walking through Bungendore's quiet streets, I tried to imagine him here decades earlier, a younger, more vigorous man involved in the cultivation operations that would later become part of Australian criminal lore. According to locals and online reports, this quaint little town remained a drug hotspot.

From there, I drove to Griffith, the flat and fertile country town known as a stronghold of 'Ndrangheta families. This was where anti-drugs campaigner Donald Mackay had been assassinated in 1977 – a case that had haunted Australian criminal history. His body was never found. Walking through Griffith's sunbaked streets, I felt a strange connection to a bloody history I hadn't known was mine until days earlier.

While in Griffith, I received another call from Joe. He was on his way to a nephew's wedding and sent me photos of the celebration. The juxtaposition was jarring – these ordinary family moments occurring against the backdrop of the criminal history I was literally driving through. *How many family celebrations had occurred while he was involved in these dangerous enterprises? How had he compartmentalised these different aspects of his life?* As easily as depicted in *The Godfather* series. Business is business. Steel cold and meticulously executed. I would later wonder if Joe had been mentally scarred from trauma inflicted or trauma witnessed.

A few days later he sent me a text telling me that he would be going to India soon on a business trip and an acknowledgement that I was indeed his daughter:

> '...*Because of your intelligence I can tell you are my real daughter, you almost reason like me. Your Old Man.*'

His compliment about my intelligence brought mixed emotions. On one hand, it was gratifying to have this connection acknowledged – to recognise familiar cognitive patterns across the genetic divide. On the other hand, knowing what I now did about his history, the comparison carried uncomfortable implications. *How similar was I really to this man whose life had ventured into territories I'd never imagined? What parts of him lived in me, beyond the physical features we shared?*

As I drove back to Melbourne from my Queanbeyan and Griffith pilgrimage, I realised that finding Giuseppe had not ended my journey of self-discovery but transformed it. The question was no longer '*Who am I?*' but '*What will I do with all I now know?*' The fragments had not disappeared; they had multiplied, becoming more nuanced, more complicated. But they were mine to arrange now – mine to integrate into a self that encompassed both inheritance and choice, both nature and nurture I had created for myself.

The road stretched before me, leading back to Melbourne where Joe waited – no longer just a name or a concept or even a criminal figure in a documentary, but a living connection to my origins. For better or worse, he was my Father. And I was his daughter. After 60 years of separation, that simple fact felt like both miracle and burden, challenge and gift.

Aunty Bruna – lawyer and barrister

19

Sinful Uncle Andrea

(2023)

Then, welcoming a familiar shame

On Sunday, 9 April 2023, the screen of my phone lit up with a notification that would prove more significant than its simple appearance suggested. Uncle Andrea had sent me a text via Messenger for the first time – a digital connection that carried the weight of formal recognition:
'Welcome Mirella to the family / clan.'
Five words that transformed my status from biological curiosity to acknowledged relative. This simple message carried extraordinary weight – the first official welcome from the most senior member of the Verduci family, an unambiguous acknowledgment of my rightful place among them. Uncle Andrea's immediate embrace stood in stark contrast to the hesitation from others, particularly my half-siblings. Where they had offered conditions, and lingering suspicion, he extended unconditional recognition – a gift whose value I couldn't yet fully calculate.
Those few words radiated a warmth that transcended their digital medium, suggesting that somewhere in Melbourne, an elderly man I had never met was thinking about me, acknowledging me, preparing a place for me in the family narrative. There was something achingly poignant in this virtual embrace from a man who had shared a childhood with my

Father – who had known him before the hardships and choices that would eventually lead to my conception and abandonment. Uncle Andrea represented more than just another relative; he was a living bridge to the past – to the Italy they had left behind, to the brothers they had been before becoming husbands and fathers, to the shared experiences that had shaped the man who had contributed half my DNA.

The next day he commented on my Facebook post about my search for my biological Father, soon after I had met Joe and Uncle Alfred. He added a comment.

'Search no more. You are welcome. Your great-grandfather was from Montebello. Your grandfather was Bartolomeo...'

We then corresponded via Messenger over the following months. I told him that I hoped to meet him one day soon.

He replied, 'Yes we will.'

Our exchanges, though brief, created a precious connection to my paternal heritage. Uncle Andrea – as the eldest brother and Joe's former business partner – held memories and knowledge that no one else could share. Through him, I might access parts of my Father's past that Joe himself was reluctant to discuss. Curious, I asked about the business he once shared with Giuseppe.

'Did you work in the furniture shop too in the 60s?'

He told me that they had nine shops and a furniture factory in Werribee, an outer western suburb of Melbourne.

'What was the name of the business? What happened to it?' I curiously asked.

'We had a few companies/ the Italo-Australian Credit, a finance co, and Verduci Bros, but we lost a lot with the credit squeeze of 1961 / 1964.'

'The furniture factory was sold.'

On 16 May, Uncle Andrea sent me a message that would become one of my most treasured connections to this newly discovered family. His words, poetic and dignified, offered an alternative framing of my conception that stood in stark contrast to Joe's blunt, transactional account:

'*La figlia dell'amore è il prodotto di una gentil donna innamorata di un principe di grazia e virtù per destino di una sorte ingrata.*'

'The daughter of love is the product of a gentlewoman in love with a prince of grace and virtue, of fate of an ungrateful lot.'

This lyrical description gave me something Joe never had – a romantic vision of my origins, one that afforded dignity and tenderness to the circumstances of my conception. Where Joe had described monetary costs and convenience, Uncle Andrea saw love and tragedy. His poetic framing suggested another perspective on my biological parents' relationship, one that acknowledged emotion rather than just pragmatism.

A month later, I tried to make time to meet up with Uncle Andrea. We had tentatively made a lunch booking, but he cancelled. We'd catch up another time, he said. Another month went by, and I read on Facebook that he was unwell. The last message I wrote to him was on 22 July 2023.

'I read that you are unwell. How are you doing? xo *un forte abbraccio Zio.*' (A big hug.)

That was the last correspondence I had with my dear Uncle Andrea. In a cruel twist of timing, the uncle who had most warmly welcomed me into the family was slipping away just as I was finding my place within it. The Universe, it seemed, insisted on a pattern of revelation followed by loss – a rhythmic giving and taking away that had defined my search from the beginning, as if teaching me that completeness would always remain just beyond my grasp.

My birthday soon followed. I had lunch with a friend, at Il Carretto in Carlton, the restaurant where I was supposed to have met Uncle Andrea a few weeks earlier. He had told me that it was too cold. The truth was that he was too sick. He was dying. After lunch I went to the Carlton Cemetery. I was in search of my late Uncle John's grave.

A few days later, a text from Uncle Alfred arrived: 'Sorry to say my brother Andrea passed away last night.' It was the day after my birthday. I didn't get to meet my eldest Uncle Andrea – another door forever closed.

The timing was devastating. I had found my family only to lose another member almost immediately. Uncle Andrea, the first to welcome me unreservedly to the Verduci clan, would never meet me in person. His death represented another severed connection to my past, another piece of my history lost before I could fully explore it.

After his passing, I asked for details of the funeral and if it was OK to go.

The reply wasn't 'of course you're family' – just 'I don't see why not.'

Even in grief, my place in the family still felt conditional – something to be negotiated, not assumed.

I last saw Joe the day after his birthday in July at Preston Market.

He sent me an SMS the day before the funeral.

> '*Mia cara sconosciuta adolescente figlia, spero che tutto sia di ottima salute nella tua vita, ... Un caldo abbraccio dal peccatone tuo padre. Joe.*' (My dear unknown teenage daughter, I hope that everything is in excellent health in your life. ... A warm hug from your sinful father Joe.)

The signature revealed a profound aspect of Joe's self-perception – referring to himself as 'sinful father' acknowledging his responsibility in my conception and abandonment in a way he rarely articulated directly. This small admission, made in the context of grief over his brother's death, suggested that Uncle Andrea's passing had perhaps stirred Joe's thoughts about legacy, mortality, and the consequences of his actions that would outlive him.

He didn't know I was attending the funeral. A small part of me was afraid to go.

On the Friday morning of the funeral, I left home early and drove to the church where it was to be held. I was wearing black pants and a dark-grey coat. I wore my Mother's necklace and pendant. Every time I enter a church, it feels like a homage to my deceased parents. I parked my car across and down the street on Queens Parade, Clifton Hill and then I walked across to church. It was a cold, grey, and very windy day. The weather mirrored the emotional landscape I was traversing – turbulent and forbidding, yet somehow appropriate for this threshold moment. In the congregation I saw my blood siblings, sisters-in-law, aunts, uncles, nieces, nephews, cousins, and my Father Joe. There were faces I knew and people I had met – blood family yet strangers.

Uncle Andrea's funeral represented a profound milestone – the first time I would be in the same room with most of my biological family at once. No longer seeking entrance at the periphery, I was now a recognised family member attending a shared ritual of grief. Yet as I took my seat among these strangers who shared my DNA, the complexity of my position was inescapable. I belonged and didn't belong simultaneously.

It was a large, ornate church, though not as elaborate as many I had visited in Rome, several years earlier. The walls of this church were orangey, reddish brick colour. It had a fancy altar. The music that had been played during the service, chosen by Uncle Andrea, floated up and reverberated throughout the vast vaulted ceiling.

I knew it would be emotional for me at the church. Funerals always remind me of my parents' passing. I didn't realise how much this one would affect me. I cried through the service – not quietly, not stoically, but with the aching rawness of a daughter mourning a man she never met. Luckily, funerals are places where it is acceptable to openly cry.

I cried tears of kaleidoscopic grief – sadness for the warm and welcoming Uncle I didn't get to meet, happiness for finally having found my clan, regret for not having found them earlier, guilt as at times I felt like an imposter at a stranger's funeral, and hope that one day I would truly connect to this sprawling family whose blood I shared. Sitting among the congregation were members I hadn't met – their faces familiar only from scrolling their social media pages only a few months earlier. And now, here I was sitting among them at my first family funeral.

I listened to the eulogies read by the two youngest living uncles. Their words revealed crucial pieces of my paternal history that helped me understand both Uncle Andrea and Joe. I learned that the business empires I'd only glimpsed in fragments had been more extensive than I'd imagined.

Joe and his brother, Andrea, the eldest of the nine children, opened their first furniture and electrical business in 1959 in Charles Street, Seddon, and a furniture factory in Werribee. Joe was 22 at the time. They later opened shops in Footscray, North Melbourne, near the Vic Market, Brunswick, Oakley, and Wangaratta. I later learnt the bedding furniture mogul Franco Cozzo worked for Joe, as did Mirabella and Scali. These three went on to have successful businesses of their own. The two brothers then opened a credit lending business. There was a financial downturn in the 1960s and the business was sold, as Uncle Andrea had told me.

Even more significantly, I discovered that Uncle Andrea had been one of the intellectuals of the family – a scholarly man whose love of literature and philosophy mirrored my own intellectual tendencies.

Uncle Andrea was the first scholar in the family. He earned the equivalent of an Arts degree in Italy in the mid-50s, after which he came to Australia in 1956, with my Grandmother Giuseppina and her seven youngest children. Uncle Andrea had a great love of literature, philosophy, history, and music. He later became a teacher of history, worked for TAA in the finance department, and opened a Manchester store on Sydney Road, Brunswick. During the 60s he was the President of the Juventus soccer club. The eulogy also revealed an unexpected side to this serious, scholarly man – a glimpse of the mischievous boy he had once been that helped humanise the Uncle I would never meet.

At one time he was studying to be a priest from about the age of 10. However, that path was thwarted when one day, he and a friend decided to paint a sleeping priest's face with shoe polish. His Mother was summoned to the seminary and told that perhaps Uncle Andrea was not suited for priesthood.

At the end of the service, the coffin was carried out by family members. I recognised my half-brothers among them. The large family followed the coffin. Grizella, my half-sister saw me in the crowd and gave me a smile. No one else saw or recognised me. I wanted to follow the coffin too, but I was not part of the clan. I left the church alone.

I arrived at my car feeling sad that I had never met Uncle Andrea. I drove to Preston Cemetery, listening to Sinead O'Connor. She had died recently, too. I was alone, attending a stranger's funeral.

Why was I there?

Perhaps to give my grief a burial. A resting place.

This question captured the peculiar position I still occupied – grieving a man I had never met in person, mourning a relationship that had barely begun before it ended. Uncle Andrea's death represented the loss of a potential relationship, and knowledge about my Father that only he, as Joe's eldest brother and former business partner, could have shared.

At the cemetery's car park, the family congregated together. I stood and walked by myself. Still alone, despite being surrounded by blood relatives – an island of solitude in a sea of genetic connection.

I made my way to where the coffin was to be buried. I stood next to a woman. We made small talk. I learned that she was a friend of Uncle Andrea's daughter. She had worked at Lifeline with her. I saw siblings, nieces, and nephews in the crowd when we all walked back to the chapel. I entered the hall, feeling apprehensive and out of place, and sat on one of the chairs that lined the room.

Among the 100 plus people there, I recognised many faces, but only knew a handful. Faces like mine. Most didn't know who I was. I met my sister-in-law, a deeply compassionate person, Lina for the first time. She gave me a warm embrace and said, 'It's nice to meet you.'

Her warm greeting marked a crucial turning point in my relationship with the family. This first expression of genuine welcome from Diego, my half-brother's wife, suggested that some family members might be open to accepting me, creating a path to potential relationships with other relatives.

She introduced me to others. They were shocked to learn who I was. I was introduced to Uncle Claude for the first time, who was also shocked, but welcoming. I said hello and my condolences to Uncle Alfred. Then I searched for Joe, who was sitting with his older cousin. He introduced me as his daughter. I saw my siblings in the distance, mingling with others. I grabbed a wine and spoke to a small group of women who said they were 'in-laws.'

I laughed and introduced myself as 'a member of the outlaws.' Someone warmly put her arm around me and said, 'No, you're not. You're welcome here.'

This simple correction – 'No, you're not' – represented another significant shift. Someone in the family was explicitly rejecting my outsider status, insisting on my legitimacy as a family member. These small moments of acceptance were building, person by person, into something more substantial.

What struck me was that everyone spoke in English, not Calabrian, even my elderly aunts and uncles. If they did venture to the mother tongue, it was Italian and not Calabrian. This was a very educated and cultured family.

I went back and sat with Joe and his sisters Angela and Stella. Both were lovely, friendly, and warm. Joe soon left with his youngest son Jacob, his wife, and their son, who I hadn't been introduced to. Then I met Aunty Joanne. She was very sad about her brother's passing, but she also had her own deep sorrow. She didn't have any children and her late husband, Frank Trimboli had died a few years earlier.

The older cousin sitting with us, asked me, 'How did you find Joe?'

I told my DNA story again and my Aunty shed tears as I talked about my long and convoluted decades long search for Giuseppe. Diego and Lina soon left. I had seen photos of Diego. He's far more handsome in person. The handsomest of my half-brothers and apparently has Joe's yesteryear charm. Diego is tall and a very fit-looking 57-year-old. He walked past and said goodbye. He shook my hand. That was our first encounter. Although, I don't think he knew who I was.

A few times that afternoon, I had been told 'You look familiar.' I replied with a smile. 'That's because I'm a Verduci, Joe's daughter.'

Shock and surprise ensued.

Each time I claimed my identity as 'Joe's daughter,' I wasn't merely informing others – I was reclaiming a piece of myself long denied. After decades of uncertainty, I could now state my paternal connection with a conviction that felt like triumph. The shock on people's faces affirmed what I already knew in my bones – my physical resemblance to the Verduci clan was unmistakable, biological reality overriding decades of social construction and denial.

The crowd thinned and my uncles, an aunt, sisters, their spouses, and some cousins remained. We were told to vacate the hall. I moved outside. Stood to one side. Alone.

Stasia , my other half-sister, was loading up the car. She is very industrious. She reminds me of a good Catholic school prefect, proper, polite, conservative, and restrained. Unlike Grizella, who can be warm, friendly, jolly, and light-hearted. I saw Aunty Joanne whisper into Uncle Alfred's ear while glancing in my direction. Then Uncle Alfred came over and invited me to his place where they were heading. It was a lovely welcoming gesture by my Aunty and Uncle.

This invitation represented the most significant acceptance I'd received from the family thus far. No longer merely tolerated at a public funeral, I was being included in the private family gathering afterward, crossing the threshold from obligatory civility to chosen inclusion. Whatever Aunty Joanne had whispered to Uncle Alfred had apparently convinced him that I belonged with the family in this moment of mourning.

By this time, my head was spinning and bursting from all the conversations and introduction stories, and meeting so many of my large Verduci clan. I felt happy and relieved that I had been warmly and lovingly welcomed into the clan by so many. I drove through Melbourne's peak hour traffic following Grizella's car.

We finally got to Uncle Alfred's house in Carlton. As I walked into the house, I chatted to Uncle Andrea's daughter. She was warm and friendly. I walked through a side gate. Through the garden, up the steps to a glassed area and into the big, lavish, but not over-the-top home. I walked into the living room. The house was bright and airy. The walls were white. I briefly stood in front of the gas fireplace to warm up and then sat in a corner sofa chair next to the youngest aunt, Aunty Stella. We had a long chat. Stasia was transmitting the old family photos shown at the funeral to the large black-framed flatscreen TV sitting on a long cabinet. On the white walls, I saw family photos of children – I guessed they were Dr Rosemary's children and grandchildren, and those of other cousins.

When the family photos were being shown on the TV, I kept asking who was who in the photos. We watched the video about three times so that they could pause and tell me who everyone was. I saw late Uncle John in a big family wedding photo. I asked my Aunty about him. She also said that he had studied arts at uni and was a poet. My Aunty got up and moved and Uncle Andrea's widow took her place, and we chatted for a long time.

Meanwhile, Uncle Alfred's wife brought out warm chicken and veggie soup in mugs – the rich fragrance dancing in the air. Others were sitting in the adjoining dining room around a very large dining table. We joined them and sat next to each other, with our backs to the glass panel behind us, looking into the room. I chatted some more to Uncle Andrea's widow. She was forthcoming with information and happily and readily answered all my questions about Uncle Andrea.

Sitting at the table with the Verduci clan, I observed the subtle cultural choreography that had, unknowingly, shaped both my adoptive and biological families – the way food was offered as love before words, the hand gestures that punctuated conversation, the unspoken protocols of respect and deference. These Italian ways had surrounded me from birth, through both nature and nurture, creating an unexpected continuity in my otherwise fractured identity.

Next to me, on my right, sat an old man, Carlo. Apparently, the maker of the best cannoli in Melbourne. He was the husband of one of the widow's sisters and he was Sicilian. We chatted. I told him how I was connected, my search story, about my adopted parents, and what I did for work. Carlo told me that Joe might have stomach cancer. Later, I quizzed Uncle Alfred about it. He was upset that Joe wasn't there. He wondered why Joe kept away from the family. He didn't think Joe had stomach cancer but had had some kind of stomach problem. I told him to tell me if was ever sick.

He said, 'We gave Joseph a home to live in.'

I didn't know any of them well enough to feel that I could comment. I was curious as to why Joe seemingly kept away from his family.

The comment about giving Joe a home revealed ongoing tensions between him and his siblings – tensions that might help explain why he had kept his distance from most of the family. I was beginning to see that Joe's isolation wasn't just about his own choices but about complex family dynamics that had evolved over decades.

Stasia remained in the background. Grizella sat in the opposite corner with the other cousins. People changed seats and now I was talking to late Aunty Bruna's daughter, who lives in Canberra. She was slim, had short hair and is an artist and potter. She was sitting to my right and Uncle Andrea's daughter sat to my left. We chatted about ourselves and our work. We spoke about trailblazing Aunty Bruna, a mother, a solicitor, and a barrister.

At one point I said, 'This is the caring end of the family table.' The potter had studied social work, Uncle Andrea's daughter is a counsellor, and I'm the psychologist. Many of the other cousins are lawyers. Most of the cousins have university degrees.

This observation highlighted an important revelation – there were distinct clusters within the large Verduci clan, and I had naturally gravitated toward those who shared my helping profession orientation. This wasn't just coincidence, but evidence of inherited temperaments and values expressed across generations, sometimes skipping the intermediate generation. The intellectual, empathic tendencies I'd always thought came from nowhere suddenly had context in this branch of the family.

Aunty Joanne arrived sometime later in the evening with Uncle Claude and his wife. I didn't get the opportunity to speak to Aunty Joanne directly, but she was attentive to conversations that I was having with the others, especially when I spoke about Joe. I showed her the photo I had of a young handsome Joe in a fancy suit and bow tie and Grandfather Bartolo.

I felt very relaxed being there amongst my DNA clan. It felt surreal that this was my blood family. Unlike my adopted family, these people were not loud or overly boisterous. There were no emotional or angry outbursts. There was intelligent, interesting, and somewhat more serious conversation. I could see similarities with myself in others. I felt like I had finally reached home. Among these thoughtful, more serious relatives, I felt a tug beneath the surface – a quiet music of reflection, a cadence I couldn't yet name. It would be much later that I would recognise it: the souls of poets and philosophers, running like an underground river through the Verduci bloodline. Even then, without knowing, I was already standing in the current my Father had once stirred.

In that moment of integration – surrounded by relatives engaged in thoughtful conversation about politics, literature, and history – I experienced the most profound sense of belonging I'd ever known. It manifested not as emotional fireworks but as quiet recognition: the distinctive Verduci temperament – intellectual, somewhat reserved, given to serious discussion rather than emotional display – matched qualities I'd always possessed but had found difficult to trace to my adoptive family's more demonstrative, pragmatic nature.

This recognition represented the final piece of unification in my reparation journey. Here among these relative strangers, I recognised myself in ways I never had before. In physical features, in cognitive patterns, in conversational rhythms, in the way thoughts were formulated before being expressed. The vessel of self that had shattered on that Melbourne bus decades earlier was now reassembled, transformed – its golden seams connecting fragments in a pattern that honoured both breakage and continuity.

The symbolism was unmistakable: seated at Uncle Alfred's

dining table, I was literally and figuratively at the family table from which I had been excluded for six decades. The arrangement of bodies in that domestic space – the physical configuration of belonging – mirrored the internal arrangement of identity fragments I had been assembling since 1980. As plates were passed and wine poured, as conversations flowed from politics to philosophy to family history, the metaphorical golden lacquer lattice work was being applied to the final cracks in my fractured sense of self.

This wasn't a naive fantasy of perfect belonging or complete restoration – several family members remained distant, some actively resistant to my presence. The vessel remained visibly broken, its history of fragmentation evident in the golden seams that now connected some of its pieces. But this was precisely the beauty of kintsugi – not the pretence of unmarred perfection but the honest acknowledgment of brokenness transformed into distinctive beauty.

The integration I experienced in that moment wasn't despite the fractures and absences in my history but because of how they had been acknowledged, honoured, and ultimately incorporated into a new kind of wholeness.

Uncle Andrea's daughter told me that her father was a complex and complicated man, his own person. After my Facebook post, a friend of mine told me she had known Uncle Andrea. She said he was an opinionated man, not afraid to express himself.

A lot like Joe. Perhaps a Verduci trait.

When I left, I was making my way through my goodbyes. I spoke to another cousin Bart. There are so many Barts and Josephines, it's hard to know who's who. They spoke about being called Bart. Grandfather Bartolo pressured Joe to name one of his sons Bart, as if there weren't already enough Barts and Josephines in the family.

Was that conceit? I wondered.

Grizella had left earlier looking happy and jolly after a few more wines with the other cousins. She said goodbye to everyone, including me, and we gave each other a warm embrace. I felt so at ease with this softly spoken gentle, warm family – unlike Mum's family, who are at times too loud, critical, judgmental or close-minded; more conservative and still holding the old Vizzini values and mindset of the mid-50s. I love them all dearly, but they're not my blood. They're not my kin. We don't share the same soul and spirit or DNA history.

Finally, I left, got to my car, and headed home, exhausted once again.

The aftermath of Uncle Andrea's funeral revealed a significant evolution in my relationship with the family. Despite my initial solitary position at the church, by the end of the day at Uncle Alfred's home, multiple family members had welcomed me in various ways – a dramatic shift from the cautious distance I'd encountered in earlier interactions.

The following day, on a Saturday, I got a text from my Uncle Claude. He wanted to catch up for a coffee and a chat. My sister-in-law, Lina, also checked in on me. I also got a text from another cousin, welcoming me to the family. Overall, I felt warmly welcomed into the clan.

I had many texts from friends and family. I had been regularly updating everyone on my ongoing adoption search. Everyone was keen to follow my story and they've been so supportive and so interested. Many encouraged me to write a book about my search.

Just when I thought I had discovered all my possible siblings, another revelation would expand my understanding of the Verduci family – and confirm a troubling pattern in how the brothers treated women and their 'illegitimate' children:

2024

At the beginning of 2024, on a hot, sunny and muggy Queensland day, I was sitting at a car park near the Outpost Café, Canungra.

Ping! SMS.
A random, unknown number. I read the message.

> *'Hi Mirella, I hope this email does not upset you. I think you may be my cousin. We may have a similar background story. I would like to chat to you. I live in Coburg if you would like to have coffee sometime.'*

I was somewhat taken aback, but not completely surprised given what I now knew about these promiscuous and carefree Verduci brothers.

I texted back and asked how we were related. I ended up calling her and we talked for about one hour. Uncle Andrea was her father. He had loved her mother – who coincidentally shared my forename. She remembered her father visiting their house when she was a child.

We were born in the same year – 1964 – months apart, the year Uncle Andrea married. Her mother kept her despite the stigma. Raised by a single mother and a loving grandmother, my cousin grew up facing the harsh judgment reserved for 'illegitimate' children. Her childhood was tough.

Perhaps I would have had a similar fate had Ursula kept me. When my cousin was 16, her father wanted to meet her. She refused so as not to upset her mother. A teenage conundrum I well understood. Years later, she tracked him down. They met briefly, but suspicion shadowed the reunion – Uncle Andrea, wary, thought she was after money. They never met again. Sometimes she would glimpse him wandering Sydney Road alone, sad, and hollow-eyed. Sometimes, the first cut is the deepest and some wounds never heal.

This discovery represented the most significant revelation since finding Giuseppe himself – evidence of a family pattern that transcended individual behaviour. The story of Uncle Andrea's daughter, born the same year as me to a woman who worked for the Verduci brothers, confirmed that Joe's treatment of Ursula wasn't an isolated moral failing, but part of a troubling pattern shared with his brother.

Both men had fathered children with vulnerable teenage women, both had chosen marriage over acknowledging these children, both had left these women to face society's harsh judgment alone.

Later, my Father Joe, confirmed this story, and he remembered her mother. He confirmed her forename. She had worked for the Verduci Brothers during the early 1960s. He also remembered forcing Andrea at gunpoint to go back to his wife and young child.

Joe's casual admission – forcing his brother back to his wife at gunpoint – laid bare a bitter irony: he had insisted on family duty for his brother, yet abandoned it when it came to his own child. When I questioned this inconsistency, his response suggested genuine regret:

I asked, 'Do you think your brother loved her?'

'Yes, she was a very intelligent woman. More Andrea's type. Maybe he always hated me for dragging him back. Perhaps I shouldn't have done that, but I was looking out for his wife and child,' he replied with a tone of great remorse. His legitimate child, I thought to myself.

A Verduci brother went to his grave broken-hearted.

Joe also told me that divorce would have been out of the question for the Verduci seniors. His Father would not have allowed it. Grandfather Bartolo sounds like he was a tyrant, ruling with a stern Calabrian backhand, worse than Joe's own tyranny.

So feared that one of his sons didn't tell him for years that he was dating a non-Italian. A man who finally mellowed after a son took his own life, into a loving, kind, and gentle grandfather who made pancakes for his grandchildren.

These stories of Grandfather Bartolo's tyrannical rule finally explained the powerful forces that had shaped Giuseppe's decisions around my birth. The fear of paternal disapproval, the rigid expectations around marriage and family, the terrible consequences that had befallen John after defying these expectations – all had likely influenced Giuseppe's choice to offer Ursula money rather than marriage, to deny my existence rather than acknowledge responsibility.

My new cousin and I have remained connected since that first surprise text message. In the 1990s, we unknowingly lived a mere few streets from each other in Coburg. Sometimes, when I look at her, I'm taken aback by how much she looks like Uncle Andrea.

Our parallel stories created an instant bond – both of us products of Verduci men's affairs, both born in 1964 while our fathers were about to marry other women, both raised without paternal acknowledgment.

The key difference was that her mother had chosen to keep her while mine had given me up for adoption – a divergence in paths that had shaped our entire lives differently despite our similar origins. But while our origins were similar, our current relationships with the Verduci family were developing quite differently.

Finding her was another piece of my puzzle – proof that the Verduci men had left more than just furniture and TV sets as their legacy. But while Uncle Andrea's daughter welcomed connection, I was learning that not all my newly discovered siblings shared her openness.

The discovery of this cousin provided the final, undeniable confirmation that my abandonment wasn't due to unique circumstances but to established family patterns. Understanding this didn't erase the pain of what I'd experienced, but it placed it in a context that was less personal and more cultural and generational – a tapestry of patriarchal entitlement and familial shame woven through decades.

The Verduci men had treated women in similar ways, made similar choices, and left similar consequences for their children to navigate decades later. What had felt like my singular story was one thread in a larger family tapestry of secrets, shame, and denied paternity that stretched across generations.

20

The Compassion of Strangers
(June 2023)

Outsiders mending wounds kin dare not touch

At the end of a long June day in 2023, I was bone-tired – not just in body, but in hope. While I was still absorbing the revelations about Uncle John and processing my newfound relationship with Joe, I received an unexpected message that would reveal yet another dimension of my biological family's complexity.
It landed quietly, but its consequences would radiate outward in ways I couldn't yet imagine.
The evening had begun unremarkably – dinner at my kitchen table, the familiar comfort of solitude that had become neither enemy nor friend but simply the contours of my life. Outside, a winter rain tapped against the windows, the Melbourne chill seeping beneath doorframes despite central heating's efforts. I was scrolling through photographs of my recent meetings with Joe, studying our similarities with the methodical attention I'd developed through decades of searching for signs of myself in strangers' faces.
Then –
The notification appeared without warning – a Facebook message that made my heart leap into my throat. It was my half-brother's wife.

Lina: *Hi... I'm Diego's wife. Giuseppe's son.*
The words glowed against the dark background of Messenger, simple in construction but seismic in implication. Five ordinary words that threatened to rearrange my understanding of family once again. Time suspended momentarily as I processed them. What could his wife want? The familiar cocktail of hope and dread surged – the one I'd come to associate with family. My fingers hovered over the screen, uncertain whether to embrace or defend against this unexpected outreach from a branch of the family that had shown little interest in grafting me onto their tree.

Me: *I'm surprised to hear from you.*
I finally typed, the words deliberately neutral, neither inviting nor rejecting whatever might follow. Her immediate response cut through my careful diplomacy:

Lina: *'Why would you be surprised to hear from me?'*
The question itself contained multitudes – revealing the vast gulf between our perspectives, the fundamental asymmetry of our positions. To me, every connection to my biological family felt like a gift that could be withdrawn at any moment, every message a potential landmine or treasure. To her, perhaps, this was simply reaching out to a newly discovered relative – extraordinary, but not fraught with the accumulated weight of decades of rejection and yearning.

Me: *I have been trying to connect with family members since about March, when I finally found my biological father, Giuseppe, after not knowing who he was. Thank goodness for DNA tests. I know that people can react in various ways to the news that they have a sibling or child they didn't know about.*

The words appeared on screen, carefully measured despite the tremor in my fingers. I crafted the response diplomatically, sharing facts while withholding the emotion beneath. Some vulnerabilities were too raw to expose.

There it was – the unspoken truth behind my surprise. After months of tentative overtures and mixed responses from my newfound siblings, I had learned to expect rejection as much as welcome. Lina's next question arrived quickly, direct, and understandable:

Lina: *How do you know 100% Giuseppe is your father?*

A cold ripple of dread ran through me. I knew this moment would come – the moment I would have to defend my very blood. The familiar challenge – the burden of proof that falls invariably on the outsider claiming connection. The question that every adoptee dreads yet expects, as if our very existence requires more substantiation than those born into acknowledged relationships. I had prepared for this, armed with the evidence I'd assembled over recent months and through decades of searching:

Me: *I can send you photos of me when I was younger. His granddaughter looks like me.*

Lina: *You definitely have a family resemblance.*

Her quick agreement startled me. So many times in my life, I'd had to fight to be believed, to justify my questions, to defend my search.

Yet here was immediate acknowledgment, offered without the resistance I'd come to expect.

Something softened in my chest – a hardened knot of defensive readiness beginning to loosen just slightly.

Me: *When I met him, he mentioned my birth mother by name. He knew her age when I was born. She told me in 1990 his name was Giuseppe, he lived in Carlton. He was involved in his father's business. He had brown eyes and brown hair. Then when I thought I had found him, I checked with a maternal uncle, and he asked his other sisters, and they knew his full name and that he had a sister who was a lawyer. He is definitely my father. We think alike. Although not completely. Obviously, my upbringing*

> and my parents had an impact on who I am. I know
> he has had, let's say, a colourful, notorious history. I
> was not expecting this stuff.

The words tumbled out, perhaps more than necessary, but I needed her to understand the certainty behind my claim – that this wasn't wishful thinking or a desperate grab for family connection, but documented fact assembled through painstaking research and confirmed through multiple sources.

Her response was measured but curious:

> **Lina:** *Colourful, yes. When did you meet him? Has he acknowledged you're his daughter? It's never been mentioned to us. I'll tell you what I've heard over the years. I know families have secrets (I've got plenty in mine).*

Her mention of secrets – delivered matter-of-factly, with casual acceptance of their existence – created an unexpected bridge between us. Here was someone who understood the complex topography of family narratives, who recognised that what is spoken often matters less than what remains deliberately unsaid. The parenthetical confession about her own family secrets offered a quiet solidarity: we were both cartographers of uncharted familial maps.

The revelation that my existence had never been mentioned to them stung, though it wasn't surprising. Six decades of silence wouldn't be broken easily. Another missing piece in the mosaic of my fragmented origins – I'd been erased from Ursula's narrative and from my Father's family history as well. I felt a surge of gratitude for her openness about family secrets – a refreshing contrast to the denials and deflections I'd encountered elsewhere.

> **Me:** *Once you dive into family history/DNA, you can discover all sorts of things. Yes, he has definitely acknowledged that I am his daughter.*

I hesitated before adding my next question, the one that mattered most for establishing credibility with my siblings:

> **Me:** *Would a DNA test by Joe reassure Diego and the others?*
>
> **Lina:** *We didn't know that Giuseppe acknowledged you as his daughter.*
>
> **Lina:** *Your bio mother. Is she still alive?*

The question about Ursula opened another chamber in the labyrinth of my fractured origins. While Joe had acknowledged me, however belatedly, Ursula remained the keeper of a door firmly closed against my entrance. The contrast between their responses – his unexpected welcome and Ursula's persistent rejection – created yet another asymmetry in my understanding of my own story.

> **Me:** *Yes, she is, but her husband is an asshole and wants her to have nothing to do with me. Then she wouldn't tell me anything more about Joe.*

Each time I recounted Ursula's rejection, the wound scalded fresh again. The memory of her voice on the phone, cold with dismissal and territorial rage – *'You keep away from MY family!'* – with that possessive emphasis that excluded me entirely from what was, by blood, partially mine. The recollection of her husband's influence – a man with no biological connection to me wielding the power to sever the one that existed – still burned with a particular injustice that time had not cooled. I'd found acceptance from Joe but continued exclusion from my maternal family – a contradiction that highlighted how arbitrary these connections could be.

To my surprise, Lina's response radiated warmth:

> **Lina:** *That's sad for you. I'm so excited. I've always told Diego he has siblings out there.*

Her excitement – genuine and unexpected – caught me off guard. After months of navigating tentative welcomes and outright rejections, her enthusiasm felt like rain in a drought. It was as though a window had suddenly opened in a stuffy room, letting in fresh air and possibility.

This stranger – this woman connected to me only through her

marriage to my half-brother – was offering more genuine welcome than many who shared my blood. There was something profound in this: the recognition that sometimes, the most meaningful connections come not from those obligated by genetics but from those who choose compassion without obligation.

>**Me:** *I grew up as an only child, it has been a little overwhelming.*

In those brief words lay the condensed reality of my experience – the jarring transition from solitary existence to suddenly having siblings, nieces, nephews, cousins; the cognitive dissonance of being simultaneously a newcomer and a blood relation; the emotional vertigo of navigating relationships that were both brand new and decades old.

'Overwhelming' barely captured the kaleidoscopic disorientation of finding oneself suddenly inserted into a family narrative at its middle chapters, expected to understand references, dynamics, and histories that others had absorbed gradually over lifetimes. From there, our conversation flowed more naturally. We exchanged background information – how she'd met Diego at school in Canberra, Joe's business activities, the *colourful* histories on both sides of our families. When I mentioned her relative Maurizio, Lina quickly clarified:

>**Lina:** *No. We don't talk to Maurizio.*

The swift, definitive statement revealed yet another fault line in the family geology – another estrangement, another complicated relationship. Each family member existed within their own intricate web of alliances and estrangements.

I ventured a more personal question:

>**Me:** *It certainly is a very interesting family. I'm curious, was I born before or after Joe was married? Joe speaks very highly and proudly of all his children. Do you have any photos of Joe when he was young? My biological mother told me I looked like him.*

Lina: *You looked like your sister.*

The comparison to my half-sister sent a peculiar thrill through me – concrete evidence of shared genetics, of visible belonging. After decades of searching for reflections of myself in strangers' faces, here was confirmation that my features existed in others, that my physical self had connections beyond my singular experience. The validation was both trivial and profound – a simple observation that confirmed what DNA had already proven, yet somehow more tangible, more real.

My message grew more vulnerable as I continued:

Me: *Seeing blood family is very emotional for me. I thought I would die not knowing.*

Lina: *You have a right to know.*

Six simple words – *'you have a right to know'* – yet they struck with the force of revelation. So many people throughout my life had treated my search as an inconvenience, an intrusion, a disruption to family secrets carefully maintained for decades. Her acknowledgement of my basic right to my own history felt revolutionary.

In that moment, I recognised the profound ethical clarity in her position – not complicated by blood loyalty or personal history, she could see what others had obscured: that knowledge of one's origins is a fundamental human need, not a privilege to be granted or withheld at others' convenience. Her recognition of this right, stated so simply and directly, validated my current search and the decades of questioning that had preceded it.

Me: *For my whole life, I knew nothing and now I have all of these blood relatives. It is very overwhelming and surreal, as it happened very quickly.*

Lina: *I can't even imagine, we must put ourselves in your shoes.*

'We have to put ourselves in your shoes.' The phrase – so simple in construction yet so profound in implication – contained more understanding than I'd received from some people who had known me for decades. After years of having my experience dismissed or minimised, here was someone genuinely trying to understand what it meant to live without knowledge of your origins.

This empathetic leap – the willingness to imagine an experience so different from her own – represented the purest form of compassion and emotional insight. Not pity, which condescends, or sympathy, which remains distant, but genuine empathy that attempts to cross the bridge between separate experiences. In that moment, she became more than just my brother's wife – she became an ally in my search for belonging, a witness to its legitimacy.

    Me: *Joe is a frail old man now.*
    Lina: *When I heard your birth mother didn't raise you, I was taken aback.*
    Me: *I was told accidentally when I was 16. My world turned upside down. Since then, I've been searching for my real identity. I love my adopted parents (both are deceased), but I always felt like I didn't quite fit.*

As I typed these words, I felt the familiar constriction in my throat that always accompanied this part of my story. How to convey in a few sentences the seismic impact of that moment on the bus? How to explain that with a stranger's casual remark, the very foundation of my identity had shattered, leaving me to spend decades reassembling the pieces? The inadequacy of language to capture such rupture has always been part of the adoptee's burden – how to make others understand an experience so fundamental yet so difficult to translate.

Even her question itself revealed genuine interest – not the polite, distant curiosity I'd encountered from so many, but an authentic desire to understand the contours of my experience. This wasn't just social pleasantry, but authentic human connection, offered freely across the distance that separated our lives.

As I sent that final message, I realised how much I had revealed to this virtual stranger who was simultaneously family. The core of my experience – the accidental revelation at 16, the instant fracturing of my reality, the decades of searching, the persistent sense of not quite fitting – was laid bare in a few lines of text. The ensuing months passed, with occasional check-ins maintaining our connection.

A new day dawned in January 2024, bringing with it a message that would expand my understanding of the Verduci family patterns in ways both validating and troubling:

9 January 2024, 6:29 am

> **Me:** *Hi Lina, how are you? I have just been contacted by one of Uncle Andrea's love children, who was born in 1964 like me. It makes me wonder, how many of us are out there? I'm heading back home via Sydney on Thursday. Xo*
>
> **Lina:** *What proof do they have? Maybe you should speak to your father, he'll probably know more info. What do they want to do?*

Her cautious response reflected the protective instinct of someone who had witnessed the complex dynamics of this family firsthand – who understood that claims of connection needed verification, that appearances could be deceptive. Yet beneath the caution lay genuine interest, a willingness to engage with this new development rather than dismiss it outright.

> **Me:** *Perhaps the siblings don't know, and they might want to know. Proof: she knew lots of things about the business. The mother worked for them. Andrea looked for his child when she was 16. They met when she was 30. He thought she was after money. We're not after money. All we want is to know who our real birth parents are and our biological history. Money can*

> never replace what was taken from us. All the significant occasions that we have missed. Birthdays, weddings, achievements, etc. I was told that the two Verduci brothers had to pay off lots and lots of women. I know this is hard for you to understand.

The words poured from me with an urgency that surprised even myself. I was responding to her questions and addressing the unspoken assumptions that had framed my entire experience of seeking connection. The implication that financial motivation might drive such searches. The suggestion that biological connection was something that needed to be proven rather than a fundamental reality. The presumption that those seeking their origins were asking for something beyond the basic human right to know their own story.

In a moment of vulnerability, I dropped the careful diplomacy I'd maintained in our earlier exchanges. This wasn't just about Uncle Andrea's child or even about me specifically, but about a pattern of denial and dismissal that had shaped so many lives like mine – a pattern I needed her to understand if she was truly going to *'put herself in my shoes.'*

> **Lina:** *I'm very sad to hear that she was rejected. Wrong decisions were made, and you suffered for it. So did this other person.*

Her response transcended mere sympathy to achieve that rare quality of true understanding. *'Wrong decisions were made, and you suffered for it.'* The acknowledgement contained no qualifications, no excuses, no deflection – just the clear recognition of cause and effect, of harm done and consequences endured. After decades of secrecy, dismissal, and denial, here was someone willing to name the truth – that the choices made by others had caused real suffering, and that suffering deserved acknowledgement.

The simplicity and directness of her validation stood in stark contrast to the evasions and justifications I'd encountered throughout my search. She didn't attempt to explain away the pain or minimise its impact but simply acknowledged its reality and legitimacy. In doing so, she offered something more valuable than information or even connection – she offered validation of my lived experience. She had offered me a golden thread. Her kindness had begun to fill one of the many cracks in my fractured sense of belonging – not erasing the damage, but transforming it into something that might, eventually, be whole in a new way.

Lina's compassion stood in stark contrast to what I would soon experience when meeting another member of my biological family – a reminder that blood connections don't automatically translate to understanding or acceptance.

This contrast reflected a truth I was slowly coming to understand, that meaningful connection isn't necessarily determined by shared DNA but by shared humanity – by the willingness to recognise another's experience without defensiveness or denial. Lina, connected to me only through marriage, had offered more genuine understanding than many who shared my blood.

Her compassion reminded me of those rare moments of true connection I'd experienced as a child – particularly with my cousins during those blissful years after my Father's death. Like Lina, my Cousin Francesca had shown me what families could be when not poisoned by rage or secrets: circles of warmth where I was drawn into the centre rather than hovering at the ragged edges. These brief experiences of healthy family dynamics had given me a template against which I could measure my later attempts at connection.

These memories – of my eldest cousin's warm embraces, of being welcomed into her home without reservation, of belonging without question even for brief periods – had sustained me through decades of searching. They had provided evidence that family could be a source of nurturing rather than wounding, of unconditional acceptance rather than conditional tolerance. That early template of belonging had given me something to seek, a standard against which to measure the connections I encountered.

Now Lina was offering something similar – not the complete integration I'd sometimes fantasised about, but a genuine acknowledgement of my reality and my right to it. In a journey marked by rejection and dismissal, such moments of authentic recognition shone like beacons, illuminating possibilities I'd sometimes feared didn't exist.

In the days that followed, I found myself returning to her messages, rereading them for the comfort they provided. Her empathy offered a glimpse of what family could be at its best – a place of understanding, of seeing and being seen, of acknowledging both connection and harm without requiring one to cancel out the other.

Another sister-in-law – someone I had known long before – also reached out. I told her that I had finally discovered my Father's identity.

Her reply showed deep insight and empathy: '*Oh gosh. I'm so happy for you that you have finally been able to do this. A missing link for so long. The more I think about it, I feel quite emotional. I hope you are okay. You must be excited and nervous.*' I went on to say that Uncle Bru helped me with my search. I told her of my relief, gratitude, excitement, and anxiousness to be meeting him – that he was still alive, and he had wanted to meet me.

The sister-in-law acknowledged my feelings: '*Oh! There are so many parts to this that are heartbreaking. But how lovely that he has been searching for you too. Now I'm welling up!*' She was shocked that I was threatened with defamation, simply for mentioning truths, even if they had been lifelong secrets. '*I'm not shocked by this reaction though. They've never really appreciated how heartbreaking this must be for you.*'

Her response – emotionally raw, unguarded in its empathy – created another small bridge across the chasm of misunderstanding that had so often separated me from those who hadn't experienced adoption firsthand. The simple acknowledgement that my situation was 'heartbreaking' validated what I had felt but so rarely heard expressed: that the separation from one's origins represents a genuine loss deserving of grief.

Most striking was her recognition that Joe had been *searching for me too* – a perspective I hadn't fully considered. In my narrative, I had been the lone seeker, the one bearing the burden of separation. The suggestion that he too might have wondered, might have searched in his own way, added a dimension to our story I was only beginning to comprehend. This wasn't just my search – but perhaps a mutual one – a connection severed that both parties had tried, in their different ways and timeframes, to restore.

This second instance of empathy – coming from someone connected to me through marriage rather than biological ties – further reinforced that understanding could transcend blood connections. These rare moments of genuine compassion served as stepping stones across the chaotic river of my identity journey, offering stable footing when everything else seemed to shift beneath me.

August 2023

As I prepared for my upcoming travels to Sydney, where I would potentially meet Diego and Lina in person, I tried to steel myself for all possibilities. The fragile hope sparked by Lina's kindness warred with the caution born of previous disappointments. Blood relatives, I was learning, weren't automatically allies – but occasionally, like unexpected blessings, they could become friends.

As I folded clothes into my suitcase, I realised I was packing more than the essentials. I was carrying hope – stitched together from the kindness of strangers and the golden threads of newly discovered kin. And for once, it didn't feel fragile. It felt hard-won, stitched from loss and luminous hope.

21

Casting the First Stone
(July 2023)

Familial blood dripping from unforgiving stones

My first meeting with my youngest paternal sibling occurred in July 2023, the day after Joe's 86th birthday – a coincidence that felt both fitting and ironic, as though the calendar itself was participating in the orchestration of our belated connection. He had called me in a jovial mood, his voice carrying the lingering warmth of birthday celebrations, and mentioned that he was meeting his nephew at the Preston Market. Would I like to join them for lunch? I readily agreed, unaware I was about to walk into a family confrontation that would crystallise both the possibility and the pain of these newly discovered connections. The Preston Market hummed with multicultural energy – vendors calling out prices in various languages, the complex aromatics of global cuisines mingling in the air, and shoppers navigating the narrow aisles with practised familiarity. I arrived early, claimed a table in the bustling food court, and waited, my body simultaneously relaxed and alert in that peculiar state of anticipatory tension I'd come to associate with Verduci encounters. Joe arrived first, his distinctive figure unmistakable even across the crowded space – the slightly stooped posture, the careful shuffling gait, his eccentric fashion marked him as a man who had long ago passed caring about appearances. He wore a traditional Indian orange hat perched atop his white hair, and beneath his long dark grey winter coat, a colourful silk orange scarf provided a flash of vibrancy – an eccentric peacock among the market's drab pigeons.

'Buongiorno, *mia cara bimba*' (my dear child).

We embraced warmly, the physical contact still novel enough to create a small shock of recognition – this was my Father, my blood, my DNA made manifest in another body. As we separated, I noticed his eyes tracking movement behind me, a slight shift in his expression signalling recognition. I turned to follow his gaze and saw them approaching – a woman and teenager moving toward us with purpose.

I knew immediately, with the bone-deep certainty that comes from studying photographs and family resemblances, that I was about to meet my youngest half-sister, Grizella. The recognition must have shown on my face because her expression immediately hardened; her steps became more deliberate, her posture tensing visibly as she closed the distance between us.

Joe made perfunctory introductions, his casual tone belying the momentousness of the occasion. Her face remained rigid, her eyes cold and evaluating as they swept over me, measuring my claim to connection, calculating my threat level. When she finally spoke, her harsh words hit with the precision of carefully aimed daggers:

'You represent one more thing that our father has done. One more trauma to add to the list of traumas.'

Her words pierced, unravelling decades of cautious hope. My body absorbed the blow, quietly bearing the force of her inherited pain. The warmth of Joe's earlier embrace drained instantly, leaving only the stark isolation I had known intimately since birth.

Her voice held neither malice nor compassion – just the weary detachment of someone who had long ago sorted their father's actions into a taxonomy of harms, with me now classified as the latest specimen.

'Don't take it personally if I'm not interested in you.'

Another physical blow – just as Ursula's had punched decades earlier.

I stood frozen in the arctic blast of his legitimate daughter's rejection.

I did not reveal that my chest tightened as if something were constricting around my heart.

This moment I had both anticipated and dreaded was unfolding in the worst possible way – not with curiosity or tentative acceptance, but with immediate hostility.

I felt simultaneously visible and erased – acknowledged only as an extension of Joe's sins rather than as a person who had suffered her own traumas, her own lifetime of absence and not-knowing. The bitter irony crushed me: in her eyes, I was the trauma, when I had been the abandoned one, the one who grew up without knowing my own story, my own blood.

I tried to dismiss her brutally insensitive reaction, but the words burrowed deep. These were the first words that one of my half-siblings expressed to me, and they carried the weight of six decades of family history I had never known.

I thought silently: *I'm not responsible for Joe's past sins. I'm not responsible for the trauma he has caused his family. I didn't ask to be born. In fact, there have been many days when I wished I hadn't been.*

Behind her anger, I glimpsed something familiar – the pain of a child who had lived with Joe's volatile nature, his unpredictability, his capacity for harm. And a loving mother she had lost, like me, at a young age. She had grown up with a father whose presence had wounded her, while I had grown up wounded by his absence. Our traumas were mirror images, both reflecting the same source. Understanding this didn't make her rejection less painful, but it framed it in ways I couldn't fully articulate.

She described our Father as crazy. I'd say wildly eccentric, not crazy. I've known crazy. Perhaps he was once crazy. Men sometimes mellow with age, their sharp edges worn smooth by time. The harsh and violent Giuseppe she grew up with is not the kinder, old man that I know. Our relationship does not have the usual parent–child emotional baggage.

'Has he told you about his time machine? Have you met his partner? She should fix her teeth.'

I deflected her sharp barbs. I had learnt to accept that not every family member would welcome me with open arms.

In contrast, her teenage son was warm and friendly. He said he and his sister were excited to hear that I existed. The generational difference struck me – this young man unburdened by decades of accumulated pain, able to see me simply as a newfound relative rather than as evidence of family wounds.

I asked Grizella if we could take a photo, and she agreed. It's a happy-looking photo, which belies the details of that day. The forced smiles mask the tension beneath, visible only to those who know what transpired before the camera clicked.

After the two left, Joe and I made some small talk. That was our fourth meeting. We gave each other a very warm embrace. Like me, he's glad that we have met. But like me, he laments the fact that we have met so late in life.

I struggled with this encounter on multiple levels. On one hand, joy surged through me – that I had found him alive, that we had met, that we had confirmed our connection. On the other, grief overwhelmed me for all I had missed – knowing him, siblings, aunts, uncles, cousins, and grandparents. And that they had lived only five minutes away from where I once lived saddened me even more. This new grief, sharper and more immediate, overtook the old chronic ache.

I would spend the next few years navigating this newfound grief – an ocean of tears I hadn't known still waited.

As I drove home, the harsh words of my half-sister played over in my mind. I wonder what nightmares haunt her sleep, what wounds our Father had inflicted that made her see me purely as 'one more trauma.'

Had she been told about me before?
Did she resent my sudden appearance in her father's life when she had struggled with him for decades?
I tried to imagine growing up with Giuseppe as a father – not the mellowed elderly man I know, but the volatile, sometimes violent figure my siblings describe. Perhaps her rejection wasn't about me at all, but about the pain she associates with the man who connects us.

The day after our first meeting, Grizella asked me via text when my birthday was. I told her.
She replied, 'Nine months before my parents were married.'
It's folly to think that a playboy of 10 years' standing would suddenly become monogamous upon marriage. Joe, along with some men of his generation, had a sense of entitlement and showed a total lack of care. All the blame and responsibility were put on the women they procreated with. Not a skerrick of care was given to the bastard offspring they were producing – not a thought to what their children's lives would be like without fathers and without blood family.
I asked her when her eldest siblings were born and when they lived in France.
She gave me the dates.
She replied, 'I'm sure you have many questions. But we must deal with the trauma of our father. And he left a lot of pain in his wake. I'm sorry.'
I sensed in her words a slight softening, a crack in the wall of hostility. The acknowledgement implied she recognised my search as legitimate, even if she wasn't prepared to participate in it.
This marked another subtle but significant shift in our relationship. Her apology, though brief, acknowledged my position for the first time. Where before she had seen only her own pain, perhaps now she was beginning to recognise mine as well. The bond between us was evolving from pure antagonism

to something more nuanced – a mutual recognition that we both carried wounds inflicted by the same man, albeit in very different ways. Though we were far from close, the emotional distance between us had narrowed.

I sent a brief reply acknowledging her pain.

Her reply pressed against old scars – tender, but no longer raw. I braced quietly.

It's a harsh reality that adoptees face repeatedly: not everyone will greet you with open arms. One must be mentally and emotionally prepared for all outcomes. During this period, I was feeling emotionally strong. There were times when I had not been, and I had to take time out from this exhausting emotional rollercoaster. There were times when I backed away after contacting biological family members. In those times, I had to grieve the multiple and ongoing losses.

A few days later, my phone pinged. It was Grizella again. I did not expect to hear from my angry half-sibling so soon after her last message.

'Hi Mirella, I just spoke to my sister, and she is fine to catch up for coffee this weekend if it suits you... Are you available?'

The message stunned me. *What had caused this sudden turnaround? Had her sister influenced her? Or was this simply part of the complex push-pull of family dynamics I was now entangled in?* Whatever the reason, this unexpected opening created a flutter of cautious hope – perhaps not all bridges were burned, perhaps connection was still possible.

This shift in her approach signalled the first major change in our nascent bond – from outright rejection to tentative outreach. The text message, simple as it was, represented a bridge being extended across the chasm of family secrets and resentments. Though I couldn't yet know if this bridge would hold or collapse beneath us, the fact that it existed at all seemed significant. Something had softened in the days since our hostile first meeting – either her heart toward me or her resistance to knowing me. Either way, a door once slammed shut was now being cautiously reopened.

We met that Saturday, on 8 July. 10:00 am at Cobrick Coffee, surrounded by the bluestone walls of what was once Pentridge Prison, Coburg. The walls that once held criminals were now containing past hurts.

My hands fidgeted with the edge of my jacket as I walked toward the café, heart jittering like keys in a pocket.

Why had she had a change of heart?
Why did the other sister want to meet me now when she had been told about me back in March?
What would we talk about?
What questions would I ask?

I played these questions in my mind that restless, sleepless night. As I walked toward the café, I couldn't know that this meeting would open yet another door to my complex heritage – this time leading me to question who my Father was and the entire lineage that had produced him.

I was the first to arrive and I sat down facing the counter, while being attacked by the fake plastic green fern plants that lined the side of the coffee shop. I was arm-wrestling with one of the plants when Grizella arrived. She was much warmer and more friendly this time, unlike our first meeting.

Then Stasia arrived. She had bluish, sad eyes. Much like our Father. She doesn't have the Verduci look. She looks more like her mother. I look and am more like the younger, feistier Grizella. How weird it was to be sitting across from two women who were simultaneously strangers and close blood relatives.

We had lots of questions for each other. They told me bits and pieces about Giuseppe. He was a harsh man, a harsh father, prone to anger outbursts.

I was sometimes prone to anger outbursts. I had always assumed it was due to witnessing domestic violence. Perhaps it was nature and nurture dancing their complicated tango.

As they shared stories of growing up with Giuseppe, I searched their faces for hints of myself. At the same time, their stories painted a picture of a father I hadn't experienced – and perhaps wouldn't have wanted to. The paradox struck me: I had spent decades yearning for a father I never knew, while they had spent decades recovering from the father they knew all too well.

Their father would pick up whatever was closest – a shoe, a belt, a washing machine hose – and hurl it across the room or use it to strike his children. But never his wife. Though I believed what they told me, it clashed painfully with the image of the gentle, poetic old man I had only recently begun to know. The stories didn't feel like lies, but they belonged to a man I had never met. And yet, somewhere deep in my bones, I understood.

Men of Giuseppe's generation didn't speak tenderness. They wielded power through silence and control, through gestures that passed for love but often landed as fear. It was the old Italian way – forged in hardship, shaped by war, and calcified within patriarchy. Their love, if it came at all, came laced with discipline and delivered with the back of a hand.

What struck me most was how his children spoke of their mother, Alice. Their voices softened when they said her name, as though the memory of her offered sanctuary. She had been the quiet centre of a storm – the thread that held the family together while everything else was fraying. In their stories, she emerged not as a martyr, but as a kind of quiet alchemist, transforming chaos into survival.

I listened, heart aching for the children they had been, trying to reconcile the father they knew with the man I had so desperately searched for. The man who had wounded them had given me life. And in that impossible equation, I felt the full weight of inheritance – its sorrow, its silence, and its strange, enduring pull.

I told them I knew about the darker chapters of Giuseppe's story, which I'd unearthed online in the weeks following our reunion. The articles painted a man both reckless and cunning – details that clashed with the frail, poetic figure I had come to know. One of my sisters recalled being a teenager, hosting friends in her room, when she glanced out the window and saw marijuana drying on the decking outside. The three brothers had worked with Giuseppe on his plantation, drawn in as boys to a world that blurred the lines between enterprise and danger.

I was shown a video of a niece. I asked if I could see some family photos and they kindly obliged.

Some of our cousins are single, unmarried, and childless, like me. They mentioned that some might be gay. But none have come out to the family yet. More forbidden secrets.

I thought: *how tragic that even now they must hide. The family, trapped in amber – preserving outdated prejudices like prehistoric insects.*

At times, as my half-siblings spoke, I could see their eyes become bloodshot. Welling with tears, especially when I told them that their father spoke proudly and was full of praise of all his children. They asked me when I found out I was adopted and about my birth mother. They knew that adoption records were sealed back in 1980 and opened in 1984. They must have done their research before our meeting. It wasn't common knowledge.

I told them that Ursula was married to an asshole of a man and that she didn't and wouldn't tell me much about Giuseppe and that I would never forgive her for withholding information about the identity of my Father.

One gently said, 'In time, you might forgive her and speak to her again.'

I resolutely replied, 'Never.'

In that moment of defiance, there was a strange connection with my half-sisters. Despite our very different experiences of family, we shared a stubborn streak, a capacity for both holding grudges and fierce loyalty. I wondered if this trait came from Giuseppe – if his influence on us transcended presence or absence, if DNA carried not just physical features, but also temperaments and tendencies as well.

I mentioned that I had lived in Coburg. They told me that they used to live in Coburg in some dead-end street near Moreland station in the 1970s. They came back to Melbourne in 1983, when Giuseppe was arrested. My gap year.

In the late 60s, 'someone died,' they said, and the family suddenly had to leave Australia. Giuseppe sent his wife and three children to Italy without any money or support. She had to fend for herself. This story didn't gel with Joe's story.

We spoke about Uncle John's tragic story.

Back in Melbourne in the 80s, Alice and Giuseppe had a Manchester business, Koala Manchester, near Sydney Road. Alice was the bookkeeper. They claimed that Giuseppe didn't have much of a business head. He always had crazy business ventures and ideas – he still does. Apparently, he's invented a machine that gives endless energy.

When Alice died, the youngest children were still living at home. Giuseppe brought his mistress into the home after two weeks and then married her two weeks later. The siblings had to move out of the family home as it had to be sold.

As they shared these stories, I began to understand the source of their initial hostility. Their rejection wasn't just about me being unwelcome evidence of Giuseppe's infidelity – it was about a lifetime of experiencing his selfishness, his impulsivity, his disregard for others' feelings. In their eyes, I represented just one more example of Giuseppe prioritising his own desires over family needs, one more manifestation of harm done to those who depended on him.

They described our Grandmother Giuseppina as a witch – literally, practising witchcraft. Giuseppe and his siblings grew up mistrusting doctors, fearing death, clinging instead to superstition.

The sisters said that the Verduci clan prized hard work above all. I didn't inherit that compulsion – life is too short, after all, to accumulate wealth you can't take with you to the grave.

Carpe diem!

Apparently, Giuseppe called his daughter a *puttana*. I thought to myself, *Wouldn't he have thought the same of me back in the 1980s?*
Thankfully, I was spared the same shame and rejection.
They told me that they have a big Verduci pre-Christmas get-together. It's a very big family. I wondered if I would ever get an invite.
I told them about my family here and in New York.
They asked, at least three times.
'What do you want from us?'
A repeat of Ursula's suspicion, that old accusation that seeking truth must mean seeking something else.
The repeated question revealed their underlying anxiety – a fear that I had an agenda beyond simple connection, that I might demand something that would further disrupt their already complicated lives. For someone who had experienced Giuseppe's self-centred behaviour firsthand, my appearance might seem like the prelude to yet another family upheaval.
I find it perplexing that people would ask such a question. I can't imagine turning away anyone that I knew was my blood family. *Perhaps it's because I don't have family. Perhaps because they are bigoted and holier than thou. And I've always carried that longing. Perhaps because they come from such a big family, they don't need another family member.*
This time there was no deep longing for connection, just opportunity and information. I said, 'I just wanted to meet my relatives, find out about them and myself, my history, my biological roots. And whatever happens, happens. I'm not after anything.'

There was something in my simple desire for connection, free of demands or expectations, that seemed to ease their wariness. The question had been a test, and my answer had passed.
In that moment of candour, our connection deepened perceptibly. The wall of suspicion between us began to crumble

further as they recognised my motives were genuine. With each honest exchange, the nature of our bond was transforming – from strangers united only by DNA to cautious acquaintances beginning to see each other as people with legitimate needs and feelings.

Their body language shifted subtly throughout our conversation; shoulders that had been tense and raised now relaxed, arms that had been tightly crossed now rested more naturally. These small physical changes reflected the emotional distance we had travelled in just a few hours together.

As we parted, Grizella said, 'Let me give you a hug goodbye.' She is the warmest and friendliest of the siblings, in her unfriendly kind of way. That hug, offered so unexpectedly after the hostility of our first meeting – a small miracle. It wasn't a full embrace into the family, not by any measure, but it was acknowledgment – a tentative opening where before there had been only walls.

In that embrace, I sensed a shift. What had begun as outright rejection just days earlier had become something warmer, more complex. Not friendship, not sisterhood in any conventional sense, but a mutual recognition – an acknowledgment that despite the complication between us, we were irrevocably connected by blood. The distance between us had not vanished, but it had narrowed enough to allow this moment of human contact.

After visiting my older cousins and recounting the day, I left feeling drained and raw. On the way home, I bought cigarettes and a bottle of wine – small comforts for a night of exhaustion too deep for sleep.

The meeting had been neither the warm welcome I'd once imagined nor the rejection I'd feared. It was something messier, more human – wariness giving way to curiosity, hostility softening into something closer to recognition. Like the fragments of identity I'd been piecing together for decades, this emerging relationship with my half-sisters would be imperfect, but real. *But perhaps the very acknowledgment of brokenness might create something quietly beautiful.*

Our bond had evolved in just days – from 'don't take it personally if I'm not interested in you' to a voluntary hug goodbye. While we would never share childhood memories, we had begun to forge something else: an adult connection rooted in mutual curiosity and tentative respect. The arc gave me hope – that hurt might yield to something more enduring. Not the idealised version I once dreamed of, but something authentic, with all the complexities that come with genuine human connection.

I had yet to fully absorb it all. My emotions were still raw from the shock of finding Giuseppe alive.

22

The Kintsugi Poet: Giovanni 'John' Verduci

(11.5.1947–18.4.1969)

A broken heart, that refused to betray.

On one of our very early meetings – those delicate beginnings now blurred together like watercolours left out in the rain – I continued my careful excavation and stitching together of the Verduci family history with Joe.
As we sat across from each other at his favourite hotel restaurant, the afternoon winter light casting long, trembling shadows across our table, the background noise of clinking glasses, the clashing of cutlery, children's laughter, and muted conversation formed a foreboding hush between us.
I gently leaned in, lowering my voice as though speaking to forbidden ghosts.
'Tell me about your brother Giovanni,' I asked, watching his face closely. My question stirred the sediment of buried years.
He momentarily looked into a distance long gone.
His eyes reddened immediately – a quick, involuntary flash of pain, as if my words had brushed against a wound not yet scarred over.
Some truths arrive like strangers at the front door – uninvited, undeniable, impossible to turn away.

What he shared with me that day was not just a story but a wound – a gash still tender, still weeping beneath the brittle scab of time.
Another tragedy woven into the Verduci bloodline.
A sorrowful aria, played again and again, each generation altering only the key, never the melody.
Here again: forbidden love.
Here again: patriarchal wrath.
Here again: catastrophic consequences.
It unfolded with the brutal precision of an old tale – Luigi Da Porto's *Giulietta e Romeo* – a story later softened and stolen by an Englishman, as my Father Joe would later remark with a mixture of bitterness and pride.
In John's story, I saw a mirror.
A mirror reflecting the circumstances of my own creation, blurred but unmistakable.
My Father spoke, his voice low, almost reverent:
'John was torn. He didn't want to upset my Father, but he couldn't bear to disappoint his pregnant Jewish girlfriend.'
Desire and duty – twin faces sharing the same sorrow, wrestling within the chest of a young man barely out of boyhood.
'My Father forbade John from marrying her. We were only allowed to marry Italians. We could not contradict the iron fist of our Father,' he said solemnly, the sadness in his eyes deepening into something rawer, older.
I could feel it – the ancient pulse of shame and honour that had governed their lives.
It would have been seen as an unthinkable disgrace – a great mala figura – for a proud Verduci son to marry a woman already carrying a child, even if it was his own.
Only good Catholic virgins were considered marriageable.
The old Italian codes had been carried across the ocean, tucked tightly in their bones, fossilised by distance, stubbornness, and fear of losing identity in a foreign land.

It would take decades for those hard traditions to thaw.
Grandfather Bartolo – the ghost presiding over these choices – would be horrified to see the melted, modern Verduci family of today.
My Father's next words fell like stones into a well:
'John shot himself.
In his room.
Used my hunting gun.'
I felt the air thicken around us.
Sunlight from the windows seemed to hesitate, turning the restaurant into a dim cavern of memory.
I watched my Father carefully – saw the rare fracture in his normally impassive face.
A flicker of the young man he had once been, trapped in the moment the gun shattered the world they knew.
Grief, I realised, rarely speaks in full sentences.
It flashes – sudden, jagged – like lightning briefly revealing the vast, dark landscape it rips across.
I asked gently, almost whispering, 'Was he sensitive?'
My father nodded, his voice catching for a moment.
'Yes. John was the most intelligent one. Studying law. A poet.'
A poet.
The word sat between us like a candle, flickering quietly as the night kissed the day.
John's description – academic, considerate, tender – stood in stark contrast to the hardened, pragmatic persona my Father had forged to survive.
I wondered if, in some secret place inside him, he had once been like John – before duty and calling chiselled away the softer edges.
Perhaps he had envied him.
Perhaps he had mourned him long before John even pulled the trigger.

The tenderness with which he spoke of John suggested a complexity I was only beginning to glimpse – a man who valued sensitivity and intellect even as life had demanded their suppression.
I asked softly, as though intruding on sacred ground, 'What happened to the child?'
My Father's voice dropped further.
'I don't know. I think the girlfriend – died. Maybe – a year later.'
Somewhere out there, I realised, was – perhaps – another Verduci orphan.
Another shadow-branch of the family tree, growing wild and unknown.
No name.
No face.
Just a possibility stitched onto the invisible tapestry of our hidden past.
Later, I learned that two of John's siblings had been home that day.
They heard the gunshots.
They found him.
Afterward, the family left their Carlton home.
The walls had absorbed too much sorrow.
Their Mother – that iron-willed woman – never spoke of it.
Grief, in their world, was something to be buried deep, never exhumed.
The image haunted me – those siblings, frozen at the threshold of the unspeakable.
Trauma layered silently into their bones, sedimented by decades of silence.
A gun had gone off, and John had been shot dead.
And then – more secrets.
More fragile retellings.
I learned that the family told a different story – of an intruder, a stranger breaking into the house, bringing death.

At first, the fabrication enraged me.
But as the anger ebbed, something softer rose in its place.
Perhaps, the lie was not meant to deceive.
Perhaps, it was meant to protect.
Perhaps, it was easier for a mother to imagine her son a victim of violence, rather than a casualty of despair.
Easier for siblings to breathe if they could place the unbearable grief outside the family walls.
Sometimes, love does not speak in truths.
Sometimes it weaves gentler fictions – not to betray memory, but to allow survival.
I thought then of my own story – how my adoptive parents were told to say that my biological parents had died in a car accident.
A lie – yes.
But also a mercy.
The same impulse:
to hush sorrow into shadows,
to create stories survivable by fragile hearts.
When I later asked Joe if my stern Grandfather Bartolo had ever shown any remorse, he answered with a shrug heavy with old bitterness:
'Well... after John died, another brother was allowed to marry his non-Italian girlfriend.'
One son's death had been the price of another's freedom.
It chilled me.
Change had come, yes – but only after irreparable loss.
And I wondered – *if I had been conceived a decade later, when those rigid walls had begun to crumble – would I have been allowed to stay?*

Would my Father have chosen differently?

The realisation hit me with quiet, devastating clarity:
John had died because the old rules were unyielding.
I had been abandoned because, for a time, they still held sway.

The same shame that had driven John to despair had erased me from my Father's life.
It was not personal rejection – it was cultural obedience.
Later, standing at Carlton Cemetery, I found John's voice – etched into stone, still speaking across time:

> *È la vita*
> *È una lunga disperata corsa*
> *Dove il tedio eterno*
> *È il mezzo scambio*
> *È la vasta immensità dell'aldilà*
> *Che insegui.*

Life is a long, desperate race.
The words struck me with the sorrowful beauty of a cracked bell, reverberating deep in my chest.
John had glimpsed the eternal weariness, the impossible chase toward the vast unknown – and had chosen to step into it, to surrender rather than endure.
His despair resonated with me.
It wasn't just his sorrow I recognised – it was his questioning.
The same relentless search for meaning that had driven me for decades – seeking belonging, identity, wholeness – now seemed less a personal affliction than a Verduci inheritance.
John's poetry was a trace I hadn't known I was listening for.
He was, I realised, a kintsugi poet – his broken heart illuminated by golden seams of truth and vulnerability.

~ ~ ~

When I spoke with other relatives about John, I heard more fragments – more carefully tended half-truths.
Yes, they said, he had fathered a child.
Yes, he had died.
But the how, the why – those details were still smudged, still hidden beneath layers of protective retelling.

One relative, speaking hesitantly, said:
'He came through to me once... through a medium.
He said he died of a broken heart.'
A broken heart.
Not by taking his own life.
Not despair.
A broken heart – softer, more romantic, and somehow more unbearable.
It wasn't just the rewriting of facts that struck me – it was the aching tenderness behind it.
How fiercely they had all wanted to believe that John had died of love, not shame.
Of sorrow, not failure.
And perhaps, in a way, that was true.
Perhaps John had simply broken – under the impossible collision of love and law, desire and duty.
And so, in the mythologies they built, they preserved something of his innocence – even as they erased parts of the story.
I often thought about the unborn child – about the girlfriend John had loved, and lost.
Nella.
And about the child they had created together – a cousin I might never meet, wandering somewhere under another name, another history.
A parallel life, mirroring mine.
Both of us born of forbidden love.
Both of us erased by fear.
Both of us carrying the silent weight of generations.
The Verduci family, like the Di Benedettos, had learned to survive by erasing their own pain.
Rewrite the story.
Protect the heart.
Move forward.
Never look back.
And yet – here I was.

A living fracture.
A fault line where the old myths cracked open.
A breathing, questioning reminder that truth, once buried, still finds a way to grow.
In time, I came to see my elderly Father more clearly – not as a villain, not even as a failed man – but as a survivor.
He had lived by different rules.
Rules that demanded silence, demanded loyalty, demanded sacrifice.
He had watched his brother break under those rules.
He had chosen to survive instead – to bend, to compromise, to compartmentalise.
He had built walls inside himself, and behind those walls, hidden all the forbidden things – love, regret, tenderness.
When he abandoned me, it wasn't out of cruelty.
It was the only language he knew.
A man doesn't burn down the house he was born in – he learns how to move through it without knocking down the walls.
Where John had chosen to die, Giuseppe had chosen to endure.
Where John had clung to his poet's heart, my Father had hidden his own – tucked it into a box marked *Too Dangerous to Touch*.
I was not simply my Father's lost child.
I was also John's living reflection –
the one who had chosen poetry over pragmatism.
John, who had spoken truth even when truth was lethal.
John, who had broken under the weight of love denied.
And I – I had survived the same weight.
I had turned the silence into song.

Later, visiting John's grave again, standing beneath a sky too wide to hold the sadness,
I whispered, 'I found you.'
I found your sorrow. Your poetry.
Your unbearable heart, still refusing to betray.

In finding Giuseppe, I found my lineage.
But in finding John, I found my inheritance.
The right to question.
The right to remember.
The right to crack the silence wide open and let the light flood in.
The right to live – not neatly, not quietly, not obediently – but fully, fiercely, vulnerably.
I am John's living poem.
I am Giuseppe's golden seam.
I am the song that shame will not silence.
And I will carry all of it – the sorrow, the silence, the secrets, the shattered love – with an open heart, and without fear.

23

Papà: The Philosopher and the Father

Musings reflected in enigmatic eyes.

Over the next few months, Joe and I had a buffet-style dinner a few times at a pub. The first time we got our meals, I noticed that Joe's plate of food was like mine and also covered in chilli flakes. I smiled to myself.

Joe and I had an instant rapport – we think similarly. We're not so into small talk, preferring to discuss life's bigger questions. It consolidated my growing sense of identity.

How did the Universe start?
Does love exist?
Does God exist?
Is there life after death?
What is the meaning of life?

These philosophical discussions revealed another dimension of my Father – the autodidact, the self-taught intellectual whose curiosity spanned cosmic questions despite limited formal education. This was perhaps the version of him I connected with most deeply – the one whose mind moved in patterns I recognised in myself and whose hunger for understanding transcended the circumstances of his life.

He left high school at around 16 and trained to be an electrical mechanic, electrician, and repairer of refrigerators and washing machines. Shortly after arriving in Australia, he taught himself English in six months, studying well into the night, as I often did and do when engrossed in something. His English vocabulary is as big as mine, if not bigger.

He later showed me the 10 cm thick Collins English dictionary that he used to study. Bits of paper with notes sticking out from the book, words were underlined, and pages were dog-eared. He was very widely read – history, philosophy, geography, astronomy, physics, politics, poetry, and literature. There was no topic that he didn't know something about. His mind was a sponge like mine, although I don't have his extraordinary memory for detail. Clearly, he passed on his intellect, imagination, and curiosity.

It was during these conversations that I began to reconcile the criminal with the intellectual – to understand how the same man could have been involved with marijuana plantations and Mafia connections while simultaneously contemplating the cosmos and memorising poetry. His criminality, I slowly realised, wasn't born of ignorance but of a complex set of choices, cultural influences, and economic opportunities within the immigrant experience. The Joe who quoted philosophers while describing drug operations was the same man who had taught himself English from that worn-out dictionary – resourceful, determined, and unbound by conventional limitations – traits I recognised in myself.

He often made comments such as: 'Men are the stronger sex. Women are weak. Women are inferior. Men are more intelligent'. As I got to know Joe, I gently challenged his outdated views and as I got to know him better, not so gently. His sexist pronouncements both repelled and fascinated me – relics of an old-world mentality I recognised from my childhood but had long since rejected.

Yet even as I challenged him, I felt a strange gratitude for having been raised apart from him. I had emerged from the crucible of suffering with a fractured but sharpened self-awareness. Had I grown up as Giuseppe's daughter, these toxic attitudes might have shaped me differently, might have crushed the independence and feminist values that were central to my identity. The separation that had caused so much pain had also, paradoxically, allowed me to become someone who could now sit across from him as an equal, challenging rather than absorbing his outdated worldview.

Over the following year, in many wide-ranging conversations that jumped from topic to topic, I learnt the following personal history.

Giuseppe and his eldest brother, Andrea, owned several businesses. They were making lots of money, they were single, well dressed 'playboys', the term that society fondly uses for men who sleep around, without any responsibility or care for the bastard offspring they might create. Giuseppe had a new suit, and shoes made every month. He drove around in a fancy Pontiac. He met Ursula sometime in 1963. Supposedly she wanted to place a message on the radio for her Father's birthday. The Verduci Brothers used to advertise often on 3AW, a local Melbourne radio station. Giuseppe helped her with the message and then they went out until she found out she was pregnant with me.

Was this just a convenient ruse to meet a wealthy Italian businessman?

The Verduci Brothers, originally known as *Fratelli Verduci*, forced to anglicise the name, were very successful. And liked to splash their money around – Giuseppe in particular.

As I pieced together the circumstances of my conception, I felt a strange emotional distance – as though I were investigating someone else's origin story rather than my own. Joe described his courtship of Ursula with the same detached tone he used for business transactions: she approached him about a radio message, they dated briefly, pregnancy resulted. There was no mention of love, of connection, of any emotional foundation that might have created me. Just two young people, one wealthy and irresponsible, the other perhaps seeking security, whose brief encounter resulted in an 'expensive' complication.

During one of our dinners, brazenly, I asked Joe for specific details regarding my conception. He told me he used to take Ursula out to night clubs in St Kilda, now a trendy suburb of Melbourne. Alone, unchaperoned. He then would drive her home around midnight.

Supposedly she said to him, *'Wait here'*. And then she would go into her house. She then snuck back out. They drove to a nearby park. So, I may have been conceived in a park, under the stars somewhere near Ursula's home, near the Yarra River, in Kew. But I was not a love child – a moment of frenzied desire on his part. Joe does not believe in love. He claims to have never been in love. He says that love is just desire. Perhaps romantic love is just that – hormone-fuelled desire. And yet, I know that he has an unwavering affection for his homeland and his family.

The revelation that I was likely conceived in a parked car in a suburban park under a canopy of twinkling celestial bodies was strangely fitting – a clandestine beginning for a life that would remain hidden for decades.

There was something poetic about it: under the cover of darkness, away from watchful eyes, a moment of connection that would have consequences neither participant could have anticipated. Joe's dismissal of love as 'just desire' struck me as a defence mechanism – a way of distancing himself from emotional responsibility. Yet his actions since our reunion – the poetry-filled text messages, the meals he insisted on paying for, the hours spent in conversation – suggested a capacity for connection he was reluctant to name.

During a few other conversations, I was able to discern further information around the time of my conception. Ursula had told me that she knew she was pregnant when she was about four months gone. She told Joe. Joe didn't want to have anything to do with her. Uncle Bru had been told that Joe had told her to piss off and to never contact him again. Over time, Bru shared other revelations too - including reasons why Ursula couldn't include me in her life that went beyond her own choice. These constraints helped explain the brittle defensiveness I'd encountered in that Camberwell café years earlier.

Joe told me that Ursula's mother, my Grandmother, wanted him to marry her daughter. She was a feisty Neapolitan woman, set in her Italian ways as Giuseppe was in his Calabrian, male chauvinistic, sexist, and bigoted ways. Giuseppe refused to marry Ursula, as he was already promised to his future wife.

It was a firmly held societal view back then; they are women you marry and women you fool around with. Instead of marriage, Joe claimed that he offered to put Ursula up in a house in Geelong, not too far from Melbourne, and offered to pay for her accommodation and my upkeep. The Grandmother rejected the offer.

Sometime later, he was taken to court by Ursula. Allegedly, she had gone to the police and told them that he wanted her to have an abortion. I questioned her motives. Abortion was illegal back in 1963. The penalty was 12 years in jail. Initially, Ursula pleaded not guilty to the charge. Then she changed her plea and said that she was guilty. The judge then sent her away into remand. Joe said he paid for her bail so she could get out of jail. Somehow, he won the case and avoided a conviction or going to jail. At the time he had a very expensive lawyer and barrister.

He said that the case cost him the equivalent of a few houses.

It was a very expensive sexual encounter.

I was his most expensive baby.

'One of many,' he said.

As he recounted the legal battle, I realised my life could have taken a very different turn. Had Giuseppe been convicted, he might have been imprisoned during my early years – another timeline in which our eventual reunion would have been even more improbable.

The intersection of personal decisions and legal systems helped determine my fate left me dizzy with the sheer contingency of it all.

More startling was his casual mention of other 'illegitimate' children – half-siblings I hadn't known existed, who had preceded me in the constellation of Giuseppe's unacknowledged offspring.

We were a scattered tribe, the collateral damage of his youthful irresponsibility.

Did they know about each other?
Had any of them found him, as I had?

The thought of these unknown siblings – potentially searching as I had been, potentially unaware as I once was – added new complexity to an already tangled familial web.

Nine months after I was born, Giuseppe married.

During a much later meeting, about a year after our first, Joe said, 'Perhaps I would have married your mother, if she had agreed to stay with you in Geelong, with my upkeep.'

I was puzzled by his comment but then thought perhaps he regretted our missed years.

At one of our early dinners, Joe had said, 'I have one regret in life.'

I looked at him and said, half-joking, 'Only one?'

He replied, his eyes misty, 'Yes – that we did not meet each other sooner.'

The admission caught me off guard – a rare moment of emotional transparency from a man who typically veiled vulnerability beneath bravado and an inherited code of silence. His misty eyes revealed what his words often concealed: that somewhere beneath the criminal history, the philandering, and the cavalier attitude toward fatherhood lay a capacity for genuine feeling. This wasn't the 'Ndrangheta middleman from the documentary, or the playboy from his stories – this was simply an old man confronting the consequences of choices made decades earlier.

I gently took his hand, swallowed hard, smiled, warmly and said, 'At least, I found you – and it's a miracle that you are alive!'

In that moment, he became my Papà Joe.

Sitting across from my Papà Joe, I felt a strange dual awareness: here was a crucial missing piece of my identity mosaic, the man whose genetics I carried.

Yet he was also becoming a new thread in the tapestry I had been weaving all these years – not replacing what came before but adding to it, creating new patterns where he intersected with the existing fabric of my life.

He likes to call me 'Mia cara bimba'.

He insists on paying for all my meals when we go out, and I keep telling him he doesn't have to. He won't let me pay for anything. He says, 'I couldn't feed you when you were young, at least I can feed you now.'

The simple statement contained multitudes – acknowledgment, regret, and a tentative offering of the only kind of care he seemed equipped to provide and in a culture where food represents love. Food became his language of atonement, each meal a small instalment on an emotional debt he could never fully repay.

I accepted these offerings for what they were – sustenance, symbols of a connection and love being carefully constructed across the chasm of six lost decades.

I asked him about his involvement with Winchester.

Casually, he replied, 'He was my boss.'

The simple four-word answer concealed layers of complexity. In that moment, he acknowledged what the documentary had revealed – his connection to the investigation that had become one of Australia's most notorious unsolved crimes.

Yet the ease with which he referenced this relationship was jarring, as though being supervised by a high-ranking police officer who would later be assassinated was merely another job detail rather than a pivotal chapter in Australian criminal history.

According to public records and the documentary, there were numerous people who had reason to kill Winchester. David Eastman – the man accused, charged, and convicted for

Winchester's murder – spent decades in jail before being acquitted and he was awarded millions in compensation.
The details of the case and witness testimony had been suppressed – explaining Papà Joe's earlier comment about being 'a suppressed man.'
He couldn't legally discuss the case, and I discovered that much of this information was only available through intense research – or through media like the documentary I'd stumbled upon.
'Didn't they make a TV drama about it? *Police Crop*?' I asked.
'You probably can't find it now,' Papà Joe replied. That too has been suppressed, it seems.
I searched extensively online but found no trace of this series, leading me to wonder if it too had been suppressed.
The ease with which history could be erased or altered – both personal and public – was unsettling.
How many other stories remained hidden?
How many connections were undocumented?
The Winchester case revealed another dimension of Papà Joe's complex past: he had been arrested in the early 1980s for marijuana cultivation but avoided conviction because of his role as a police informant.
He had been working both sides – criminal and law enforcement – in a dangerous balancing act that could have cost him his life.
On a dark Canberra night around 9:30 pm, Winchester had pulled into his neighbour's driveway in his white sedan.
As he was about to exit his vehicle, he was assassinated – two bullets to the head, the assailant vanishing without a trace.
I found these connections to Australia's criminal underworld simultaneously fascinating and disturbing. The man who now sent me poetic text messages and insisted on paying for my meals had once moved in circles where violence was currency and loyalty was constantly questioned.
How had he survived?
What had he witnessed?

The questions multiplied with each revelation, even as answers dissolved on contact. I was left bewildered.

I asked Papà Joe about his deceased sister, Bruna – the lawyer and barrister.
He said Bruna had wanted to complete high school and go to university to study law, but his Father Bartolo didn't want her to go.
Women were supposed to get married and have Italian babies. Apparently, Joe convinced their parents – particularly his Mother, whom he described as the more intelligent of the couple, to allow Bruna to complete high school and go on to study law at RMIT.
This story revealed a surprising contradiction in Papà Joe's character – the same man with deeply sexist views had once advocated for his sister's education pushing against prevailing family attitudes.
When I pointed out this inconsistency, he shrugged.
'Bruna was different. She was very intelligent,' he said.
Back in Motticella, as a child, she was known as *l'Avvocata* (the barrister).
Yet the fact remained: he had recognised his sister's intelligence and supported her ambitions at a time when such support was rare.
This glimpse of a more enlightened perspective suggested that beneath the bravado and chauvinism lay a more complex moral understanding – one capable of transcending, however imperfectly, the cultural limitations of his upbringing.
Giuseppe and his family moved to Canberra around 1969 because of his 'business' activities. He didn't go into detail.
During this time, he was also a member of the Australian Labour Party and became involved in the Italo-Australia Club – a highly influential organisation, frequented by politicians, lawyers, barristers, and police officers of the time.
Members could leverage the club to enter Australian politics.

Al Grasby was once a member.

Giuseppe aspired to get into politics.

The intersection of organised crime and politics was another dimension of Giuseppe's life that the documentary had hinted at, but our conversations began to illuminate more fully.

His political connections and ambitions suggested a man constantly seeking legitimacy and influence – someone for whom criminality wasn't an end in itself but a means to achieve status and power within a system that often marginalised immigrants.

'I could have been somebody in politics,' he told me once, a hint of wistfulness in his voice.

'What happened?' I asked.

'I wasn't Australian enough. The 1970s were a more racist time.'

What kind of father would a Parliamentarian Giuseppe have been?

Would he have acknowledged me then, or would I have been an even more meticulously guarded secret?

I found his connections to Australia's underworld scarily fascinating.

What began as mere curiosity about my Father had inadvertently led me into a shadowy world I'd previously encountered only in crime documentaries and news headlines.

I was the daughter of an Italian immigrant – a man whose name appeared in books about organised crime, whose testimony had influenced major criminal investigations, whose life had intersected with one of Australia's most notorious unsolved murders.

How far back did the criminal connection stretch?

Back to the homeland?

This knowledge transformed how I understood Papà Joe and myself.

The DNA I carried, the genetic inheritance I'd sought to understand for decades, came with a more complex legacy than I could have imagined.

Yet strangely, this revelation didn't destabilise me as the original adoption discovery had.

Instead, it added another dimension to my self-understanding – another piece of the puzzle that made me who I am, shaped by the strange twists of fate that had both connected me to and separated me from this complicated man.

As our relationship developed in the months and years following our first meeting at the Kent, I found myself getting to know Papà Joe as he was now. Piecing together the man he had been throughout his life – the ambitious young immigrant; the businessman; the electrician; the playboy; the husband; the son; the brother; the philosopher; the poet; the informant; the exile; the scholar; the gardener; the father of many children, both acknowledged and unacknowledged.

He contained multitudes, and in understanding his complexity, I gained a deeper appreciation for my own.

In one of our conversations about his past, Papà Joe mentioned something that stayed with me: 'We're all saints and sinners, *mia cara bimba*. Anyone who says different is selling something,' he said, his weathered hand gesturing toward the empty space between us – the 60 years of absence suddenly compressed into inches across a restaurant table.

In that moment, I glimpsed a truth that philosophers have wrestled with for centuries: that moral purity is a fiction we create to comfort ourselves – that humanity exists not in perfection but in the complex interplay of virtue and transgression.

His casual wisdom mimicked Machiavelli's assertion that human nature is fundamentally inconsistent – a tapestry of contradictions rather than a coherent moral narrative.

This understanding didn't excuse his abandonment but contextualised it within the messy reality of human existence. Perhaps wholeness wasn't about achieving moral perfection but about integrating our contradictions into a more honest self-conception.

The simplicity of this philosophy, coming from a man whose life had traversed such extreme territories of both legal and moral boundaries, struck me as profound.

It offered a framework for understanding both him and myself – a way of reconciling the contradictions we all contain, the capacity for both harm and healing that exists in every human relationship.

Perhaps this is why, despite the shocking revelations about his criminal past, I found myself continuing to build a relationship with him.

The man I was coming to know was neither the 'Ndrangheta figure from the documentary nor the plaster saint I might have imagined in my decades of searching.

He was simply human – flawed, complex, capable of both cruelty and kindness, shaped by choices both good and bad, just as I had been.

Like a condemned man, he bore within him both the seeds of destruction and the possibility of grace. In his contradictions, I found a strange comfort – a reminder that wholeness comes not from perfection but from the integration of all our aspects, even those we might prefer to disown.

As time passed, our connection deepened – in words, in presence.

My Papà Joe transitioned into my second Father.

He had been Giuseppe, my enigmatic biological father, but over time, he became my Papà.

He has difficulty walking and struggles to hear. Even with his hearing aids. He says this is a product of learning to fire guns at a very young age with his Uncle Giuseppe, the one accused of murder.

Apparently after World War II, the soldiers had left ammunition and guns behind. Great–Uncle Giuseppe found a gun and showed my Father how to use it. He was about seven at the time.

During our regular weekend lunch dates or shopping outings, I constantly asked my Papà about his and my family history. One Sunday while we were shopping for fruit and veggies at the Preston Market, I asked my Papà about the i 'ngùrii in his family. In Calabrian tradition, these nicknames often revealed more about a person than their given name. The young boy Giuseppe was *Giuseppe u Mulinov* – after the Russian General Malinovsky – he used to walk around his village with a gun in his trousers, as the leader of his pack.

His Father was *Bartolo u Melito*, named after the town he was from.

His Grandfather Giuseppe was *Peppe u Mastru* (master), and his Uncle Giuseppe was '*Giuseppe u Muzzo*,' because he carried a cut-off gun.

Each nickname contained a story – another thread connecting me to my heritage.

Through the telling of stories – and the weaving of family history – I was learning about my culture – and myself.

My Mother had once told me similar stories – her culture became my adopted culture.

Now, I was discovering my inherited culture – the one written in my blood.

I had inherited his eyes, his intensity, his intellect – and now, too, I could bear the knowledge of his shadows.

And I would carry it – without fear.

Young Giuseppe and Nonno Bartolo Verduci

24

Meeting Diego
(August 2023)

Unsettled by mirrors too heavy to bear

While millions watched the Matildas battle through their World Cup journey, bodies moving across manicured fields in choreographed pursuit of fleeting victory. I sat on an airplane bound for Sydney, my stomach knotted with a different kind of anticipation. The semi-final between Australia and England, my official reason for travel, had receded in importance compared to the meeting I'd arranged with my sister-in-law and my eldest Verduci half-brother, Diego. Soccer's fleeting drama paled in comparison to the lasting consequences this encounter might bring.

The harbour glittered in the afternoon sun as I navigated my rental car through the affluent eastern suburbs, the late winter sunshine casting long shadows across sprawling mansions with private jetties – a world apart from my Melbourne reality.

The GPS guided me through streets where houses presented perfect façades to the world, much like families themselves often do. Diego's home, when I arrived, was an elegant residence with water views, a prosperity that both reflected and complicated Joe's legacy.

This meeting had required delicate diplomacy. Diego had initially declined my indirect overtures. It was only his wife Lina's intervention, her quiet insistence that family connections should at least be acknowledged, that had secured my invitation.

In this branch of the Verduci family tree, the truth was in plain view: it was the in-law rather than the blood relative who recognised the moral imperative of connection, who understood that shared DNA created responsibilities that superseded personal preference.

Standing at their imposing front door, finger hovering over the doorbell, I reminded myself that blood ties create obligation rather than automatic welcome – a lesson I'd learned repeatedly throughout my search. The door swung open before I could ring, and there stood Lina – warm smile, appraising eyes – the intermediary between myself and the brother who had never known I existed until months ago.

Her immediate embrace contained a generosity that transcended the awkwardness of our situation, a humanity that acknowledged the fundamental strangeness of meeting siblings in middle age after a lifetime of separation.

I wasn't interested in forcing anyone to meet me – if they wanted to, great; if not, so be it. As Doris Day sang, *Che sarà, sarà* – whatever will be, will be. It might have disappointed me, but life offers no shortage of such moments. Life can also be wonderfully exciting, and you'll never have such experiences unless you move out of your comfort zone and test the waters.

During our visit, I also met my 5-year-old grandniece, who was only interested in watching her children's TV programme and eating green olives. We gathered around a large table in Diego's expansive home, sharing cheese, crackers, and a fine red wine. As conversation flowed, I found myself with countless questions about the father whose DNA I carried but whose life had been a mystery to me for nearly six decades.

Diego seemed puzzled by my interest in Joe, regarding my curiosity with wariness and incomprehension. His furrowed brow and shifting gaze betrayed the most significant revelation of our meeting: while I was seeking connection to a father I'd never known, Diego was wrestling with the trauma of having known him all too well. Our shared blood had produced vastly different relationships with the same man. He hadn't spoken to Giuseppe for close to 30 years. His children did not know they had a living grandfather.

'What do you want to know about him for?' Diego asked, his fingers tightening around his wine glass, knuckles whitening against the crystal. His voice maintained a studied casualness that his body betrayed – shoulders tensed as if bracing against an invisible blow.

Each question about Giuseppe seemed to reactivate old neural pathways of vigilance, his body remembering what his conscious mind worked to forget. The question revealed a profound gap in our experiences – where I saw a missing piece of my identity puzzle, he saw painful memories better left undisturbed.

I am an inquisitive type of person. I want to know how and why – it's always been part of my nature. And Joe, for better or worse, is my biological Father.

As our conversation deepened, Diego revealed disturbing details about Giuseppe that transformed my understanding of what it might have meant to grow up as his acknowledged child. Far from the gentle, philosophical old man I'd recently met, the Giuseppe of Diego's childhood had been harsh, violent, and terrifying. Far worse than my other Father, Vastiano, who to my recollection, only ever hit me once. I can still feel the burning sting of that smack across my face in public view.

'He belted us. He'd throw things at us. He made us kneel on grains of rice for punishment,' Diego said, his voice flat with old pain. These stories emerged haltingly, each revelation more disturbing than the last – a father who had once tied his son up beneath the house for days, who had compelled his children to commit acts of violence against animals and other children. I had seen hints of the old man's temper. It rarely shows itself now. At least not in my presence.

The most chilling moment came when Diego fell silent, his eyes distant, shaking his head, as if to cast the memories aside. 'There were other things,' he said quietly. 'Things I couldn't possibly share with you.' The weight of those unspoken horrors pressed against my chest, a shadow across our tentative connection.

In these revelations lay the most profound insight of our meeting. My lifelong yearning to know Giuseppe occurred alongside my siblings' struggle to recover from knowing him. The void I mourned may have shielded me from storms they survived. This paradox – that my loss might have been, in some ways, a protection – forced me to reconsider the narrative of abandonment I'd carried for decades.

Diego's stories aligned with what I'd gathered from Grizella and Stasia, and other members of the family, but provided darker, more specific examples. When he told me about Giuseppe throwing a chair at Stasia after she expressed interest in becoming a nun, shouting 'That's not what I educated you for!' I glimpsed the controlling, explosive man my siblings had endured – so different from the reflective elder who now cooks pasta in his cluttered kitchen and sends me poetic text messages. The Giuseppe who might have raised me.

The Giuseppe I had been spared. The Joe I was only now discovering.

All existing simultaneously in that Sydney dining room, time collapsing like an accordion, playing the strange music of our belated connection.

I asked Diego if Giuseppe had beaten his wife. 'No,' he said, but went on to say that Giuseppe had a gambling problem and other destructive behaviours. The boys had been taken to the races from a young age, and later worked with Giuseppe in Bungendore with the marijuana crops – linking them to his criminal activities and placing them at great risk.

With a sardonic smile, Diego shared a telling anecdote from his youth. When he was about 14, driving his father's car illegally with Giuseppe beside him, they were pulled over by a policeman. Giuseppe immediately feigned ignorance of English, asking his son in Italian, '*Cosa vuole questo cretino?*' (What does this idiot want?) When the officer explained that the underage boy was not permitted to drive, Giuseppe switched places until they were out of sight, then returned the wheel to his underage son: an apprenticeship in misdirection passed from father to son – a fleeting glimpse into a lifelong legacy.

As our visit ended, I found myself in the disorienting position of feeling grateful for my abandonment. The Giuseppe who rejected me had, perhaps unintentionally, spared me. I was deprived of a father but protected from a perpetrator of harm. This complex realisation – that abandonment might have been, in some ways, a blessing – represented the most significant shift in how I understood my origin story.

Diego's testimony had fundamentally reframed the narrative I'd constructed around our Father, requiring a complex psychological integration. The idealised father-figure I had occasionally imagined during childhood – the phantom parent who might have understood me better than my adoptive Father – dissolved against the concrete reality Diego described.

The man I had spent decades searching for had, during those same years, been inflicting wounds on his acknowledged children – wounds that stitched themselves into their bodies and psyches, scars that time could not erase. Their resentment was not abstract or philosophical – it lived in the muscles, the memories, the very architecture of survival, just as profoundly as his absence had shaped mine.

This cognitive dissonance initially created psychological turbulence. *How could I simultaneously mourn an absence and feel grateful for it?* It required a complete cognitive restructuring: what I had categorised as unambiguous injury needed to be reconceptualised as potentially containing elements of inadvertent protection. The integration of these seemingly incompatible realities demanded psychological flexibility beyond what most identity formation requires – the capacity to hold multiple contradictory truths simultaneously without attempting to resolve their fundamental opposition.

As I drove back to my hotel, Sydney's harbour twinkling in the distance, I felt the fragments of my identity shifting once again – not shattering as they had on that bus decades ago but rearranging themselves into a more complex pattern. The kaleidoscope of my identity turned, forming new constellations of understanding.

The father I had found was neither the monster of Diego's childhood nor the gentle philosopher of our recent lunches, but somehow both simultaneously – a man capable of cruelty and tenderness, of abandonment and connection, of harm and healing.

In this layered complexity lay perhaps the most important truth of my search: that no single story could contain the reality of biological connection. The same blood that had given me my eyes, my intellect, my determination had also carried the capacity for both creation and destruction. In accepting this contradiction – that Joe could be both wound and balm – I moved one step closer to the integration I had been seeking since that day on the bus in 1980.

25

A Seat at the Christmas Table
(November 2023/2024)

Building a bridge between theft and reckoning

Late 2023 brought a milestone – one I never dared name, yet recognised instantly. This was more than a meal: it was a cartography of identity, a carefully choreographed performance of family mythology where each gesture, each glance carried the weight of decades of unspoken narratives. This wasn't just a table but a tribunal of memory. And I – the unclaimed artefact – was placed in full view.

The restaurant hummed with a particular energy – that intricate ecosystem of family gatherings where obligation and affection dance their perpetual, complicated waltz. I was strategically seated next to Aunty Joanne, a placement that felt less coincidental and more like a carefully considered diplomatic positioning.

At over 80, Aunty Joanne remained a formidable presence. Her hands – mapped with blue veins, sun-freckled skin, the set lines on her face, and the slight tremor of age – told stories more complex than words could capture. She spoke of her late husband, whose absence still resonated in the quiet spaces between her words.

Her story unfolded like a delicate piece of family archaeology – each memory a fragment revealing deeper layers of pain and resilience. Her husband had been a successful real estate agent, then an instructor at university, embodying the immigrant narrative of generational ascension through education and professional achievement. Yet beneath this seemingly triumphant story lay a profound, unhealing wound – their inability to have children. Like my Mother's. Like mine. We were all childless.

The silence around their childlessness was a landscape of its own – a terrain of grief meticulously maintained, its boundaries marked by cultural expectations and personal sorrow.

I was later told that Aunty Joanne hadn't wanted to adopt – a detail that struck me with a peculiar resonance, given my own adoption story. *Was this a personal choice, or another manifestation of the cultural stigma that had shaped so many lives like mine?* The question hung in the air, unanswered but palpable.

Aunty Angela sat nearby, her sadness a tangible presence. I was told she was depressed – a condition possibly stemming from a previous illness, compounded by her husband's recent death. Her daughter's estrangement from the family added another layer of unspoken complexity, another fracture in the family's carefully maintained façade. So many questions still unanswered.

The arrival of a half-sibling brought an unexpected tension – a reminder that not every member of this clan was comfortable with my presence.

'I heard you're writing a book,' she announced with gusto, her words contumelious. 'You need to get everyone's permission.' I wondered if she was merely the messenger. I felt my body become tense – demanding a cordial restraint, given the setting. The irony was not lost on me – after decades of being denied my own story, I was now being told I needed permission to tell it. My inner response was a quiet defiance: I would not be silenced again, not by the very mechanisms of secrecy that had defined my existence. I smiled and replied, 'Really?'

Uncle Claude approached, his presence a welcome respite from the earlier confrontation. Now I sat between my Father's youngest brother and his eldest sister – perhaps not an accident, but a quiet acknowledgment that I belonged at the table. In that moment, I felt a warmth that transcended the complicated family dynamics – a connection both fragile and profound.

As I sat among my biological relatives, I was acutely aware of the 50 chairs that represented missed Christmases, lost connections, stolen moments of shared history. Each chair a birthday missed, each chair an Easter celebration where my absence wasn't even noticed, each chair a milestone where my achievements echoed in silent rooms where no Verduci heard them. These weren't just absences – they were entire universes of potential connection, systematically denied, erased, and stolen – from me, and from other bastards like me.

The laughter, the toasts, the birthday cakes uncut in my absence. For a moment, I saw an entire phantom table set just for me: place cards with no names, dishes never passed, glasses never raised in my honour.

Yet despite the bittersweet awareness, this gathering represented something remarkable – a tentative belonging. I was no longer an outsider desperately seeking connection, but a recognised, if not entirely embraced, member of the clan.

The Verduci Christmas lunch was more than a meal. It was a negotiation of identity, a delicate dance of inclusion and exclusion, a living testament to the complex ways families construct and deconstruct belonging.

As the afternoon light filtered through the restaurant windows, casting long shadows across faces both familiar and strange, I understood that my journey was not about finding a perfect, uncomplicated family. It was about understanding the beautiful, broken complexity of human connection – about learning to belong not by erasing differences, but by holding them with grace and compassion.

In this moment, surrounded by the familial cacophony, I remained in-between – not guest, not kin, just seated. I was becoming something else entirely – a bridge between what was lost and what might still be found.

But what was lost can never be retrieved. It can never be undone. In the months that followed, grief returned. Not the loud grief of death, but something quieter – an invisible loss, like a miscarriage.

Mine was a miscarriage not of nature, but of law. Of brutal societal norms that denied me my birthright – my place at the table.

The following year, 2024, I wondered if I would be invited to the Christmas gathering again. In the in-between year, I had met a cousin for coffee in Melbourne, I met another in Italy, and received a few birthday wishes. So, I was very surprised to find myself at Aunty Joanne's house for another family gathering. The invitation had arrived via my Papà, a casual invitation to dinner that belied the significance it held for me. His words contained no hint of the complex emotions they stirred – apprehension, hope, gratitude, and trepidation.

Aunty Joanne had cooked all the food. The kitchen benches groaned under the weight of tradition – handmade pork sausages, slow-simmered ragù, and antipasti arranged with an artistry that spoke of generations of practice. The now familiar sweet aroma of red roasted peppers and eggplant filled the air. The same dish Joe had cooked for me many times during the year.

Some of the dishes I was eating were probably passed down from her Calabrian Mother, and her Mother before that. I was experiencing generational cuisine. Each mouthful connected me to culinary lineages I had never known but somehow recognised, my palate responding to flavours that spoke to my DNA rather than my upbringing. I still felt like an outsider, an intruder, but most people made me feel very welcome.

A couple of siblings were there, whom I chose to circumspectly eschew, their tacit repudiation hanging palpably between us.

While I was deeply engrossed in a lengthy conversation with her daughter, my niece, my half-sibling approached and handed me a glass of champagne. I felt a knot in the pit of my stomach. Her sardonic words echoed still: *'Don't take it personally if I'm not interested in you.'*
Hesitantly, she clinked my glass, her eyes locked mine. She smiled apprehensively and said, 'Merry Christmas.' Confused, I replied, 'Merry Christmas.' She was a perplexing contradiction. Sometimes inimical – sometimes convivial. My hand hesitated for a beat. A flicker of something primal – an old, limbic hesitation – surged through me. *Was this a truce or a trap?* My smile came half a second before my nervous system caught up. The glasses touched, but something in my gut remained clenched, unconvinced.
She had been hovering – shooting nervous glances our way while her daughter revealed more family secrets.
This small gesture – the offering of champagne from a sister who had previously rejected me – carried more weight than casual observers could possibly understand. The glass, cool against my palm, represented a tentative bridge across a chasm of mistrust and resentment. Not reconciliation, not acceptance, but perhaps the first, fragile recognition that bonds of blood might eventually transcend bonds of resentment.
Someone passed me a dish of roast eggplant, and I thought of all the Christmases I'd spent with my adopted families – generous, warm, often joyful. I was never alone, but I was always aware of what was missing. Love was present; blood was absent.
Now, seated among my biological kin, I felt the strange, disorienting sensation of being both participant and observer – invited in, yet somehow peripheral. A simple gesture – a plate passed, a glance exchanged – carried the weight of 60 years.
I joined other conversations and eventually felt more relaxed. The wine softened the edges of my caution, and the familiar cadence of Italian-Australian English – that music of immigrants' children – washed over me like a forgotten lullaby.

I learnt that soon I would become a great-aunt again. This child would be born 'out of wedlock,' such an archaic and judgemental phrase. However, there was no suggestion that the child would be hidden away in a cold and harsh institution for spurned, sinful women or that the baby would be handed over to the upbringing of total strangers, never to be seen again.

No, this child would be warmly embraced and cared for by its village.

The revelation struck me with poignancy – this unborn child, conceived in circumstances that would have once brought shame and secrecy, would be welcomed into the family fold without question. The contrast with my own beginning could not have been starker. *What fundamental shifts in cultural norms, in family values, in societal expectations had occurred in the 60 years separating my birth from this child's? How many women's lives had been irreparably altered, how many families permanently fractured, by attitudes that now seemed as antiquated as horse-drawn carriages on modern highways?*

As I looked around – faces young and old, some known for decades, some only recently discovered – I reflected on how the Verduci family's hidden stories had shifted across generations. Once, children born outside marriage had been erased, denied, or hidden away – adopted out like me, kept by brave mothers like my cousin's, or perhaps lost altogether. Yet, here we were in 2024 – the descendants of both sanctioned unions and forbidden liaisons – gathered side by side. What shame had once scattered us, time and courage had begun to heal. The bloodlines that had splintered were, in their imperfect way, beginning to reweave themselves.

My vessel hadn't just been mended – it had become a chalice, brimming with hard-won belonging. It was filling – slowly, tenderly – with love and connection. Perhaps this is what healing looks like after decades of fracture – not a perfect restoration of what might have been, but the quiet creation of something new from the remnants of what remains. My place in this family would always bear the seams of our separated history, yet those very marks were beginning to form the outline of a new narrative – one that acknowledged brokenness, but refused to be bound by it.

As I watched my niece and nephew circulate through Aunty Joanne's living room, their movements casual and unselfconscious, I recognised that my integration into this family would always be different from theirs. They had been born into this belonging; I had fought for it, excavated it from decades of secrecy and denial. Their place at the Christmas table was assumed; mine had required archaeology, persistence, and courage.

Yet, there was something valuable in this difference – a perspective they could never possess, an appreciation for connection they could never fully understand. The seams showed, but perhaps that was the point. I was beginning to understand that fractures weren't something to hide – they were the very lines along which this strange, shimmering mosaic of family might eventually hold. My place in this family tapestry was distinctive – stitched through fracture and repair, the golden seams no longer hidden but essential to its enduring beauty.

A month later, I was celebrating my first, and perhaps only, Christmas with my Papà. The three of us huddled in his tiny kitchen as he prepared a lavish lunch. The smell of roasting bacon, resting atop oysters, seeped through the oven door. Big, fat prawns danced in a pool of olive oil. He added a sprinkle of this and that – slowly, but deftly – revelling in his culinary creation.

On the small kitchen table sat a carefully arranged salad: chopped home grown tomatoes, sliced red onion, capers, artichokes, nasturtiums from the garden, dressed with olive oil and red wine vinegar. The aroma of roasting red peppers and eggplant, an obligatory addition to most meals, filled the air. As I lifted the wine glass to take a sip, the fruity waft of Italian red tickled my nostrils.

The moment was the best Christmas gift I had ever received. All the more so, as the next drama unfolded.

My Papà and his partner had an altercation. She had been in a foul mood all morning. In his pent-up frustration – the anger I knew was always just below the surface but well-contained in my presence – my Papà said some fiery words. As he fiercely turned towards her, he lost his balance and fell to the ground with a heavy thud, hitting a makeshift shelf along the way. Papers, books, and knick-knacks came flying and tumbled to the ground, scattering in all directions.

His partner went to his aid. He roared, '*Vattene via!*' (Get out of here.) She leapt out of her seat and ran out the door, down the long, darkened hallway – never to be seen again.

For a moment, I was frozen in stunned silence. Not like the helpless child, but as a shocked adult, still getting to know my Papà. The shock quickly passed, and I helped him up. Then I took a big sip of wine. A lunch for three became an intimate moment with my Father on our first Christmas together.

As usual, I asked, and he shared fragments of his former life – as Giuseppe, that enigmatic figure who had been surreptitiously kept from me. He mentioned Mark, Chopper Read, Winchester, Arthur Calwell, Jim Cairns, Malcolm Fraser, Ian Sinclair, Don McKay – names dropped casually, interspersed with tales of his earlier life as Giuseppe u Mulinov. He had been an altar boy and later joined the Communist Party after an altercation with a priest. I sat eating and drinking, like a child listening in wonder to fairy tales.

Our eventful and intimate lunch ended in a warm embrace. I then drove to my second Christmas lunch with my first family. I sat at the table where I had always been welcome. My spiritual family – their love forming the first golden seams that held me together.

Across the decades, their quiet, steadfast affection stitched invisible threads through my life, keeping me from completely unravelling. Without knowing it, they had tethered me to belonging – a delicate weave of memory, loyalty, and unconditional love.

These threads, though often stretched thin by distance and time, had endured. And now, surrounded by those quiet, enduring threads of connection, they gathered around me again – not to erase what had been torn, but to reinforce what remained.

On that day, I was finally able to weave in some previously lost fragments. The vessel mending, glowing and becoming unified.

Papà Joe's Christmas lunch (2024)

26

Carpe Diem (2024)

Wounds carved in the chambers, where wisdom dwells

When I hadn't heard from Joe for some time after our initial meetings and the first family Christmas gathering – a silence that once might have triggered abandonment anxiety – I stayed steady. I persisted with gentle tenacity, sending soft nudges: 'When can we catch up again?'
We exchanged messages over the Christmas holiday while I endured Queensland's oppressive summer heat. I sent photos from my trip, maintaining the thread of connection with the Father I had just discovered.
Each photo, a fragment in the mosaic of rediscovery. Each reply from him, a fragile bridge across the chasm of time that had separated us.

When I returned to Melbourne's milder climate, he invited me to his home for lunch – a significant escalation in intimacy from our neutral restaurant encounters. When I arrived, he was outside attending to his vegetable garden. The scent of tomatoes ripening on vines unfurling skyward, the musty odour, and the fragrance of autumn lingering in the air. This was the father I had imagined – not the complex person with the long and varied history that I had read about online. I couldn't help but contrast the younger, violent man of legend with the gentler vegetable gardener before me.
'I'm going to teach you how to cook pasta,' he announced with the certainty of a man who knew some roots run deeper than the

span of lost time. Some inheritances, especially those passed down over a stovetop, defied time. In our world, food was love. It had always been the way.

I smiled at the irony – the father who had missed every milestone now teaching me how to boil pasta. Papà Joe still saw me, on some level, as the child he had never known. Still believed there were fatherly roles he could fulfil – even now.

His home revealed aspects of his character that our restaurant meetings had concealed – the organised chaos of his kitchen, the eclectic collections reflecting diverse interests, the arrangement of furniture that accommodated his reading habits and preferences. Open books lay scattered across every surface – philosophy, science, history, law, politics, astronomy – each one a quiet declaration of the rich and varied world within the old scholar.

He cooked an elaborate lunch in his overstuffed kitchen, navigating between counters and appliances with the practised movements of someone who had transformed necessity into art. Olive oil splattering in a frying pan made the chopped onions dance about. A pinch of oregano. A dash of salt and pepper. Cans of tomatoes. The pan's contents danced the Tarantella. In a small griller oven, he was roasting red peppers, eggplant, and potato. The combined aroma, a perfect match. 'I amuse myself with cooking,' he said with characteristic understatement, but the complexity of his preparations belied this casual framing. This wasn't mere sustenance but expression, communication through ingredients and techniques rather than words.

He explained that his maternal Grandmother, Francesca, had taught him to cook – a detail that added another strand in the web of family connections I was slowly mapping, another point of heritage that had unknowingly shaped my own culinary preferences.

The meal unfolded in courses: fried prawns for an entrée with a dipping sauce he had concocted – a hint of mango rose from the

dish; red fried onion with chopped tomatoes transitioning to meat that had been slow cooked to tenderness; flat fettuccine coated in a sauce whose recipe spanned generations and continents; fresh Italian bread to accompany each element.
We had a glass of Italian red wine, its tannic complexity matching the layered conversation that unfolded over hours, him doing most of the talking while I listened with the eagerness of someone making up for decades of silence. Sometimes he lurched into highbrow Italian, reciting poetry or passages from Machiavelli's *Il Principe* – one of his favourite books. Often, I had to stop him and ask for translations.
My knowledge of Italian is limited to everyday conversations I had with my Mother. Then he segued into discussing how the Universe was formed and emphasised that Calabrians were responsible for many inventions. Quizzing my knowledge of these topics – there is only ever one correct answer which infuriates my sensibilities. He is completely stubborn and proud.
It was a stinking hot Melbourne late summer's day, the kind where the air feels thick and immobile, where even breathing becomes a conscious effort. The heat intensified the aromas emanating from the kitchen – garlic, basil, tomato, olive oil – scents that transported me across hemispheres to a homeland I'd never known but somehow recognised in my marrow.
When I finally left, my friend picked me up and we went to Carlton Cemetery looking for Uncle John's grave. I developed a severe, twisting pain in my gut, spreading like wildfire through my abdomen. I was desperate to go to the toilet, but the cemetery offered no facilities, no respite from this sudden biological urgency. The pain increased; I was desperate. I hurriedly walked to the nearby old section of the cemetery. I found a secluded spot.
Relief.
We left and went searching for the old family home on Lygon Street, Carlton. We drove past Princes Hill High School, where the younger uncles went to school.

More pain erupted in my gut, sudden and violent. Cold sweat beaded on my forehead despite the heat. My body was revolting, betraying me in this moment of ancestral pilgrimage. It was peak hour traffic time – I would not make it home. I desperately had to relieve myself again. We were near Princes Park, and I knew there were public toilets there. I had a bout of severe gut-aching gastro.

Had my Papà Joe tried to poison me?
The thought flashed through my mind, unbidden and alarming – a primitive fear response connecting ancient taboos about food and family with my physical distress. The trained psychologist in me recognised the irrational thought pattern even as my body continued its revolt.

I've never told him.

A few weeks later, soon after that eventful day, we lunched at his favourite hotel again.

There, he told me that he thought I might kill him. I didn't tell him that I had harboured the same primitive fear – that perhaps he might have tried to kill me. A darkly comic symmetry: he feared I might shoot him for abandoning me as a child, while I had briefly wondered if he'd poisoned me at our first shared meal. I laughed. I'm not the violent vindictive type, even though at times I've had many an evil thought, but not about him.

'Revenge is a waste of time,' we both agreed.

Sitting across from Papà Joe, I could simultaneously hold three realities: the abandoned infant I once was, the searching adult I had been, and this present moment of connection. Past, recent past, and present no longer blurred painfully into each other but formed a coherent timeline I could navigate at will.

The Sunday lunch at Papà Joe's became a new ritual between us. He insisted on cooking, preparing elaborate multi-course Italian meals that seemed to compensate for 60 years of absence. 'I couldn't feed you when you were young, at least I can feed you now,' he said, placing another helping of homemade pasta before me. The simple statement contained volumes –

acknowledgment, regret, and a tentative offering.

As we ate, he would tell stories of Calabria, his eyes brightening when describing his Grandmother's kitchen, or the village paths he'd roamed as a boy. These weren't merely anecdotes but offerings of heritage being passed across the chasm of our separation. In these moments, I glimpsed what might have been, had circumstances been different.

Sitting in the ramshackle old run-down kitchen, watching his strong but slow hands prepare pasta with the same movements my adoptive Mother had used decades earlier, I saw how identity forms like sedimentary rock – layer upon layer of experience, biology, choice, and chance, compressed into something solid yet still containing the evidence of its formation.

The recipe wasn't identical – his contained pieces of pork on bone and chillies where hers had used minced meat and sweet basil – but the meaning was the same. Food represented love. This culinary language transcended our decades of separation, creating a bridge between the Mother who had raised me, and the Father I had found too late, but much better than never.

At our next lunch at Papà Joe's favourite hotel, he said that I was to pick him and his partner up and drive to the hotel. I figured he was now certain that I wouldn't kill him.

When I dropped him off, he suggested that the following week, we would go for a country drive to Ballarat, to which I eagerly agreed. I love road trips.

He asked me to come in. We went to the back garden of the empty house next door. There were two big old fig trees, their twisted trunks and gnarled branches reaching skyward like arthritic hands seeking the sun. I caressed the big gnarly bark, tracing the round knobbly contours. Their shade created a small oasis of coolness in the summer heat.

The fragrance and taste of the figs dripping with sticky sweetness took me back to my old Faraway Tree. I smiled to myself as I reminisced. My Papà Joe collected figs and gave me a bag of them.

The following Sunday, I drove us to Ballarat. We went to Sovereign Hill – and then we had a picnic by Lake Wendouree. We feasted on fresh Italian bread, mortadella, salami, ham, cheese, tomato, and Italian sausage – a spread that could have been transported directly from a Calabrian hillside. It was a beautiful sunny autumnal day. Ballarat streets were a symphony of autumn colours – yellows, reds, oranges, and browns – backlit by a clear blue sky that seemed to celebrate our belated connection. Papà Joe gently fed the black swans, alert to the scent of food. The gesture – this man who had once abandoned me now nurtured creatures with such tenderness – stirred something profound within me. Warm fuzzy feelings arose.

The following week, a public holiday beckoned us toward Mildura, a border town where two states meet – an apt metaphor for my own existence between identities. The journey stretched before us, kilometres of Australian landscape rolling past our windows, creating space for conversation to unfold at its own pace, without the constraints of restaurant hours or social expectations.

In Mildura, we went to an Orange Farm. While sitting in the car park, Papà Joe told me about his past enemies. I told the Calabrian lady inside the small shop how I eventually found my elderly Father. She was intrigued by my story.

On our way from Mildura to Swan Hill, I asked Papà Joe, 'Why did you choose your first wife?'

'She was very, very religious and I wanted an obedient woman,' he replied. He sadly recounted her tragic death following a stroke. 'She was left blind and did not have the will to live on…' he told me. Like many of his stories, I wasn't entirely sure where fact ended and embellishment began, but the choice of details – what he emphasised and what he glossed over – revealed as much about him as any verifiable truth might have. He spoke of her fondly and I noticed his eyes reddening and a slight shake in his voice as he told the story.

Papà Joe told me that he wanted to have at least six children. In 1969, with three children and a wife pregnant with her fourth, he had to suddenly go overseas. He had to leave Australia. I was told that *'someone had died'*.

When I questioned him about this story, he told me that he was on 'work business'. He was chasing someone, and he couldn't tell me any more information. He was on secret business. *'Silence is my master,'* is his mantra. It has also become mine to a certain degree. Some aspects of his storytelling I cannot share.

His cryptic references to 'business' and 'silence' carried ominous undertones given what I now knew about his criminal connections. The timing of his sudden departure from Australia coincided with periods of heightened law enforcement attention to organised crime – *was he fleeing potential prosecution? Had he witnessed something he shouldn't have?*

I'm left to surmise what his secret men's business may have been about.

He went to Paris, and he was able to learn some French. Just before his younger brother John died, prophetically, he had told Giuseppe, 'You need to learn French because one day you're going to need it.' Later Papà Joe told me that while he was in France he went to 'spy' school and that he has worked for Russia, the USA, the UK, and ASIO. Sometimes his stories are so elaborate and fanciful, yet some of them are also there in black and white on the internet for anyone to read.

The more outlandish claims about spy school and international intelligence work strained credibility, yet I couldn't dismiss them entirely. The documented connections between organised crime and intelligence agencies during the Cold War period made even these fantastic stories potentially plausible.

Was he embellishing to impress me? Confusing fantasy with reality in his advanced age? Did he have an overactive imagination that now confused fact with fiction? Or had his criminal connections intersected with the shadowy world of international espionage?

The uncertainty was another fragment in the already complex mosaic of his identity.

The following week we went on another day trip and another picnic at Hanging Rock – that mysterious geological formation immortalised in Australian literature as a place of disappearance and transformation. The ancient form loomed above us, its presence a testament to time's patient power to reshape even the most resistant materials. The symbolism wasn't lost on me as we spread our picnic near the ancient stones. This place of vanishing and return seemed appropriate for our story – I too had disappeared from my biological narrative, only to reappear decades later, changed by the journey.

Those months became a season of discovery, a rare, fertile period when connection and memory blossomed alongside the autumn leaves

Soon followed the first lunch at my house – I let Papà Joe do the cooking, roast peppers, eggplant, sausages, and potatoes, in the same way his Grandmother had prepared for him.

We went to see *Tosca* – the performance disappointing, voices straining where they should soar, staging static where it should flow. They whinged the whole time, Papà Joe and his partner, their critical commentary a running counterpoint to the opera. I found myself entertained more by their biting analysis than by the performance itself, another unexpected inheritance from this man whose DNA I carry: a critical eye, an unwillingness to accept mediocrity, a certain imperviousness to social pressure that manifests as blunt honesty where others might offer polite silence.

The next outing was to the *Festa dell'Italia* at the Calabria Club in Bulla. We listened to opera and Italian folk music, the melodies stirring something in me that transcended conscious memory – perhaps some cellular recognition of sounds that had shaped my biological heritage for generations before my birth. As the sounds of the 'Tarantella' began and people rose from their seats to dance to a cultural song about snake bites and frenzied dancing, I caught Papà Joe watching me – gauging my reaction, perhaps wondering if music might be another inheritance he had unknowingly bestowed.

The music created a temporal bridge, connecting me to him. A lineage I was only beginning to understand.

I would relish these rare outings with my elderly Father, each one adding another tile to the mosaic of our relationship. With each encounter, I felt a stronger connection with him and a greater sense of belonging to the Verduci clan, even if I would never be fully welcomed by the whole family. These shared moments far exceeded what I could have imagined in those decades of searching – finding a father, building an actual relationship with him, creating memories to partially fill the vast empty space of our shared history.

Papà Joe had a sudden change of heart – 'Stuff it! We can't take it with us!' We talked about going to Italy later that year in September, where we would see a real opera in Verona.

I pinched myself, a childlike gesture to verify this wasn't merely another dream of connection – like those that had sustained and tortured me through decades of searching. A genuine relationship unfolded day by day, month by month, year by precious year, each encounter added another thread to the tapestry of our belated bond.

More lunches followed with my friends and adopted family. They were eager to meet this eccentric old man, this missing piece of my biological puzzle.

On a cold, dreary, and wet Melbourne winter's night in July, Papà Joe and his partner attended my 60th birthday. It was a small gathering of my closest family and dearest friends – an intimate circle now expanded to include the Father I had found just in time. His presence represented something profound – the first time a member of my biological families had attended a significant event in my life. His face flickered in mine – a silent inheritance the candles could not hide. After 60 years of absence, he sat among those who have chosen and have been chosen by me, bearing witness to this milestone that marked my age and the extraordinary journey that had brought us to this moment. I was proud to be able to integrate all aspects of my social life – old friends, the family I had always known, and the new, recently acquired family. My identity was like a mosaic: the distinct pieces of my history arranged into a coherent image, each element influencing and being influenced by the others. The arrangement showed the journey of these fragments – not disguising the breaks where they met but honouring the unique path that brought them together.

As my relationship with my Papà Joe deepened, I began to realise that my story wasn't ending with finding him – it was evolving into something new. The search that had defined so much of my life was transforming into a different kind of journey – one of integration, understanding, and eventually, inner peace, acceptance, and letting go of past hurts, loss, and trauma – simply appreciating the present moment.

What had begun as a quest for origins was becoming something far more profound: a meditation on the nature of forgiveness, the elasticity of human connection, and the possibility that even the deepest wounds might, with time and courage, become sources of wisdom rather than only pain.

Those early blissful years after my Father, Sebastiano's death, before my Mother's remarriage, had given me a template for what peace might feel like. Though brief, that period had shown me that identity could heal and reconfigure after trauma – that new patterns could emerge from brokenness. It had taught me that integration was not only possible but inevitable – when broken pieces are held with care and time is allowed to work its quiet miracles.

27

Redemption
(September 2024)

Fractures mended with golden seams

The journey that began with shattered fragments was approaching its completion – not an ending, but a transformation – the broken pieces not discarded but integrated, not replaced but recontextualised within a larger whole. Whole yet marked, a vessel reborn through its breaking.
After decades of searching, after finding Giuseppe and building a fragile but meaningful connection with him and parts of the Verduci clan, one final pilgrimage remained – to the ancestral soil from which all displacement and reunion had sprung.
I had meant to travel to Italy with my Papà Joe, his partner, and a friend – a journey of generations returning together, multiple perspectives witnessing the same landscapes through different historical lenses. Instead, I found myself travelling alone, the solitary nature of the trip both a disappointment and opportunity.
After picking up a hire car at Roma's Leonardo da Vinci Airport – named for another Italian known for both artistic and scientific precision, a duality I recognised in myself – I drove through rugged, mountainous Italian countryside toward the seaside town of Maratea.
There, on a solitary walk through the town, I realised how profoundly my relationship with my once-fragmented identity had transformed. The pieces hadn't disappeared – the adopted

child, the abandoned infant, the searching adult, the professional woman, the newly discovered daughter, sister, and niece – but had been acknowledged, examined, and carefully arranged into something new that honoured rather than denied their distinctiveness.

The breaking had been necessary for the rebuilding.

After two nights, I meandered southward, driving along the Amalfi Coast – a drive that mirrored my journey: slow, frustrating, and beautiful. I took a deliberate detour via Eboli, Campania – Ursula's hometown – but I didn't linger. I continued further south to Reggio.

I checked into my hotel on the calm water's edge, looking across the Messina Strait to Sicily – the land that had shaped the emotional geography of my childhood through my adoptive parents' origins. A place to which I felt an inexplicable, deeply spiritual connection, despite having no biological ties.

In the distance, Mt Etna sat – majestic, watchful, and calm. From my balcony, I could see three places forming a geographic triangle: Reggio Calabria, Eboli, and Sicily – an unholy trinity that had made me who I was, through a complicated alchemy of presence and absence, connection and severance, inheritance and choice.

This triangle mirrored the psychological one I had navigated for much of my life: my biological heritage, my adoptive upbringing, and the self I had constructed in the space between.

Standing at this confluence of bloodlines and histories, I felt a strange sense of completion – not because all questions had been answered or all wounds healed, but because I could finally hold all these contradictory truths at once, without splitting.

Although I was tired and anxious, travelling alone in Calabria, I made my solitary pilgrimage with intent – tracing a path through southern Italy to Motticella, a village now reduced to a ghost town. Bordered by the Bruzzano River – the birthplace of my paternal Bisnonni (great-grandparents).

As I slowly drove through the sun-drenched, rugged countryside,

I compared the woman I was now to the girl I had been. On that bus in 1980, it had felt as though the earth cracked beneath me with every step. Now, my hands gripped the steering wheel with quiet certainty, guiding me along unfamiliar roads with a sense of groundedness I'd once thought impossible.

The girl on that bus had watched her world collapse when a stranger shattered everything she thought she knew about herself.

The woman in this car felt the earth hold her steady – driving toward a village where DNA had originated but not destined her. Along the way, I passed signs for Anna di Melito di Porto Salvo and Montebello Jonico – towns where my Bisnonno Andrea, and my Nonno Bartolo had once lived.

These names – once abstract – now belonged to real places, warmed by sun, shaped by hills, and grounded in earth.

With each kilometre, biological heritage shifted from concept to experience.

I approached a sign that read Motticella – the letters faded by sun and weather, a marker separating the world I'd always known from the one that shaped my blood.

The countryside unfolded in undulations of olive groves and vineyards, punctuated with contorted prickly pears, their twisted forms reaching skyward with arthritic hands. Once foreign to this soil, now flourishing – these plants mirrored my own adopted existence.

Another sign marked the entrance to the village proper, population 155 according to the faded numerals beneath the name.

I stopped the car and stepped out onto the hard, dusty ground. The engine's ticking was the only sound disturbing the profound rural tranquillity. The dry, warm air carried scents both unfamiliar and strangely recognisable – wild herbs, sun-weathered stone, the distant saline tang of the Mediterranean. A deeper blue Calabrian sky stretched above me – more saturated and intense compared to the lighter blue that had witnessed my shattering, that spring day in 1980 on bus route 534. The northern Mediterranean sun beamed down, warming my skin in a way that felt ancestral – as though my cells remembered this quality of light falling once on relatives who never knew I existed.

The solid earth below my feet was dry and brown, sandy-coloured pebbles pressed into my sandals – grounding me in this place.

As I stood on the dusty soil, I felt the last of my seven enigmatic fragments click firmly into place.

The cultural heritage I'd sensed but couldn't name now had geography, architecture, light, and air. I breathed in the same Calabrian air my ancestors had, squinted against the same Mediterranean sun, heard the same church bells that had oriented their days.

The fifth fragment – cultural origins – was no longer abstract but palpably real beneath my feet.

The seven enigmatic pieces that had defined my search were now assembled into something resembling a whole. Not perfect, not unmarked by their separation – but recognisably complete:

1. My physical appearance – eyes, build, mannerisms – now had context in the faces of my Papà, my half-siblings, aunts, uncles, and the photographs of ancestors.
2. The name 'Giuseppe' had transformed from a whispered secret to a flesh-and-blood Father with a complex, human history.
3. My biological heritage had expanded from a void to a rich tapestry connecting me to this ancient village and its people.
4. My medical history, though still incomplete, was no longer entirely blank.
5. My cultural inheritance had taken root – in this soil, in these stone houses, in the air I breathed.
6. My family history – once absent – now held names, faces and relationships I could finally trace.

7. My psychological self had gathered these fragments and shaped them into something coherent: a whole that honoured both fracture and healing.

Seven – a sacred and mystical number. A symbol of completeness, introspection, spiritual awakening, and the pursuit of inner wisdom.

I took photos with my phone and sent them to my Papà Joe, back home in Melbourne. As I pressed send, I marvelled at the technology that could bridge hemispheres in seconds – a connection that transcended absence.

There I stood on the soil that had formed him, capturing images he would view in a country that had transformed him. The photos travelled instantly across a distance that had once taken months by ship – connecting the old world to the new, the past to the present, the Father I had only recently found to the ancestral village he had left seven decades ago.

This digital bridge collapsed 60 years of separation into mere seconds – creating yet another form of integration: a shared experience of place, across vast distance.

I imagined him walking through these streets as a young boy – gun in hand, Giuseppe u Mulinov, as the leader of his pack – or carrying goods beside his Father as they travelled from town to town on foot.

I surveyed the undulating landscape, letting my gaze follow the hills to the dazzling, jewelled sea in the distance. I breathed in the hot afternoon air – slowly, deliberately.

A stillness settled in me.

My heart was full, my body at ease, my mind clear – mindful and present, a gentle and peaceful whole.

Standing on Calabrian soil in Motticella, I realised how profoundly my understanding of family had transformed.

The girl on the bus – whose world had fractured in an instant – could only see in binaries: real family versus false family, truth versus lies, belonging versus alienation. Black and white. Either/or. Mine or not mine.

That fragmented perception shaped decades of my life – my relationships, my decisions, my very sense of self. It had been a prison built from opposites, each wall an impassable dichotomy. But here, beneath the same sky that had once witnessed my ancestors' lives, I recognised the spectrum that lived between those absolutes.

Family, I realised, was not a binary – it was a palimpsest. Layers of truth, concealment, inheritance, and invention.

Identity was not whole or broken, but evolving.

Belonging was not complete or absent, but partial, contextual, and self-authored.

Now, I saw family as a constellation of connections – biological and chosen, present and absent, harmful and healing. The very capacity to hold these contradictions marked the journey from fragmentation to integration.

I could trace the evolution in my own writing: from the fractured syntax of my journal entries after the bus revelation to the reflective clarity I now carried. The fragments had not vanished; they had been acknowledged, honoured, and reassembled into a mosaic – a beauty born not despite the breaking, but because of it.

The girl on the bus, who had once felt her foundations crack beneath her, now stood rooted in a more complex truth – that identity was neither singular nor fixed, but multiple, evolving, alive.

I was Mirella Di Benedetto.

I was Anna Zunica.

I am now Mirella Anna Verduci.

I am my Mother Michelina and my Father, Sebastiano's daughter, and Giuseppe's *cara bimba*.

I was all of these, and more – determined, resilient, psychologist, friend, seeker, finder.

I was the product of both nature and nurture, of presence and absence, of truths told and secrets kept.

The seven fragments that once seemed impossible to reconcile now formed a mosaic – a beauty perhaps more compelling for having been broken.

The golden seams between my fragments no longer symbolised possibility; they had become reality. They didn't diminish the whole – they enhanced it. They told the story not only of breaking, but of mending: of deliberate reassembly, more beautiful for acknowledging its scars.

No longer a fragmented enigma, my parts were now intertwined with golden strings of hope, love, and joy.

And in that multiplicity, I had finally found wholeness – a wholeness greater than the sum of its parts.

The prodigal offspring was finally home.

The psychological paradox revealed through my siblings' testimonies continued to reverberate through my consciousness as I stood in Motticella:

I had spent decades yearning for the father I never knew, spinning elaborate fantasies about what life might have been had he claimed me – while they had spent those same decades recovering from knowing him too well.

Standing on these ancient stones, breathing this Mediterranean air, I saw Giuseppe's journey with new clarity.

The harshness my siblings described – his volatility, his cruelty – took on different dimensions here. This village, with its stark beauty and unforgiving terrain, had forged men who survived through toughness, who carried the weight of familial expectations across oceans.

Had I grown up as Giuseppe's acknowledged daughter, I would have experienced that same hardness – the discipline he imposed on my siblings, the rigid boundaries he inherited from his own Father, the brittle love shaped by survival, not tenderness.

The narrow streets of Motticella – where everyone knew everyone's business, and survival had long depended on family loyalty and strict adherence to tradition – helped me understand how Giuseppe became both the charismatic businessman and the tyrannical father my siblings described.

The same Mediterranean sun that now warmed my face had once hardened his resolve; the same village gossip that might have followed an unwed mother and her child had pushed him toward denying my existence.

Soon after, I returned home and went to visit my Papà Joe. His immediate joy at my unexpected arrival, after a month's absence, was touching.

As I stood in his driveway surrounded by a myriad of trinkets – some rusty, some broken – hanging from fences or scattered on the ground, an old artefact caught my eye. It shimmered in the evening light like a wound made visible.

He said he had found it at a trash and treasure market.

The object was oval-shaped and rounded, flat at the bottom, so it could stand. The top tapered up and was cut off at an angle. A teardrop-shaped hole pierced the centre. Its surface was covered in a fine lattice of delicate cracks.

It was a literal metaphor of my journey.

I lifted it off the fence and traced its fractures. I decided I would take it home and honour its damage with gold, bronze, and silver metallic paint.

My brush followed lines in deliberate strokes, each golden seam an act of recognition, each fracture a quiet hymn to resilience. As the gold began to softly shimmer, I recognised my reflection in every fissure – not broken but remade.

It now proudly sits on my writing desk – a constant reminder of my life's odyssey.

I looked at it and thought: *Perhaps this is what Nietzsche meant by amor fati – not merely to accept the cracks, but to love them. To see their necessity in the shape of who I've become.*

Not because I remembered it all.

But because I finally spoke.

Me and my Papà Joe (2024)

Interlude 3

A Message from my Papà Joe

È sempre bello leggere i tuoi messaggi. Si sta vivendo un periodo di tempo transitoriale, a volte anche incompreso, per le sue memorie o per il periodo del tempo in cui esse sono avvenute. Malgrado tutti gli eventi che il tempo ha presentato, oggi, in quel fascio che avvolge il tempo passato, ci siamo avvolti anche io e te. Memorie gioiose e periodi deplorevoli. Il sentimento di averti incontrata sotterra tutte le avversità. Hai superato il male dei mali. Hai sofferto umiliazioni impossibili da descrivere tutte.
È glorioso che oggi è possibile che io e te possiamo essere in comunicazione. Ti voglio bene come tutto il resto dei tuoi fratelli e sorelle.

It is always beautiful to read your messages. We are living through a transitory time – at times misunderstood, both for its memories and for the period in which those memories occurred. Despite all the events that time has presented, today, in that bundle that wraps around the past, you and I are also now wrapped within it. Joyful memories – and deplorable periods. The feeling of having met you buries all adversity. You have overcome the worst of evils; you have suffered humiliations that are impossible to fully describe. It is glorious that today it is possible for you and me to be in communication. I care for you deeply – just as I do for all your brothers and sisters.

Author's Interlude

My story arrived in fragments – some jagged, some hidden, others buried.
For decades I raged against the silence, holding the fragile pieces together.
Writing this memoir flung open closets full of skeletons.
Memory came like ash – light, fragile, formed by intention.
Sifting. Recalling. Piece by piece. Syllable by syllable.
Each brushstroke revealing the past.
The narrative was not orderly. No triumphant happy end.
Bits – held together by metaphor, DNA, and the need to know.
As the story unfolded, I understood that I was forming a whole from what was taken. Stolen.
Reclaiming hidden voices, once shamed.
A reckoning.
This memoir is my kintsugi – a vessel that can now speak its truth.
The lacquer while golden – is also rage, and grief-stricken.
If you carry your own scars – may you find the courage to gently hold them.
If you choose, as I have, to caress them into narrative, may it be your own – a reckoning with truth. A letting go.
This was my journey.
The mirror I broke open – to finally be at peace with myself.

Driving to Motticella (September 2024)

Looking out to the sea from Motticella

Looking out from Reggio to Mt Etna (2024)

Motticella

Epilogue: Blood Memory

Every ending becomes a new beginning.

The golden light of Calabria warmed my skin with an ancestral familiarity, as if my cells remembered this sun long before my mind could. It didn't erase my fractures; it revealed them – gilded and gleaming – as essential elements of a reconstructed whole. The vessel that shattered on that Melbourne bus has been rebuilt into something more complex: a consciousness that can hold contradiction without disintegration.

The Golden Seams: A Kintsugi Reflection
Kintsugi: Breaks mended by gold, celebrated – becoming the most precious part of the vessel's history.
My life had been such a vessel. Each fragment – my adoption, the bus ride that shattered my identity, the years of searching, the rejections, the discoveries – represented a break. But these were not weaknesses to be concealed. They were the golden seams that connect my disparate experiences, threading meaning through what could have remained irreparably broken. The golden lacquer of understanding seeped through the cracks of my experience. My birth mother's silence, my adoptive parents' complicated love, my Papà's complex history – these were not flaws to be ashamed of, but essential elements that give me a unique form and strength.
Transformation didn't come from erasing the breaks, but from illuminating them. Each golden weave represented a moment of resilience, a choice to integrate rather than hide, to understand rather than judge.
I was not whole despite my fractures. I was whole because of them.

Truth, I discovered, was never singular – not a name on a certificate nor a single biological fact, but a mosaic of silences, guesses, contradictions, and recognitions. Some truths were withheld, others distorted, and some only emerged when I was strong enough to receive them. In the end, the search for my Father was also a search for what truth could survive abandonment – and what kind of truth I could live with. Beneath the same sky that witnessed my ancestors' lives, I understood that the gold connecting my fragments wasn't external validation or perfect knowledge, but *meaning* – forged from decades of seeking, from absence remade into presence, from loss remade into discovery.

Standing on Calabrian soil, I realised how my understanding of home had evolved. The peace I'd briefly known in those years with my Mother after my Father Sebastiano's death had been my first lesson in belonging – not a place but a feeling of safety, of being seen.

That period had planted seeds of resilience that would eventually flower into the capacity to create my own sense of home amid the fragments of my identity. Those blissful years, though temporary, had been as crucial to my formation as the trauma that preceded and followed them.

The Calabrian sun differed from the Australian light I'd known all my life – softer, more golden, casting shadows that whispered stories across ancient stones rather than declaring them with harsh clarity. The light here filtered through olive leaves in dappled patterns, illuminating dust motes that seemed to dance between centuries rather than merely marking time.

Standing on the dusty road of Giuseppe, Joe, Verduci's birthplace created a strange doubling of vision – here was the old man I'd known barely a year, his frailty and eccentricity suddenly contextualised by this landscape that shaped him, and here too was the young man who contributed to my existence 60 years ago, his presence lingering in the quality of light, the particular angle of hillsides against sky.

This doubling of time echoed the complex layering of who I had become – the adopted child with one narrative, the biological child with another, the adult who had had to integrate both into something coherent. The girl who once stood frozen on a bus aisle, world crumbling beneath her feet at a stranger's casual revelation, now stood on Calabrian soil with the steady centredness of someone who had learned to build foundations on shifting ground.

I studied the weathered stone buildings of Motticella, this small Calabrian village where my Father was born, and where his Father before him had walked these same narrow streets.

The village perched above the Mediterranean, that sent its daughters and sons across oceans for generations, their DNA travelling to distant shores, creating stories – like mine – that could never have been anticipated by those who remained.

The stone walls bore witness to centuries of comings and goings, each departure etching invisible lines across oceans, each return a completion of some ancient, unspoken promise. I ran my fingers along rough stone walls that had witnessed centuries of births, deaths, departures, and returns – feeling the texture of history beneath my fingertips.

This small Calabrian village – now home to barely 155 souls – perched above the Mediterranean like a raptor's nest, simultaneously protected and exposed. For generations, it had sent its daughters and sons across oceans in patterns of migration driven by economic necessity and political upheaval. Mine was but one such story – one strand in a complex tapestry of separated bloodlines and dispersed identity that defined the Calabrian experience of the twentieth century.

I pulled over by the side of the dusty road, stepping out to feel the earth beneath my feet, to breathe the air my ancestors once breathed. The soil crumbled between my fingers – a communion more intimate than prayer, this touch connecting me across generations to those who cultivated this same earth.

I imagined my Father here as a boy, before life's hardships carved the man he would become – running through these streets, perhaps already developing the charismatic confidence and risk-taking propensity that would eventually lead to both his success and downfall. In my mind's eye, I placed my hand over his weathered one, bridging decades and continents. His skin was paper-thin now, blue veins visible beneath the surface, but his grip remained surprisingly strong. In that imagined touch, I felt the strange miracle of our connection – a biological bond severed for decades, now restored in the twilight of his life.
I could almost hear his voice as if he stood beside me:
'*Benvenuta a casa, mia cara bimba,*' (Welcome home, my dear child).
But which home was mine?
The Melbourne suburbs where Michelina and Sebastiano raised me?
The New York apartments where maternal relatives embraced me?
The houses I'd owned as an adult?
Or here, in this ancestral village I'd never seen before today – where my blood had its deepest roots?
Perhaps the most profound insight from my decades-long search was that home wasn't singular but plural – not a place but a constellation of belonging that shifted and evolved through time. Home existed in the overlap of geographies, in the confluence of bloodlines, in the intersection of chosen and inherited identities – a Venn diagram whose centre was wherever I stood fully present with all my complexity.
Perhaps home wasn't a single place but a capacity we carried within ourselves, expanding and contracting as we moved through our lives.
Looking back on my long search, I realise now that what I was seeking wasn't just information or even connection – it was integration – the skill to weave together the many parts of

myself: the adopted child of Italian immigrants, the abandoned infant, the professional woman, the seeker, the finder.

But life didn't offer perfect coherence. Giuseppe, the father I searched for so long, turned out to be both more and less than I had imagined – a complex man with a colourful past, capable of both violence and tenderness. My birth mother, Ursula, whose body carried me but whose arms never held me, remained largely a mystery, her choices both understandable and painful. She existed in my narrative as both absence and presence – the negative space that helped define the contours of my journey, the invisible hand that pushed me toward my eventual becoming.

My adoptive parents, who gave me a home and name but kept the truth of my origins from me, were neither heroes nor villains – but simply flawed humans doing their best with the values and limitations of their time.

I was the product of all of them – their choices, their genes, their cultural inheritances – yet also something entirely my own. More than just their biological continuation, I was what I'd made of myself through my own choices, values, and persistent searching. The abandoned child became the determined seeker. The shattered teenager became the integrator of fragments. The lost daughter became her own woman.

There are days when the ache is sharp – a hollow in my chest where memories should have lived. But I also see now that absence is not always abandonment; sometimes, it is the space where resilience grows. In the void my Father left, I learned to become whole without him.

Perhaps his absence shielded me from injuries I'll never fully comprehend, even as it carved an emptiness I'll always carry. That is the paradox I must learn to live with – that love withheld may have saved me, and in saving me, it still wounded me.

This was the greatest transformation in my journey: the shift from seeing identity as something to be discovered to understanding it as something actively created – shaped, not found, from whatever materials life provided.

The voice of the younger me that began this memoir – tentative, searching, splintered – is not the same voice that concludes this memoir. That earlier tone reflected who I was: a woman chasing fragments, unsure of how or whether they might fit together. What you hear now is a voice shaped by integration, by grief transmuted into understanding.
If the early chapters tremble, these later ones hum with hard-won steadiness.
Despite all the forces that conspired to keep us apart, I found my way back to my origins. *The Clean Break Theory of Adoption* – the postwar myth that infants were blank slates, untouched by womb, bloodline, or ancestral pull – had failed spectacularly in my case. It imagined identity simply as a legal stamp on a page. But memory, it turns out, has roots that grow in silence.
I was meant to forget my origin story, as if love alone could overwrite blood. But like water seeping through concrete, truth found its way – through dreams, body memory, bone structure, and the echo of my name spoken in a different tongue.
The tidy narrative of replacement unravelled. What remained was something messier, more sacred: the lived reality that a child's need for belonging cannot be surgically removed. It curls beneath the skin, waiting for recognition. Some connections refuse to be permanently broken; some fragments insist on finding their way back to wholeness.
Growing up, I didn't know that my biological and adoptive families came from southern Italy, that they shared a nationality, similar cultural patterns, values, and religious traditions.
Some might call this coincidence. Others might call it fate. The Calabrians have another word for it: *destinu*. Destiny. Not predetermined, exactly – but a pattern woven from choices and circumstances that, in retrospect, seems somehow inevitable.
The paradox stayed with me: while I had spent decades yearning for a father I never knew, my siblings had spent those same years recovering from the wounds of knowing him too well. My

emptiness had mirrored their burden. What I had mourned as absence, they had survived as excess.

As the afternoon sun descended toward the Mediterranean, casting the village in golden light, I found a beach town overlooking the coast. I sat – connected to this place by blood, yet separated by nearly everything else: language, culture, experience, choices. And still, in that moment, the connection felt sufficient – incomplete, imperfect, and yet somehow enough. I was finally home and whole, not because I'd gathered all the scattered pieces of myself, but because I'd learned to live within the imperfect reassembly.

All seven enigmatic fragments – my physical appearance, Giuseppe's name, my biological heritage, my medical history, my cultural origins, my family story, and my psychological self – had found their rightful places in the mosaic of who I am.

The fragments had not disappeared; they have found their places within a self that embraces contradiction, loss, and discovery.

My eyes rested on the distant sea. *È meravigliosa*. And wonderful it was – the landscape, the moment, the connection, the hard-won peace. The Mediterranean stretched before me – the same waters that carried my ancestors away, now welcoming their descendant home, the circle completing itself across generations – beautiful in its imperfection, its belatedness, its fragility.

This wasn't the end. Just the closing of the longest search I've ever known – for identity, for belonging, for home. What remained was something quiet yet profound – a sense of wholeness shaped through fracture, like a mosaic whose beauty emerged from the brokenness itself. Golden resin gleamed in the spaces between my once-scattered pieces – the breaks visible, revealed and honoured. My life moved forward from that moment – formed with intention, guided by the choices that were finally mine.

Melbourne, 5 April 2025

On our way to one of our many lunches, we were talking about the themes in my memoir, and my Papà said quietly, 'We are all broken.'
Some of us more than others. It is not the brokenness that defines us – but how we choose to repair and grow from the cracks.
As we were saying goodbye, he unexpectedly took my hand and said something that caught me off guard with its depth: '*Vedere te è uno dei pellegrinaggi della mia vita.*'
(Seeing you is one of the pilgrimages of my life.)
In those few words, he acknowledged that finding me had been meaningful for him too – a sacred journey of his own, not only mine. After decades of absence, he was now calling our connection one of the defining paths of his existence – a long-delayed arrival at fatherhood.
My journey has surged and spun like a rollercoaster – breathtaking highs, gut-wrenching lows, and sudden turns I never saw coming. Each twist, a teacher.
Each plunge broke and rebuilt me – until I emerged changed. I may not have ended up where I expected.
But I learned to find balance in the freefall,
to gather meaning from wreckage,
to hold the fragments gently and still call them mine. In the end, the rollercoaster made me more than I was at the start – a tapestry of all the moments, both exhilarating and heartbreaking, which shaped me.
My story is not seamless.
Its scars are stitched with gold – not despite the breaking, but because of it.
These fragments were not the destination – they were the terrain.
This journey wasn't about finding wholeness.
It was the act of traversing that made me whole.

Author's Note on Structure

The Golden Seams Beneath the Words

This memoir is the story of a fractured identity painstakingly pieced together over decades. It is also a work constructed with intentional symbolism embedded within it.

Like the art of kintsugi, which repairs broken pottery with golden lacquer to make the breaks part of the vessel's beauty, this book was designed so that even its numbers – the chapter titles, word counts, and total pages – would become golden seams of meaning.

Some of these patterns emerged intuitively; others revealed themselves only in the final stages of writing, as if the story itself insisted on an order beneath the chaos.

A few symbolic layers:

- 27 chapters – The age my biological Father, *Giuseppe*, was when I was born in 1964.
- Chapter 9 starts on page 126
- Chapter 10 starts on page 148
- Chapter 16 – I discovered that Giuseppe was still alive.
- Chapter 22 – *The Kintsugi Poet – Giovanni 'John' Verduci* – his age at death, and hauntingly, the chapter contains exactly 1969 words – the year he died. It starts on page 347.
- Chapter 25 – *A Seat at the Christmas Table* – A tribute to my birth date, the 25th, and the holiday traditionally associated with family, ritual, and belonging.
- Chapter 26 – *Carpe Diem* – The age Giuseppe was when I was conceived and the age I was when I first met Ursula.
- The memoir was completed on 26/5/2025
- 106,308 words
- 430 pages
- 2025 – the year I turned 61

These structural choices are intentional acts of homage and reckoning – numerical echoes of people, places, and moments that shaped me.

They are a quiet rebellion against the 'clean break' adoption myth that sought to sever me from origin, memory, and meaning.

Instead, this book insists that even absence leaves a trace. Even silence has structure.

Just as my identity had to be reassembled piece by piece, this story had to be built with similar care.

Numbers, titles, pages are part of that mosaic.

The golden seams are not just in the sentences.

They're in the structure itself.

Dr Mirella Di Benedetto
Melbourne, 26 May 2025

Glossary of Italian Terms

Family Terms
Bisnonna – Great grandmother
Bisnonno – Great grandfather
Fidya mia – My daughter (Sicilian)
Mamma – Mother
Nonna – Grandmother
Nonno – Grandfather
Papà – Dad
Zia – Aunt
Zio – Uncle

Greetings and Common Phrases
Ciau – Hello, goodbye (Sicilian, equivalent to 'Ciao')
Comu stai? – How are you? (Sicilian)
È meravigliosa – It's wonderful/marvellous
Un forte abbraccio – A strong hug/embrace

Places and Objects
Bottega – Small shop, often family-owned
Chiesa Di San Giovanni Battista – Church of St. John the Baptist

Cultural Concepts
Destinu – Destiny, fate
La bella figura – Making a good impression; an essential concept in Italian culture representing proper social conduct.
Una mala figura – A bad impression; failing to maintain proper social conduct.
Maleducato – Ill-mannered, rude, uncultured
Paesani – Fellow villagers or townspeople, especially from the

same town in Italy.
Terra straniera, quanta malinconia – Foreign land, how much melancholy (lyric from a popular song about emigration)

Food Terms
Passata – Tomato purée used as a base for many Italian dishes.

Expressions and Exclamations
Bona – Good (Sicilian)
Che vergogna! – What shame!
Dio aiutami! – God help me!
Mamma mia! – My God! (expression of surprise or dismay)
Si' anormali? – Are you abnormal?

Phrases from the Narrative
'E su maritu?' – And her husband? (Sicilian)
'E tu sai ca tò patri, non era tò patri?' – And you know your father wasn't your father? (Sicilian)
'Fidya di puttana!' – Daughter of a whore! (Sicilian insult)
'Ho fatto un grande mala figura' – I've made a very bad impression.
'Lassa stari a piccirida' – Leave the child alone (Sicilian)
'Ora tu lu sai' – Now you know (Sicilian)
'Scarpi, scarpi, mamma' – Shoes, shoes, mama
'To' patri, non era to' patri' – Your father wasn't your father (Sicilian dialect)
'Tu ci l'haiu a diri' – You must tell her (Sicilian)

Other Terms
L'Avvocata – the barrister
'Ndrangheta – Calabria's powerful organised crime network, considered even more secretive than the Sicilian Mafia.
Puttana – Whore (vulgar)

Extended Phrases and Quotations

'La figlia dell'amore è il prodotto di una gentil donna innamorata di un principe di grazia e virtù per destino di una sorte ingrata.' – The daughter of love is the product of a gentlewoman in love with a prince of grace and virtue by fate of an ungrateful lot.
'Mi sembrava di aveti conosciuta tutta la mia vita, per se innanzi agli occhi miei solo per alcuni istanti lo sei stata nella famiglia Verduci ci sono altri come il tuo sia lievel vita ovunque tu cammine.' – It seemed to me that I have known you all my life, even if you were before my eyes only for a few moments. In the Verduci family there are others like you. Let your life be gentle wherever you walk.
'Mia cara sconosciuta adolescente figlia, spero che tutto sia di ottima salute nella tua vita, come ben già sei in conoscenza, domani verrà tumulata la salma di mio fratello Andrea. Mi metterò in comunicazione con te nel prossimo futuro.' – My dear unknown teenage daughter, I hope that everything is in excellent health in your life. As you are already aware, tomorrow the body of my brother Andrea will be buried. I will communicate with you soon.
È la vita / È una lunga disperata corsa / Dove il tedio Eterno / È il mezzo scambio / È la vasta immensita' dell'aldilsa'/ Che insuguo
It is life / It's a long desperate race / Where eternal boredom / Is the middle exchange / And the vast immensity of the beyond / That I pursue (poem from John Verduci's tombstone)

Che sarà sarà – *What will be, will be*. A phrase popularised in the 1950s song made famous by Doris Day. While it mimics Italian grammar, it is not an idiomatic phrase in actual Italian. Nevertheless, it carries emotional resonance in the memoir as a philosophy of acceptance and letting go.

Acknowledgments

Heartfelt gratitude to Nicole, Emily, and Papà Joe (Giuseppe) who read my early drafts and gave me constant encouragement. To my Papà (Giuseppe), who acknowledged me as his daughter and encouraged the writing of this book and gave me permission to mention his name. To my eldest Cousin Francesca and my eldest living maternal aunt, Zia Diana, who verified historical information. To Dr Rosemary for responding to my message and who helped me to contact my Father. To Uncle Alfred for contacting his brother, Joseph, on my behalf and agreeing to meet me. To all other family members and friends who helped me in this journey. To my sisters-in-law for their compassion and insight.

Many thanks to the members of the online Facebook group DNA Detectives who gave me the knowledge and support to help me trace my paternal biological family and for their encouragement in writing this personal history.

To friends, siblings, cousins, aunts, and uncles who have been a constant in my life and accepted me into their families, unconditionally.

This work includes excerpts from the National Apology for Forced Adoptions, delivered by the Australian Government on 21 March 2013, and sourced from the Attorney-General's Department. This material is used under the Creative Commons Attribution 4.0 International licence. To view a copy of this licence, visit https://creativecommons.org/licenses/by/4.0. Minor edits have been made for length and formatting.
Thank you.

About the Author

Dr Mirella Di Benedetto has lived in Melbourne, Australia, for most of her life. She has worked as a health psychologist since 2001 and as a researcher, lecturer, and academic at various universities in Victoria from 2001–2020.
She has published numerous research papers in international peer-reviewed journals and two book chapters in *Health Psychology in Australia.*
She completed her PhD in Psychology, at La Trobe University, in 2006. Prior to returning to university to complete her psychology studies, she worked as a medical laboratory scientist at various pathology laboratories in Melbourne from 1985–1996.
She is an avid photographer, traveller, gardener, musician, artist, animal and nature lover, and a writer.
When she is not creating or making music, she works as a clinical health psychologist, helping people with heart-related trauma integrate their past and present into a developing identity, with a strong focus on post-traumatic growth.

Motticella (September 2024)

Giovanni

The Kintsugi Poet

Made in United States
Cleveland, OH
26 September 2025